Arms and the People

GW00566794

ARMS AND THE PEOPLE

Popular Movements and the Military
from the Paris Commune to the Arab Spring

Edited by Mike Gonzalez and Houman Barekat

PlutoPress
www.plutobooks.com

First published 2013 by Pluto Press
345 Archway Road, London N6 5AA

www.plutobooks.com

Distributed in the United States of America exclusively by
Palgrave Macmillan, a division of St. Martin's Press LLC,
175 Fifth Avenue, New York, NY 10010

British Library Cataloguing in Publication Data
A catalogue record for this book is available from the British Library

ISBN   978 0 7453 3289 5   Hardback
ISBN   978 0 7453 3297 0   Paperback
ISBN   978 1 8496 4809 7   PDF eBook
ISBN   978 1 8496 4811 0   Kindle eBook
ISBN   978 1 8496 4810 3   EPUB eBook

Library of Congress Cataloging in Publication Data applied for

This book is printed on paper suitable for recycling and made from fully managed
and sustained forest sources. Logging, pulping and manufacturing processes are
expected to conform to the environmental standards of the country of origin.

10   9   8   7   6   5   4   3   2   1

Designed and produced for Pluto Press by Chase Publishing Services Ltd
Typeset from disk by Stanford DTP Services, Northampton, England
Simultaneously printed digitally by CPI Antony Rowe, Chippenham, UK and
Edwards Bros in the United States of America

Contents

Introduction

Mike Gonzalez

When the tanks rolled into Tahrir Square, Cairo in February 2011, the world held its breath. The crowd, however, saw the army – or at least the conscripts who were its rank and file – as their allies. 'Army and people, one hand' was the slogan painted on walls and banners, as well as on the tanks themselves. Since then the evolution of events in Egypt itself and in the rest of the Middle East has called that assumption into question. A year later, the movement has clashed with those very soldiers across the country and the Arab revolution continues to seek its future. Can a revolutionary movement defeat an army? The Arab Spring offers contradictory answers as, on the one hand, the Libyan and Tunisian regimes have fallen, while, on the other, in Bahrain and particularly in Syria an army still largely intact has unleashed and continues to unleash terrible violence against its people.

This collection of essays is a review and an analysis of the experience of those social movements across the world to have confronted the question, in their practice, from 1871 onwards. There are experiences common to each of them, errors committed and warning signs unacknowledged. At the same time, each of these experiences exists in a specific time and place. And yet the questions and debates that arise seem to recur insistently in the arguments at factory gates or on the barricades. The writers come to their topic from a shared perspective – how to change the world and transform the society we live in – and in the hope that what follows will enrich and deepen a debate at once historical and intensely, achingly contemporary.

The German revolutionary Karl Liebknecht, in his 1907 pamphlet *Militarism and Anti-militarism*, set out the problem that concerns us here in a famous passage:

> '[Modern militarism] wants neither more nor less than the squaring of the circle; it arms the people against the people itself; it is insolent enough to force the workers . . . to become oppressors, enemies and murderers of their own class comrades and friends,

1

of their parents, brothers, sisters and children, murderers of their own past and future. It wants to be at the same time democratic and despotic, enlightened and machine-like, to serve the nation and at the same time to be its enemy.'[1]

The modern army is no longer the armed citizenry of the *levée en masse*, a 'people in arms'. The shape of such a people's militia could be seen in the Commune of 1871 or in the anti-fascist committees and armed units of the Spanish Revolution. How to arm and organise the working class has rarely been addressed as a concrete question in this century of revolutions, though Venezuela, as Douglas Bravo discusses, was an exception in the 1950s and 1960s. Yet the focus of debate on the left, then and now, has been first and foremost how to divide and break the armed forces – what Mike Haynes calls 'the battle for the soul of the army'.[2]

The simplistic cliché suggests that soldiers are 'workers in uniform'. That is obviously true. A quick survey of the dead in Afghanistan will demonstrate that most of those who have fallen are young working-class men, their origins in poor working-class neighbourhoods obvious to anyone who knows the countries they came from. They are privates and sergeants. It is rare, by contrast, to hear mention of officers dying in the field. When they do, it is newsworthy and their obituaries leave no doubt as to how different is their class background. So, in that sense it is true that the bulk of the military are workers. The assumption that flows from this is that, in the event of an uprising of their class, their loyalties will automatically lean towards their own and 'go over'. From Chile and Indonesia to Syria today, it is clear that this is not necessarily the case. Many other factors intervene – loyalties, divisions, fears. And where it has happened, a series of particular circumstances have combined to make it possible, as each essay in this volume clearly shows.

Liebknecht describes, with his customary passion, how a modern army cajoles, seduces and imprisons its recruits:

'Militarism must bend the will by moral and psychological influence or by force; it must entice or compel it. The principle of the carrot and the stick is applicable here. The true "spirit" required by militarism, in respect first of all of its function against the external enemy, is chauvinistic pig-headedness, narrow-mindedness and arrogance; second, in respect of its function against the internal enemy, it is a lack of understanding and even hatred of all progress, of every undertaking and endeavour which might in any way threaten the power of the class dominant at the time. This is the direction in which militarism must guide the thoughts and feelings of the soldiers, in so far as it wants to lure with the carrot those whose class interests are opposed to all chauvinism and for whom progress should appear as the only reasonable goal until the time when the existing social order is overthrown.'[3]

The process of induction, as Hollywood has shown us, is a series of humiliations and dehumanisation, the systematic breaking of the soldier's will and his isolation from his own world:

'First of all, the proletarian in uniform is sharply and ruthlessly cut off from his class comrades and his family. This is done by taking him away from his home, which is systematically done in Germany, and especially by shutting him up in barracks. One might almost speak of a repetition of the Jesuit method of education, a counterpart of monastic organization.'

At the same time there is a corresponding ideological assault, reinforced by internal training and external media. Military discourse is rooted in an assumption that a national army exists to serve and defend the state *against external enemies*, and historically it is true that imperialist armies have been built to expand the dominion of the state, to colonise and control. Yet they exist also as an oppressive internal force, though the discourse does not change – the 'enemy within' is described in sinister and shadowy terms from one age to the next. As the pre-war situation in Germany showed, for example, the high command was equally and simultaneously concerned with both. And in the aftermath of 9/11, George W. Bush proposed the suspension of the Posse Comitatus, the legal principle that restricts the use of the military for domestic purposes, and the military have been deployed within the country since then.

To speak of workers in uniform is to address both objective and subjective factors. It is possible to have been born into a working-class family, to have grown up in a working-class area, and yet not to see yourself as part of a collective life, to be objectively a worker yet not to live that reality as part of your own consciousness and understanding. The argument about solidarity or the strength of the collective is not an abstraction, but a generalisation from experience, a recognition of how workers can defend their interests as individuals and as a social force. The training of soldiers, especially professional soldiers, but also of conscripts, consists in good measure of breaking the individual from that shared reality and persuading the rank-and-file fighter that he belongs to a different collective called 'the Nation' to whose defence he has committed his life. The Nation is an abstraction, yet ideology and ceremonial combine to give a sense that it exists and that it is an undifferentiated whole in which peasant and landlord, worker and employer, share equally. The battle for the 'military soul' must first find a way to re-establish an identity of class and unmask the falsehoods of the concept of a united nation.

That is a political task, of course. But our discussions show that it can be achieved in some circumstances and not in others. The clearest cases in this volume of the collapse of the armed forces are Germany in 1918, where the mutinies of soldiers and sailors were central to the revolution and Vietnam, where the officers completely lost control over their men. Nearly a thousand of them died at the hands of their own rank and file as the combination of the protests at home and the total collapse of morale among soldiers led to the refusal of an exhausted and disillusioned army, a disproportionate number of whom were black or Hispanic, to fight an enemy they did not understand. This did not necessarily lead, however, to a more radical perception of the realities of American life, beyond opposing the continuing war – except perhaps in black America. Chile and Indonesia, for their part, demonstrate that a mass movement is a necessary but not sufficient condition for the fragmenting of the army to occur.

It is arresting to return to the statistics of death, injury and destruction that war throws up, from Flanders Field to Vietnam. The First World War in particular left an unimaginable toll in its wake. Yet at its beginning the imperialist purposes the war set in train won general support from the majority of every country – Britain, France, Germany, Russia. Germany is a particularly dramatic case. A left working-class party of two and a half million with a history of internationalism and anti-militarism crumbled in weeks and leapt nimbly onto the bandwagon of national chauvinism. Many of those who had fought with such courage for the rights of women in Britain abandoned the field when war began. Across Europe the troops went singing into war. And yet, by 1917, there were mutinies in the French and German armed forces and the trembling Tsarist autocracy was unable to maintain its grip on its own people. The Russian revolution of 1917 produced organs of popular organisation which proudly asserted class over nation in the soviets of workers, soldiers and peasants which were the germs of a different power, and they found their echo in the German workers' councils as well as elsewhere.

In many ways the revolution in the most advanced capitalist state in Europe, Germany, was the most significant. Yet it was eventually crushed, its leaders murdered and its participants persecuted and killed in the Nazi regime, which could be seen as the final stage of the revenge of the German ruling class. In Italy, too, the enormously creative 'two red years' (1919–20) raised the spectre of working-class power eventually broken by the military dictatorship of the renegade Mussolini.

In each case, workers in uniform took key roles in these movements. To read John Reed's *Ten Days that Shook the World* is to be present at the birth of a new kind of power – soviet power. In Russia and in Germany patriotism and national pride were, as Volkhard Mosler suggests, 'wafer-thin'. The war was waged with exemplary brutality and pointless slaughter; yet the ruling classes continued their lives of ostentatious luxury in the officers' messes in Belgium and France, as well as in the court of the Tsar. And in the 'war at home' the families of soldiers experienced deepening poverty, while those who worked in the armaments factories witnessed the gleeful appropriation of huge profits by their employers. The contrast between the grand rhetoric of patriotic war and the contradictions at home opened cracks in the ideological edifice. The Russian revolution announced to the world that imperial dynasties could be overthrown by the mobilisation of the masses. In 1973, as the last Americans fought to board the final helicopter out of Saigon, the flaws and cracks in US power were exposed to the world.

It is one possible condition of the revolutionary moment that the state and its institutions of social control fail or collapse. It is clear that this happened in Russia in 1917, under a right-wing assault in Spain in 1936 and in Cuba and Nicaragua in 1959 and 1979 respectively. In the social crisis in which the old ruling class cannot rule in the old way and the working class will no longer accept being ruled in the old way – what Lenin described as a revolutionary crisis – the class struggle does not end. No ruling class in history has ever given up power voluntarily, irrespective of whether or not their rule enjoyed general support. Instead, when that manner of ruling by consensus is no longer feasible, it will turn to explicitly military solutions, creating in some cases alternative armies, as was the case with the German *Freikorps*, in others an entirely professional military enjoying special living and economic conditions, as in the case of Syria or Venezuela after 1966. In Egypt the military enjoyed very particular privileges but also controlled a significant sector of the economy, which gave them, and gives them still, a loyalty to the system at once financial and ideological.

In a revolutionary crisis the transfer of power is posed as the oppressed and exploited begin to act collectively in their own interest. The clocks are stopped and a new time begins. But since the old ruling class is already preparing its violent response, what are the options for the revolution? At the general level, it is to place arms under the control of politics. At this critical moment, politics, not arms, should prevail. But the question is, whose politics – the politics of social democracy, in whatever specific guise they appear? Where that has been the case, as the essays in this volume dramatically reveal, the consequence has been to delay or undermine the seizure of power. Organisations whose purpose was to take power *in the existing state* vacillate when that state and its institutions of oppression enter a time of crisis. The politics of reform start from the assumption of a neutral state, an instrument which can be taken and applied to any tasks, rather than an apparatus designed for the defence and maintenance of class rule.

Wilhelm Liebknecht (Karl's father) said of Germany: 'We have two peoples in Germany, one *in* arms and the other *without* arms. And the people *without* arms are kept in slavery by the people in arms.' At what point can that balance be changed? A people with arms but without political cohesion cannot match the continuing monopoly of arms in the hands of the ruling class and their allies – 29 states rushed to support the counter-revolutionary White armies besieging Russia after 1918! In the collapse of an armed force, of the kind that happened to the Americans in Vietnam and in a different way in Portugal, a political space is opened up in which the role of the military among many other questions can be posed in practice. But Portugal in particular reveals that unless there is an alternative organisation of social force, the forces of Capital will adjust and adapt and return to fill the vacuum.

It is working people who drive the tanks, fly the bombers, man the submarines. The machines cannot be disabled unless their handlers are won over from the purposes to which they have been devoted. For this to happen a range of factors have to combine – political leadership and coordination, a shared vision of a different future, the highest level of organisation that is at once coherent and absolutely open to every working man and woman. In a revolutionary moment the struggle itself throws up extraordinary new and unexpected forms and structures – the formulas are swept away in the tide of change. The political work that prepares the common purpose begins long before the crisis, but its starting point and its strength will be its ability to remind the 'workers in uniform' that they can fight for a new world or fight to defend the old because the alternatives exist before them in real time.

NOTES

1. See www.marxists.org, accessed 20 March 2012.
2. Mike Haynes, personal communication, February 2012.
3. Liebknecht, www.marxists.org, accessed 20 March 2012.

Soldiers and Revolution

1
Soldiers, Sailors and Revolution: Russia 1917

Mike Haynes

The outbreak of the First World War in 1914 seemed to unite the masses behind their respective governments, not least in Russia where 96 per cent of those called up willingly enlisted. But within three years the strain of war was being felt everywhere and several states were racing each other to revolution. Austria-Hungary and Italy were close, but it was Russia which won. In late February 1917, troops from the Petrograd garrison refused to fire on demonstrators. The mutiny turned the demonstrations into a revolution which overthrew the 300-year Romanov dynasty. The months of radicalisation which followed led, in October 1917, to a second revolution and the call to soldiers, sailors and airmen across the world to lay down their arms and cease fighting in the interests of their rulers.

A century later, this remains one of the most intense revolutionary crises in history and at its heart were the Russian armed forces. These events challenge established views, and generations of historians have tried to explain their import. Claiming to rise above the passions of the past, they too often fall prey to the prejudices of the present in questioning the nature and possibilities of fundamental change. The aim of this chapter is to contest such interpretations and show how the disintegration of the armed forces not only contributed to the democratisation of Russian society in 1917, but also prevented the old order and its generals from mustering sufficient forces to halt the revolution by the imposition of military rule or defeat it in the civil war that followed.

Whatever else states may do, they are about power. At their core is the ability to deploy military power to defend or project influence outside their borders and to contain the home population to whom (in a democratic order) they are nominally responsible but over whom, radical critics suggest, they rule. States are therefore Janus-faced – looking both inwards and outwards. Military power too is Janus-faced – capable of being used against external and internal enemies. Max Weber famously argued that as states develop they come to claim 'the *monopoly of the legitimate use of physical force* within a given territory'. 'The state,' he argued, 'is a relation of men dominating men, a relation supported by means of legitimate (i.e. considered to be legitimate) violence. If the state is to exist, the dominated must obey the authority claimed by the powers that be.' If men and women do not obey and the state cannot deploy the means of force to make them obey, then it falls apart. Lenin, following Engels, made the same point. The essence of the state is that it is 'a body of armed men'. In a class society military power cannot be based on an armed population; it must be separate from society and rise above it. A standing army and police are the chief instruments of state power. This is because social divisions mean that the control and organisation of the means of violence have to be alienated from the mass of the population.[1]

The complex links between the rise of the state system and the development of capitalism need not detain us here. Suffice it to say that the rise of a separate military force was an important element in the development of a state-based global system. States tend not to emerge as a result of any essential democratic process; they are made by force. From the seventeenth century onwards, the intermittent organisation of military forces for specific actions gave way to the development of standing armies led by professional officer elites. In the first instance armies and navies were loyal to the monarch, who was deemed to embody the state. But from the late eighteenth century, and not least with the French Revolution, a more fundamental identification was made with the (nation) state whose nature was no longer sufficiently captured in the person of the sovereign. With this, mass conscription followed and the idea of service armies based on citizens or quasi-citizens. Clausewitz recognised that that this enabled capitalist states to deploy almost unlimited resources to build up the military for war.[2] But it also allowed the development of the idea that the military itself might better express the interests of the state/nation than civilian politicians. The armed forces could then either act as arbiter or take power themselves to bring order or progress where others had failed.

The separation of the military from society as a hierarchical, disciplined force gives them the capacity to act if their leaders, or a group of them, decide to do so and sufficient members of the lower ranks can be assured to obey. The fact that the military have a monopoly of arms also makes possible the speedy imposition of order. What has been called the military 'mind' or 'ethic' also plays a role. The military see themselves as the core of the state and its guardian. They not only have a right to intervene in a crisis, but a duty to do so. This is reinforced by their sense of professionalism and lack of corruption (something perhaps belied in practice) compared to the dirty world of civilian politics.

Lenin described the conditions for a successful revolution as being where 'the "lower classes" *do not want* to live in the old way and the "upper classes" *cannot carry on in the old way*'.[3] But these were also to become the conditions for direct military interventions and coups or indirect military action associated with paramilitary forces, of which the role of the *Freikorps* in Germany in 1919 was an early example. In the early twentieth century such military actions were a new phenomenon but they were soon to become commonplace, reflecting what some called a praetorian tendency in politics (after the Praetorian Guard of Imperial Rome, who acted as bodyguards to the emperor).

When a successful revolution occurs, we have to ask not only what happened but also what did *not* happen. A successful revolution cannot defeat a united army. The army must come over to the people and in such a way that it makes it an unstoppable force, not only against the old order but also against the potential of the officer class to seize power itself. This is what happened in Russia, not because anyone had a 'plan', but because they were able, at times almost intuitively, to grope towards solutions which, it could be argued later, embodied fundamental lessons.

THE TSARIST MILITARY AND STATE POWER BEFORE 1914

In 1914 the Russian empire was the largest country in the world, covering a sixth of the earth's surface and stretching at its furthest 5,000 miles west to east and 2,000 miles north to south. Its strategic position at the heart of the global system worked in two ways – it was able to project out, but it was also threatened by powers along its extensive borders. To expand or hold on to its gains, Russia had built up the largest peacetime army in Europe, numbering at least one million in most years before 1914, as well as developing the fifth biggest navy.[4] In the nineteenth century the military had been involved in wars with other European powers – with France between 1805 and 1814, with Sweden in 1808–9 and three wars with Turkey: the Crimean War against the combined forces of Britain, France and Turkey in 1853–56; and war with Japan in 1904–5. Military action also supported the incorporation of less developed areas into the empire, though often opposed by local peoples and their overlords such as Persia, with Russia expanding to the east across Siberia to the Pacific, south into the Caucasus and south-east to Central Asia. But large forces were also needed because the army had to be deployed to contain revolution. In 1849 the Tsarist armies moved into Hungary to crush revolution there. But such actions were usually 'internal' – in 1830–31 in Poland, again in Poland in 1863 and against the 1905 revolution – in the towns in 1905–6 and the countryside in 1906–7. During the restoration of order in 1905–9 some 2,500 (estimates are conflicting) were executed after field courts martial and an unknown number summarily shot in punitive expeditions, among them troops that had mutinied. In tandem with these large-scale actions it was common to find the military involved in more local policing actions against peasants and workers as Russia had a weak police force. Thus between 1890 and 1914 the army was used 3,000 times to suppress internal disorder.[5] Finally, the size of the army reflected a growing tendency to use Russia's cheap manpower as a substitute for capital in the form of modern weaponry. Much as workers might be referred to as 'hands', it was common until quite late for these ordinary soldiers to be referred to as 'bayonets' in the assessment of military strength and less flatteringly as 'cattle'. For although Russia was the world's fifth largest industrial power, it remained largely undeveloped; the mass of its population were peasants, who made up the majority of army conscripts.

The officer class, and through them ordinary soldiers and sailors, were supposed to be personally loyal to the Tsar and the wider landowning class on whose power Tsarism initially rested. Military reform had been undertaken in 1874 to create a more modern army with new forms of conscription and organisation, but also to help define the role of the military as an expression of a unified nation.[6] But these reforms had a limited impact on the army's sense of itself. The day-to-day behaviour of troops in society at large was ordered and regulated in petty ways by the military code. Soldiers were subject to rigid, brutal and humiliating forms of discipline. Their officers saw themselves as a superior caste, reflected in part by their noble origins, but in practice they were generally anti-intellectual and had a limited interest in military theory and techniques.

Mutinies did take place, but until 1905 they had little impact. In the revolution of 1905–6 they were more widespread, but the army held together and was deployed more against the revolution than contributed to it. Trotsky, with some exaggeration, said of the workers' uprising at the end of 1905, 'the Russian proletariat in December foundered not on its own mistakes, but on a more real force: the bayonets of the peasant army'.[7]

The officer corps before 1914 was changing socially. The 1913 class of the General Staff Academy had only 9 per cent of nobles compared to 19 per cent from the peasant estate. But among the 41,000 officers of the existing officer corps, nobles still just dominated and in the high command over 85 per cent were of noble origin.[8] A minority of the newer generation hoped that the army might be a force for modernisation in its own interest. In 1908 they found a source of inspiration in the Ottoman empire, where the Young Turks revolution led by army officers overthrew the failing regime of Sultan Abdul Hamid. Their interest was reinforced by the fact that a reinvigorated Ottoman empire would stand in the way of Russian influence in the Balkans and its aim of controlling access from the Black Sea to the Mediterranean through the Straits. But those like the politician Alexander Guchkov (a 'liberal with spurs') also saw that any positive elements in the actions of an officer group had to balance the risk in Russia that a process might be unleashed they would be unable to control.

THE FIRST WORLD WAR TO FEBRUARY 1917

Russia had allied itself with France in 1894 and with Britain in 1907 against the rising power of any alliance led by Germany. The assassination of Archduke Franz Ferdinand in 1914 then set in train events in which each side claimed the mantle of right while really engaged in an imperial conflict that would lead to an estimated 8.5 million military deaths and 10–13 million civilian dead.

It is a commonplace in even authoritative discussions of the Russian armed forces to throw in bewilderingly large numbers. But to appreciate how the armed forces partly politicised and partly disintegrated, it helps to have a sense of the numbers involved. We will follow the data collected and in some cases estimated by Nicholas Golovine, a former Tsarist general writing in the late 1920s.[9] Although his work can be criticised, it remains the best attempt to track the human scale of the war effort and its costs to the Russian side.[10] Table 1.1 sets out the main components of the 'military' between 1914 and 1917.

Table 1.1   The Russian Army 1914–17

	Mobilised	Army of the Field Total	Remote Rear of which Combatants	Ministry of War and Territorials	Auxiliary supplies
1914 Oct	6,553,000	2,700,000	1,500,000 ⇕ 3,500,000		2–3 million
1914 Dec		2,000,000			
1915 Jan	5,047,000	3,500,000			300,000
1915 Aug		3,800,000		2,000,000	
1915 Nov		4,900,000			
1916 Feb	3,048,000	6,200,000			350,000
1916 June		6,800,000			
1916 Nov		6,900.000		2,200,000	
1917 Jan	730,000	6,900,000			
1917 Sept		6,000,000		1,100,000	400,000

At the outset of the war Russia had 1,423,000 troops and before October 1917, as Table 1.1 shows, perhaps another 14 million were mobilised. Those mobilised were men, though token women's battalions drew brief publicity in 1917.[11] In terms of age, 16 per cent were under 20 years, 49 per cent were 20–29, 30 per cent were 30–39 and 5 per cent over 40. They came overwhelmingly from Russia's rural poor. But even among the 20–29 age group only about half were called up. Non-Russians were excluded; others were in occupied areas; still others – perhaps as many as five million – were physically unfit to serve; and some 2.5 million had deferment for war work. Initially, this did not include many skilled workers and miners, who were lost to the front to the detriment of the war effort. It was never fully appreciated that, in the words of a memorandum of the Special Council for National Defence, 'an experienced smith . . . may be incomparably more useful doing the work on national defence in a factory than in the trenches'. At the top and middle of society, although many Russian families lost their sons, there was less evidence of any disproportionate sacrifice in the interests of patriotism and national salvation. Wartime deferments were relatively easy to obtain by middle- and upper-class men, who could show that they were needed for essential work on the home front. In reality, therefore, there was a volunteer element in conscription which depended on who you were. As Golovine noted, 'whenever [the Ministry of War] took measures against "slackers" those measures chiefly affected workers and peasants'.[12]

Before the war Russia had been divided into military districts under the command of the commander-in-chief, and non-military districts. Although the former were ostensibly border regions, in fact they covered vast areas, which expanded during the war. Troops in these districts served in what was called the Army of the Field. Those closest to the front and in the immediate rear of the front were 'troops in combat'. As can be seen in Table 1.1 these numbered between 1.5 and 3.5 million at any one time with rotation between the field and front elements. Beyond the military zones was the 'remote rear'. Here were to be found garrison troops and mobilised men undergoing training. The numbers here too represent a constantly churning group, as men were drafted, all too briefly trained, and sent to the Army of the Field. A third component was represented by Ministry of War employees and local territorial units, which protected the interior. Finally, large numbers were involved in various auxiliary activities such as the Red Cross or the supply work of the Union of Zemstvos and Towns. These did not serve as part of the military but they did come under the army supply system for rations. Beyond them, and not counted here, were the vast numbers of civilian workers employed more or less directly in making and transporting war goods.

Table 1.2 sets out the basic data for Russia's losses in the war which for Russia lasted 39 months (compared to 51 months on the Western Front). Again drawing on Golovine, the statistics here are a combination of hard data, estimates and guesses because record-keeping was poor and many records were subsequently lost.

Table 1.2   Losses in the Tsarist Army, August 1914 to October 1917[13]

	Mobilised	Killed Casualties	Died of wounds	Survived wounds	POW	Of which POW dead	Sick	Of which sick deaths	Discharged sick/wounded
1914	6,553	724	424		3,008				
1915	5,047	2,230	1368						
1916	3,048	1,980	348						
1917	730	566	277		2,062				
1914/17	15,378	1,300	350	3,850	2,417	70	5,070	140	700

Conditions at the front and the sacrifices demanded were gruelling. 'The Germans expend metal, and we expend our blood,' said one Russian general. 'This is not war, sir, this is slaughter', the British observer Bernard Pares was told. Both east and west the war was one of attrition. The victor, said a British general, would be the alliance with the longer purse and in human terms Russia was seen to have the longest purse of all. Indeed, in 1916 some 40,000 of a requested 400,000 Russian troops were shipped to the Western Front where they would subsequently mutiny in 1917.[14] The estimates in Table 1.2 suggest that 1.86 million Russian soldiers died between 1914 and October 1917. It seems likely that over 40 per cent of Russian deaths at the front were not individually recorded due to soldiers being blown to bits or left behind in retreats to be buried, if at all, in mass graves. Over four million were wounded and a further five million were sick at some time. But neither condition necessarily prevented a return to service. In Russia, although traumas like shell shock began to be recognised, as elsewhere there was a view that the 'sick' included many malingerers, who were effectively 'deserters in disguise'.[15] But a high proportion of the sick and wounded – perhaps 75 per cent – did go back, some to be killed, wounded or become sick again. Some 260,000 of Russia's prisoners of war even escaped to return to the front, though it was safer to remain a prisoner.

The most fluid period of the war was 1914–15, but by 1915–16 the various Eastern Fronts were becoming stuck fast in ways similar to the trenches of Western Europe. Yet despite huge losses, in 1917 Russia had not lost the military war. On the Northern and Western Fronts, where it primarily faced Germany, the Russian army performed badly; but as the German general Erich Ludendorff had to admit, 'the Russians always succeeded in escaping'.[16] Against Austria-Hungary on the South-Western Front and in Romania (from 1916) and against Turkey (from 1915) the Russian army often did well in territorial terms and took some two million prisoners – over 80 per cent from Austria-Hungary.

In 1914–15 shortages were rife – in transport, medical supplies, food, boots, socks, clothing, rifles, bullets, shells, etc. Weapons were often taken from the dead. In the spring of 1915 General Yanushkevich, as chief of staff, wrote that 'all our armies are crying with one voice, "Give us ammunition!"' Denikin remembered the retreat in Galicia at this time as

'one vast tragedy for the Russian army. No cartridges, no shells. Bloody fighting and difficult marches day after day. No end to the weariness, physical as well as moral. Faint hopes followed by sinister dread . . . Blood flowed unendingly, the ranks became thinner and thinner, the number of graves constantly multiplied.'[17]

In such frequent episodes of chaos, troops might be force-marched for days as their boots fell apart and hunger grew, in order to fill lines in the trenches. 'One had the impression of vast forces hurled carelessly here and there, of indifference on a grand scale, of gigantic waste,' wrote John Reed of what he saw on the Eastern Front in 1915.[18] These shortages came from both a lack of supplies and poor organisation. By 1916 supplies had increased thanks to a creditable conversion of the economy to the war effort and munitions imported from abroad via Murmansk and Archangel'sk in the far north and Vladivostok in the far east. But poor organisation continued to hinder their distribution and undermined soldiers' confidence in the support they received and why they were fighting at all.

There is considerable debate about how far the Russian armies held together *before* 1917. Sustaining an army in the face of likely death may not be easy. Troops at the front suffer from boredom and fatigue interspersed with periods of fear and terror. The bravado of the military and their chroniclers leads them to stress the role of patriotism, training and *esprit de corps* in overcoming these. In these terms the Tsarist armies suffered because patriotism was too new a force, training too brief and *esprit de corps* limited. But alongside the 'military virtues' more critical accounts recognise the use of bribes – alcohol, narcotics, sex, plunder; fear of discipline from your own side; commitment and loyalty less to some grand ideal than to the small unit of which you are a part and its gelling around a 'big man' – whether a junior officer, a non-commissioned officer or an ordinary soldier.

These were all evident on the Eastern Front. Least talked about at the time was the way that some soldiers were encouraged to terrorise the local population. In the military districts behind the front the local population was subject to wartime military control and were often abused with the tacit support of the high command. Worst treated were the Jews, who were subject to attacks and expulsion in the autumn of 1914 and the spring of 1915.[19] But in the late summer of 1915 and the early autumn during the great retreat from Poland involving perhaps two million men a scorched earth policy was pursued. 'Only those who have seen the flight of the Russian people can in any way conceive of the horror which attended it,' wrote one senior Russian officer.[20]

Discipline was imposed harshly and erratically at the discretion of local generals or commanders. The ultimate sanction of a court martial – execution – was seemingly much more widespread than on the Western Front. 'Friendly fire' incidents were probably common, but there are reports of troops surrendering, and fraternising troops (on the Eastern Front this was especially evident at Eastertime) being deliberately shelled by their own side to deter them. And there were threats at senior levels that the families of those who did not fight to the death or become prisoners of war would suffer.[21]

War had a dramatic impact on the composition of the officer class. By 1917 there were 145,000 officers serving. In 1914 the Tsar had told his officers, 'I need your lives . . . useless losses . . . may lead to serious consequences,' but by 1917 two-thirds of the 1914 cohort were dead – many in the first months of the war. Muriel Buchanan, the daughter of the British ambassador, noted that 'the men we danced with last year had lost their lives in east Prussia and the Carpathians'. Overall the officer corps lost some 60,000 and during the war around 170,000 new junior officers had to be created along with corporals and sergeants. They tended to be drawn from a broader social background and had a more limited commitment to the traditions of the old army (which lack of training did nothing to modify). Disaffection in 1917 would therefore involve a significant minority of these junior officers and NCOs, who felt a closer affinity with their men and revolutionary Russia than they did with the old order.[22]

During the war the power of the Tsar, his court and the government was undermined by their poor organisation of the war effort and the sense of general incompetence, widespread corruption and even treason. The determination to keep those who offered assistance at arm's length increased the alienation and this became more focused as the government became more camarilla-like. Forty-one people served in the top twelve government posts for an average of only nine months each between 1914 and 1917.[23] But those arguing for change were paralysed by its possible consequences. 'Our methods of struggle are double-edged, and because of the excited state of the people, especially of the workers, they may strike the first spark and kindle a fire, the size of which no-one can foresee and the limiting of which will be impossible,' Guchkov wrote to General Alekseev in August 1916.[24]

1917 AND SUSTAINED RADICALISATION

In the event the matter was taken out of their hands. On Thursday, 23 February, International Women's Day, following a lock-out at the Putilov works, some 180,000 demonstrated in Petrograd. By the 26th, 300,000 were on strike and a few hundred soldiers disobeyed orders for the first time. The next day it was 70,000 and the situation was transformed. On 28 February perhaps 120,000 were in revolt and on 1–2 March 170,000, virtually the whole of the Petrograd garrison. Their actions tipped the balance, forced out the Tsar and pushed the country dramatically to the left. It created a dual power situation in which a new, self-appointed provisional government and an elected soviet or council of workers and soldiers deputies vied to direct events.

At this point, 'the revolutionary troops . . . were still so disorganised that they could have been dealt with by a single Cossack division, untainted by propaganda, if this had been brought in from the front,' wrote Fyodor Raskolnikov, one of the leading revolutionaries in the navy. But there was now no serious will among the generals to save the Tsar.[25] However, in the army the revolution went deeper than paralysis at the top – it overturned the army's internal relations. This was 'the first revolution ever to be achieved by the soldiers going over to the people not only without the co-operation of the officers, but actually against their will,' said one contemporary. Within the army the fact that officers were forced to follow the men, said one officer, created an 'unfathomable abyss' between them and their troops who, on the streets of Petrograd, were now regarded as heroes.[26]

The problem was that the troops of Petrograd had come over to the people, but would they stay there? Order No. 1, hurriedly agreed by the Petrograd soviet, was an attempt to ensure that they did. Improvised under pressure it was, according to Trotsky, 'the only worthy document of the February revolution'.[27] Although intended only for Petrograd, the order was widely circulated at the front and the rear. Its succinct seven points opened up the possibility of a long-term challenge to the traditional role of the army and its organisation.

The order had four main elements. One was the election of committees from the rank-and-file soldiers and sailors and their sending of representatives to the soviet. The second was that weapons had to be kept under the control of 'company and battalion committees, and in no case be turned over to officers, even at their demand'. The third was that, while recognising the need for military discipline, soldiers and sailors had to be seen by their officers as citizens and not subject to the petty humiliations of military rank. The final element was that 'the military branch' would no longer see itself as responsible to the old order or itself. The soviet was to be a 'Soviet of Workers and Soldiers Deputies' to which 'the military branch' was subordinate and crucially orders from above could only be carried out 'insofar as they did not conflict with orders and resolutions of the soviets'. Separately, military discipline was also weakened by the withdrawal of the threat of the death penalty.

The political implication and logic of this order were enormous and well understood at the time. Goldenberg, an editor of the paper *Novaya zhizn*, said:

> Order No. 1 was the unanimous expression of the Soviet's will. On the first day of the Revolution we understood that if we did not destroy the old army, the latter would crush the Revolution. We had to choose between the army and the Revolution. We did not hesitate. We took a decision in favour of the Revolution and we used, I declare it boldly, the proper means.[28]

Some attempted to minimise the scale of the shift by presenting the February revolution as a Young Turks-style overthrow by the military, but this was dismissed by the economist Mikhail Tugan-Baranovsky writing in the newspaper *Birzhevoe Vedomosti*:

> The Turkish revolution consisted in a victorious uprising of the army, prepared and carried out by the leaders of the army; the soldiers were merely obedient executives of the plans of their officers. But the regiments of the Guard which on February 27 overthrew the Russian throne, came without their officers. Not the army but the workers began the insurrection; not the generals but the soldiers came to the State Duma. The soldiers supported the workers not because they were obediently fulfilling the commands of their officers, but because . . . they felt themselves blood brothers of the workers as a class composed of toilers like themselves. The peasants and the workers-those are the two social classes which made the Russian revolution.[29]

In this way Order No. 1 helped to consolidate in the army the same situation of dual power that existed in Russian society at large.

On 9 March, Alexander Guchkov, the new government's Minister of War, told the head of the army, General Alekseev, 'One may say directly that the Provisional Government exists only so long as the Soviet permits this. Especially in the military sphere it is possible now to give out only such orders as do not definitely conflict with the orders of the Soviet.'[30] For the general and his officers the same problems would be reproduced within the army and navy as the revolution developed.

At the formal level a struggle immediately began to put the genie unleashed by Order No. 1 back in the bottle. Hurried negotiations between the Ministry of War and leaders of the soviet produced Order No. 2, which recognised the election of committees but offered an 'explanation and amplification', which meant a qualification and limiting of their roles. But while Order No. 2 said that soldiers 'are bound to submit to all their orders that have reference to military service', it also said that the soldiers were bound to submit to the soviets 'in matters of their public and *political* life'. Given that the revolution was beginning to bring into question the divide between the military and the political, this qualification was of limited help. Moreover, Order No. 2 still implied that the provisional government had to work with the soviet and to reflect it. This would be reinforced in subsequent declarations in which the soviet said of itself that it 'was the highest representative of the political will and action of the mass of the soldiers'. In the army matters were clearer. The high command worked to restore its authority and that of its officers. But here too it was obvious that the rapidly spreading committees could not immediately be done away with. Instead, temporary regulations were drawn up to limit their role. Committees were to be dominated by officers with 'military and training matters . . . in no way subject to discussion'. All army congresses were allowed but would again be dominated and held at the Supreme Command headquarters.

Less formally, a struggle ensued over the extent to which the authority of the senior officers and the military hierarchy could be restored. This was played out in everyday encounters between officers and men; tensions over rule by committee (*komitetchina*) and, at the most senior levels, debate about how to move forward in relation to the war, relations with the provisional government and soviets and the restoration of 'normal' order within the armed forces.

Initially, the impact of February led many to think that the war would gain a new legitimacy. It could now be fought for 'Russia's freedom and democracy [and] that of the whole world'. At the front the immediate impact on the willingness to fight was unclear. Perhaps the war might have a new meaning and purpose, but perhaps too it might not last as long and blood be spilled so wastefully.[31] In the rear things seemed clearer. The revolution might revitalise the means of fighting. There could now be an all-class effort, a greater degree of mobilisation in Russia itself and more commitment to the front. Shock battalions of volunteers, including women, were recruited to supplement the normal call-up. These would be 'death battalions' fighting for the 'freedom of Russia'.

The wider assumption was that the provisional government, the soviets and the military could work harmoniously together. But the decisive element in the minds of the soldiers and sailors remained the role of the soviets in general and the Petrograd soviet in particular. Support for the provisional government and high command was implicitly conditional, based on the *insofar as* formula which derived from February and Order No. 1 – support would only be there *insofar as* it did not conflict with the policies of the soviets.

The subsequent story of 1917 is therefore one of overlapping dynamics – the loss of authority by the provisional government, the high command and the old soviet leadership; the growing weariness of some who, as Lenin would say, voted with their legs by beginning to walk away; and the growing radicalisation of others in the army and navy who swung to support a second revolution.

At the top, despite the fine talk of new ideals, the imperial logic behind the war did not change, nor did the demands of the allies that Russia participate fully. Russia remained a class society and those who supported the war also now saw democracy as a means to enable Russia to achieve its imperial aims. The supposed radical Victor Chernov argued that 'Russia must have a strong army to enforce the respect of friends and foes alike'.[32] Even when couched more robustly as *revolutionary defencism*, Russia's continued role in the war inevitably helped one side against the other – a point rubbed home by the Allied refusal to countenance an early peace or any constructive discussion of war aims. 'The magic of victory' in Russia would help to restore the honour of the army and instil a greater sense of discipline and unity of purpose between the front and the rear, pulling the country back from the brink of a deeper revolution. Support for the war also had the benefit that it might delay further reform at home, not least land reform. Although continued participation in the war was later seen as a 'fatal blunder', it would require a more fundamental revolution to break from it.[33]

In May and early June a lot of energy was put into preparing the Brusilov offensive, which began in mid-June. Its ignominious failure before counterattacks beginning in early July led to mutual recriminations. The generals blamed the government and the soviets, who in turn blamed the generals. Both turned on and insulted the ordinary soldiers. Alexander Kerensky, the leader of the provisional government, spoke of 'faintheartedness and contemptible cowardice' in the ranks. The soldiers, despite dying in their thousands, had, it seemed, preferred meetings to the real task of fighting. The waste of the offensive and these criticisms led to a growing lack of confidence in the provisional government, the officers and the leadership of the soviets who had supported them. The mutual concern to continue the war, reinforce discipline and then launch the offensive seemed to draw together those at the top in the eyes of an increasing number of ordinary soldiers and 'became firm with the launching of the [June] offensive'.[34]

The failure of the offensive contributed to the July Days when radicalised workers, soldiers and sailors came out on the streets of Petrograd. But the government retained enough support to crush the revolt. This pulled the political mood to the right and senior officers once more demanded discipline and the restoration of the death penalty. This was the space in which it appeared possible for a new commander-in-chief, Lavr Kornilov, as a future 'man on horseback', to try to seize his moment.[35] The defeat of his confused coup attempt in late August by mass mobilisation effectively broke the provisional government and discredited Kerensky. It disoriented and demoralised the generals (although it is in the nature of such crises that sooner or later new opportunities become available to them). A huge power vacuum was created at the top, which the soviets were strategically placed to fill. This they did in September and October as their composition changed to reflect an ever greater degree of radicalisation.

On 24–25 October, units consisting of Bolsheviks, Left Socialist Revolutionaries, the Red Guard, some soldiers and, especially, sailors moved to seize power in Petrograd in the name of the Second Congress of Soviets, which voted the next day to support their actions. The standard estimates suggest that by the end the provisional government could call on only around 25,000 armed supporters in Petrograd compared to 300,000 armed workers, soldiers and sailors who were supporting the transfer of power. As in February, decisive action by a general whose troops were prepared to follow him might have crushed the revolution. But none was forthcoming. The revolutionaries were able to resist an initial response to the events in Petrograd and overcome an attack by General Krasnov. They were also able to spread the revolution and take power across Russia – immediately in Moscow where fighting was more forced, and over the next weeks and months across Russia. To understand how this happened we need to look at the mass of soldiers and sailors, NCOs and junior officers and how the process of radicalisation was embodied on the ground.

AMONG THE RANK AND FILE

February had opened up new perspectives for soldiers and sailors no less than it did for workers and, to a lesser extent, Russia's peasants. What senior officers saw as a lack of discipline and a refusal to obey orders was also the expression of a new assertiveness. Trotsky later wrote:

> For millions of soldiers the revolution meant the right to a personal life, and first of all the right to life in general . . . In this sense . . . the fundamental psychological process taking place in the army was the awakening of personality . . . this volcanic eruption of individualism . . . often took anarchic forms . . . [a] flood of mass individualism.'[36]

1917 therefore involved a tension between new forms of collective consciousness and new individualistic forces. Russians, said Kerensky, supporting the generals, having made the February revolution, now had to stop acting like 'rebellious slaves'. For the radicals, on the other hand, these 'rebellious slaves' had to become conscious revolutionaries. Between February and October this tension was played out in both front and rear units. The mood was often volatile, with soldiers and sailors oscillating between pro- and anti-war positions, from hostility to the rear to solidarity with workers and peasants there.

A crucial role was played by the many rank-and-file committees that were formed over the year. Estimates put their numbers at some 50,000 with 300,000 or more members – a ratio of perhaps one member to every 20–25 soldiers.[37] Their authority was considerable, as can be seen in the complaints by the authorities about one guard division which disobeyed orders in June 1917. From the point of view of the army command things took a turn for the worse in May when one junior officer, Lieutenant Dzevaltovsky, returned from Petrograd where he had gone as a regimental delegate. He now argued for the committee to be re-elected and renamed a soviet, made up of only four junior officers and 32 men. The new soldiers' soviet began to

> 'take part not only in the regiment's daily life but also on military matters . . . no decision could be made without the agreement of the soviet. Lieutenant Dzevaltovsky had such ascendancy over the soviet that he became the real leader of the regiment, whose

commander could no longer give the slightest order without first consulting him.'

In these words we see reflected the role of the committees, the key influence of a radicalised individual and the link between parts of the army and the events in big cities like Petrograd.[38]

Senior officers were acutely alive to the threat that such committees posed and their role in political organisation. For General Brusilov,

'Allowing soldiers to participate in political organisations is undoubtedly harmful, because it undermines the basic foundations of military service and introduces into military units a political element, when the army should be outside it. The interference of the army in politics is a destructive influence on its necessary discipline and inevitably distracts from its direct goal, and this will always be a threat to the firmness of state power and will weaken the stability of the state organism. The army is isolated from political influences and overtures in all states, even those with the most liberal political systems.'

For their part radicals were aware of how powerful a force the committees were in their favour. 'If there had been no army committees or if they had been deprived of most of their rights, the army would have been a plaything in the hands of the counter-revolutionary generals,' argued *Rabochii put*, a Bolshevik newspaper.[39]

Political life in the garrisons at the rear merged more easily with the revolution than for those at the front, but everywhere the connection grew. As Golovine recognised:

'Pessimism at the front was communicated to the rear by those thousands of chords which unite a modern army of many millions with the people at home. The letters to relatives, the complaints of the wounded, the tales of indignant social workers, were only, as it were, so many drips. Together they became streams of gloom which finally became an ocean of general discontent and confusion.'

But for the generals and senior officers the important issue was the impact of the rear on the front. Golovine even suggested that it was 'a social and psychological law' that 'the disintegration of an army begins in its rear'. But we might argue that it is a psychological law that generals and senior officers underestimate the interaction between the front and the rear. They prefer to see their waning authority not in terms of their own failures and that of the system, but as a 'stab in the back'.[40]

Lack of enthusiasm to fight is always talked of in terms of 'demoralisation'. 'The army is simply a vast, weary, shabby and ill-fed mob of angry men united by a common thirst for peace and by common disappointment,' according to a military report of mid-October 1917. But this assumes that a disciplined commitment to mass killings in a competitive national cause is 'moral' and refusal to do so 'demoralisation'. In fact, a refusal to fight is more complicated than that and this is reflected in its various manifestations – going over to the enemy; fraternisation; refusing to go over the top or move to the front; retreating; sabotage; attacking officers; 'malingering'; deserting, and so on. There is much uncertainty and some controversy over the scale of these in 1917. Golovine was sceptical in his evaluation of the desertion and claimed it was the Bolsheviks' 'trump card', with the total number of deserters perhaps around two million by September 1917. But contemporaries often seem to have mistaken soldiers on leave or in transport as 'deserters'. Some officers even asserted that attending soldiers' and sailors' committees was a form of desertion. But all types of resistance to continuing the war increased in 1917, albeit in disguised forms – the incidence of sickness, for example, rose dramatically by 120 per cent for men and 40 per cent for officers (reflecting the latter's better, but imperfect, discipline). It was claimed that medical officers were forced to issue mass notices for medical evacuation from the front.[41]

However, organised political parties did play a significant role in the dissolution of the armed forces. Indeed, the Russian revolution is the first major revolution in which conscious political organisations played a central role. This was not the case in February when the few members of the existing parties were often found to be 'fast asleep'.[42] But then rapid political organisation took place. It is too simple to see this in terms of the actions of one party – the Bolsheviks. Despite the tendency to call agitators 'Bolsheviks', all factions of the left and even centre parties had some input into the politicisation of the army. The Mensheviks may have peaked at some 200,000, but largest of all were the Socialist Revolutionaries with up to one million members. Both had significant support and organisation in the military. Moreover, the Bolsheviks had to vie with the Left Socialist Revolutionaries to be the most radical party. Rank-and-file newspapers, pamphlets and leaflets were published. Formal and informal discussions seemed endless, in the form of meetings, conferences and congresses. Although we might estimate that no more than 1 per cent of the soldiers were linked to a party organisation (it was probably higher in the navy) those who were could play a disproportionate role. By June, for example, the Bolsheviks claimed 26,000 members in the military and by October perhaps 50,000. In June 1917 they held their own All Party Conference of Party Organisations from the Front and Rear which called for the creation 'amongst the democratic-revolutionary elements within the army, who support and work for Social Democracy, [of] a material armed backing for the revolution and for the demands that the revolution places on the agenda'. Indeed, in the July Days in Petrograd, Bolshevik cells in the military would act to some degree independently of the party itself.[43]

The importance of political demands is captured in the Bolshevik slogan 'Bread, Peace and Land', which linked the interests of workers, peasants and soldiers. For the soldiers the key issue was peace and land. Rejecting the argument that 'he who wants a good peace must wage a good war' (Plekhanov), the Bolsheviks followed the argument set out by Lenin in April. There was an 'inseparable connection between capital and the imperialist war' and 'without the overthrow of capital it is impossible to conclude the war with a really democratic, non-oppressive peace'. But just as important for many troops was the demand for land for the peasants and, by implication, peasant soldiers. Responding to peasants' demands for land was a bridge between the town and country and the front and the rear – a bridge that could avoid the fate of the Paris Commune. As the Bolshevik Vladimir Nevsky argued, 'We must fix things so that we shall not have the experience of the French Commune where the peasantry did not understand Paris and Paris did not understand the peasantry.'[44]

The overall impact on the military can be seen in the voting of soldiers and sailors in the Constituent Assembly elections immediately after October. The Bolsheviks and the Socialist Revolutionaries, especially the left Socialist Revolutionaries and their national-based allies, swept the board, splitting the military vote roughly between them. The Bolsheviks were strongest in the Baltic Fleet (57 per cent), on the Northern Front (56 per cent) and Western Front (67 per cent). In the Black Sea Fleet, the South-Western, Romanian and Caucasian Fronts the Socialist Revolutionaries and their national-based allies were equally if not more dominant. Everywhere in the army and navy, the other parties were largely rejected.

Voting is a relatively passive act. Where war support was undermined, this could also take the form of a growing unwillingness to fight and a desire simply to go home. For others it involved a readiness to take up a more explicit fight against the existing order. This radical mood was strongest in the navy and especially at the Helsingfors (Helsinki) base and Kronstadt, close to Petrograd. Sailors from Kronstadt played an increasing role in the summer and autumn of 1917.[45] Traditionally, the navy had recruited more from literate, educated and urban centres, and naval ships and bases had some similarity to the big workplaces of Petrograd, concentrating men together at close quarters. In the army, apart from the differences between the fronts, the infantry tended to be more radical than the artillery or the cavalry. The micro-history of the revolution even allows us to trace differences between armies and units within them – the XII Northern army, for example, stands out as one of the most radical, and some regiments such as the Latvian, Siberian and *Novoladozskii* (New Lagoda) are prominent.

The revolution also had a constructive element in the form of an attempt to create a new force based on urban workers. This was the Red Guard. No less than other worker militias in other countries, its development was uneven and chaotic. But conventional armies did not appear out of thin air either – their coercive formation took place over many decades. Initially, the task of the Red Guard was simply to protect the revolution and not least the factories and workers' areas from possible counter-revolution. By April there were perhaps 10,000 and, though the numbers are only rough, by October some 20,000 in Petrograd (including a small number of Chinese railway workers which put some well-to-do into a racist frenzy) and perhaps 10,000 in Moscow with other towns with fewer. But as the Red Guard grew it began to be seen by radicals as an embryonic, larger-scale workers' militia, a new revolutionary army, 'an organisation without party' but subordinate to the soviets. While the Bolsheviks played a key role in its development, as late as the start of 1918 some 30 per cent of Red Guard commanders were non-Bolshevik, as were 50 per cent of the Red Guard itself. The Red Guard would be built on what was called 'comradely discipline', with elected officers:

The strict observation of discipline and the unconditional submission to the elected institutions is based not only on the force of blind obedience but on the consciousness of the importance and extraordinary responsibility of the tasks of the

Workers' Guard, and also on a wholly free and independent democratic organisation.[46]

Its aim would not be offensive but revolutionary defence by revolutionary means. These would centre on forms of partisan warfare rather than conventional military tactics.

COUNTER-REVOLUTION VERSUS REVOLUTION

By October 1917, owing to the scale of the collapse of the army and the navy, the officer corps was isolated. When General Alekseev went south to raise a volunteer army to fight the revolution he managed to recruit only around 4,000 men, including a disproportionate number of officers. After October both those supporting the revolution and those opposing it would need to build new armies. For the revolutionaries the immediate task was to oppose the predatory grab for land, labour and resources made by German imperialism. But soon they also faced a threat from the Allies supporting the forces of counter-revolution.

The resultant civil war wrecked the society that had made the revolution and reduced the mass of the population to penury. Too often this story is told as if all that mattered were internal Russian dynamics and cruelty on both sides. Such depoliticisation lends support to the argument that revolutions always go wrong and degenerate. A no less happy consequence is that the role of Western imperialism is minimised. But another story can be told. As the historian Christopher Read has put it:

'Russia was the first test bed for what has become standard Western (that is, initially British and French, later in the century, American) counter-revolutionary tactics based on direct armed intervention where feasible, ample funding of contras if not, and "low intensity" (providing one is not on the receiving end) economic warfare in any case.'[47]

Russia was blockaded by sea and land by 'Allied intervention'; funds were given to the White opposition; huge numbers of troops were landed on Russia's borders; supplies of munitions flowed; military advisers were sent and a general political and moral backing given to the counter-revolution. Beyond the borders of Russia too a propaganda war was fought to discredit the revolution and undermine support for it as an example of radical change. But this chapter has given a different account. Historians today sometimes say that the Russian revolution has passed from politics into history. They should know better. Politics is history and history is politics.

NOTES

1. Max Weber, *From Max Weber, Essays in Sociology*, edited H. H. Gerth and C. Wright Mills, London: Routledge, 2002, pp. 78–9; V. I. Lenin, *State and Revolution* (1917), available from the Marxist Internet Archive.
2. Carl von Clausewitz, *On War*, edited and translated M. Howard and P. Paret, Oxford: Oxford University Press, 2008, passim.
3. V. I. Lenin, *Left-Wing Communism: An Infantile Disorder* (1920), available from the Marxist Internet Archive.
4. There is now a formidable literature in English on the history of the Russian military and the revolution, which can only be partly drawn on here. Two popular studies are by Ward Rutherford, *The Russian Army in World War I*, London: Cremonesi, 1975; and Nik Cornish, *The Russian Army and the First World War*, Stroud: The History Press, 2006, and more briefly his (with Andrei Karachtchouk) *The Russian Army 1914–1918*, Oxford: Osprey Publishing, 2001. Norman Stone's iconoclastic *The Eastern Front*, London: Penguin, 2nd edition 1998 is still central. For those who read Russian the literature is vast and some is easily accessible on the website regiment.ru/index.htm. In terms of the issues discussed here Brian Taylor, *Politics and the Russian Army. Civil–Military Relations, 1689–2000*, Cambridge: Cambridge University Press, 2003 offers a top-down perspective.
5. Turner, *Politics and the Russian Army*, pp. 61, 72.
6. Joshua Sanborn, *Drafting the Russian Nation. Military Conscription, Total War and Mass Politics, 1905–1925*, DeKalb, IL: Northern Illinois University Press, 2002.
7. Leon Trotsky, *1905* (1907), available at the Marxist Internet Archive.
8. Turner, *Politics and the Russian Army*, p. 73; J. Adelman, *The Revolutionary Armies*, Westport, CT: Greenwood Press, 1980, *passim*.
9. Nicholas Golovine, *The Russian Army in the World War*, New Haven, CT: Yale University Press, 1931.
10. See also Mike Haynes and Rumy Husan, *A Century of State Murder? Death and Policy in Twentieth-Century Russia*, London: Pluto Press, 2003.
11. Melissa Stockdale, '"My death for the motherland is happiness": women, patriotism, and soldiering in Russia's Great War, 1914–1917', *American Historical Review*, 109(1), February 2004, pp. 78–116.
12. Golovine, *The Russian Army*, pp. 64–6, 72.
13. Author's calculations from Golovine, *The Russian Army*.
14. Jamie H. Cockfield, *With Snow on Their Boots: The Tragic Odyssey of the Russian Expeditionary Force in France during World War 1*, New York: St. Martin's Griffin, 1997.
15. There is a growing literature on this. See Irina Sirotkina, 'The politics of etiology: shell shock in the Russian Army 1914–1918', in Angela Brintlinger and Ilya Vinitsky, eds., *Madness and the Mad in Russian Culture*, Toronto: University of Toronto Press, 2007, pp. 117–29; Laura L. Phillips, 'Gendered dis/ability: perspectives from the treatment of psychiatric casualties in Russia's early twen-

tieth-century wars', *Social History of Medicine*, 20(2), 2007, pp. 333–50; and Jan Plamper, 'Fear: soldiers and emotion in early twentieth-century Russian military psychology', *Slavic Review*, 66(2), Summer 2009, pp. 259–83.

16. Quoted in Rutherford, *The Russian Army in World War I*, p. 160.

17. Golovine, *The Russian Army*, pp. 145–6.

18. J. Reed, *War in Eastern Europe. Travels through the Balkans in 1915* (1916), London: Phoenix, 1994, p. 87.

19. M. Farbman, *Russia and the Struggle for Peace*, London: Allen & Unwin, 1918, pp. 81–8; J. Sanborn, 'The genesis of Russian warlordism: violence and governance during the First World War and Civil War', *Contemporary European History*, 19(3), 2010, pp. 195–213.

20. P. Gatrell, *A Whole Empire Walking: Refugees in Russia During World War I*, Bloomington, IN: Indiana University Press, 1999.

21. Stone, *The Eastern Front*, pp. 168–9.

22. Turner, *Politics and the Russian Army*, pp. 73–4, 82; Golovine, *The Russian Army*, p. 66; Rutherford, *The Russian Army in World War I*, p. 84.

23. Adelman, *The Revolutionary Armies*, p. 114.

24. Quoted in Golovine, *The Russian Army*, pp. 245–6.

25. F. Raskolnikov, *Kronstadt and Petrograd in 1917* (1925), London: New Park, 1982, p. 9.

26. Farbman, *Russia and the Struggle for Peace*, p. 101; Allan Wildman, *The End of the Russian Imperial Army: The Old Army and the Soldiers' Revolt (March–April)*, Princeton, NJ: Princeton University Press, 1980.

27. Leon Trotsky, *History of the Russian Revolution* (1932), available at the Marxist Internet Archive.

28. Quoted in Golovine, *The Russian Army*, p. 251.

29. Leon Trotsky, *History of the Russian Revolution* (1932), available at the Marxist Internet Archive.

30. Quoted in William Henry Chamberlin, *The Russian Revolution, 1917–1921*, Volume 1, New York: Grosset & Dunlap, 1965.

31. Wildman, *The End of the Russian Imperial Army, passim*; M. Ferro, 'The Russian soldier in 1917: undisciplined, patriotic and revolutionary', *Slavic Review*, 30, 1971, pp. 483–512.

32. Quoted in M. Farbman, *The Russian Revolution & the War*, London: National Council for Civil Liberties, 1917, p. 42.

33. Lousie Heenan, *Russian Democracy's Fatal Blunder: The Summer Offensive of 1917*, Westport, CT: Greenwood Press, 1987.

34. Ferro, 'The Russian soldier in 1917', p. 510.

35. Allan Wildman, 'Officers of the general staff and the Kornilov movement', in E. R. Frankel, J. Frankel and B. Knei-Paz, eds., *Revolution in Russia: Reassessments of 1917*, Cambridge: Cambridge University Press, 1992.

36. Leon Trotsky, *History of the Russian Revolution*, available at the Marxist Internet Archive.

37. The British liaison officer General Knox was given a spuriously accurate figure of 84,949 members of committees on the South-Western Front alone. Golovine, *The Russian Army*, p. 124.

38. The indictment is translated in M. Ferro, *The Bolshevik Revolution. A Social History of the Russian Revolution*, London: Routledge, 1985, pp. 77–80.

39. Quoted in Taylor, *Politics and the Russian Army*, p. 100; L. N. Tropov, 'Soldiers' committees of central Russia in the spring of 1917', *Russian Studies in History*, 15(4), Spring 1977, pp. 63–92.
40. Golovine, *The Russian Army*, pp. 225, 249, 252.
41. Ibid., pp. 281, 101.
42. Sergei Mstislavskii, *Five Days Which Transformed Russia*, London: Hutchinson, 1988, p. 112.
43. A. Rabinowitch, *Prelude to Revolution. The Petrograd Bolsheviks and the July 1917 Uprising*, Bloomington, IN: Indiana University Press; 1968; A. Rabinowitch, *The Bolsheviks Come to Power*, London: New Left Books, 1979.
44. Trotsky, *History of the Russian Revolution*; J. Ellis, *Armies in Revolution*, London: Croom Helm, 1973, p. 169.
45. Cornish, *The Russian Army and the First World War*, pp. 203–13; E. Mawdsley, *The Russian Revolution and the Baltic Fleet: War and Politics, February 1917– April 1918*, London: Macmillan, 1978.
46. Rex Wade, *Red Guards and Workers' Militias in the Russian Revolution*, Stanford, CA: Stanford University Press, 1984.
47. Christopher Read, *From Tsar to Soviets*, London: UCL Press, 1996, p. 292.

BIBLIOGRAPHY/FURTHER READING

Nik Cornish, *The Russian Army and the First World War*, Stroud: The History Press, 2006.

F. Raskolnikov, *Kronstadt and Petrograd in 1917* (1925), London: New Park, 1982.

R. Reese, ed., *The Russian Imperial Army 1796–1917*, Aldershot: Ashgate, 2006.

Allan Wildman, *The End of the Russian Imperial Army*, Volumes 1 and 2, Princeton, NJ: Princeton University Press, 1980 and 1987.

2
An Army in Revolt: Germany 1918–19

Volkhard Mosler

At the end of the First World War the German army consisted of nine million men, most of whom were conscripts. The death toll in the conflict had been two million, and another 2.6 million were wounded or affected mentally. Overall, nine million men had lost their lives in an unprecedented industrial slaughter.

In 1917, two events heralded the defeat of Germany and the end of the war. One was the Russian revolution in the east; the other was America's entry into the war. At first it seemed that the Russian revolution would improve the Kaiser's prospect of victory. But in fact the victory of the Bolsheviks in October 1917 and the establishment of the workers' republic in Russia rebounded on Germany with a vengeance. The morale of the German soldiers, who had watched a revolution bring an end to war, even if it was in the 'enemy camp', was profoundly affected, and this 'disease' infected the troops on the Western and Southern Fronts when they were moved westward. After all, the arguments for the 'defence of Germany and the Fatherland' against a reactionary Russian Tsarism had played a crucial part in winning workers to support for the war. August Bebel (1868–1913), the veteran leader of the German Socialist Party, the SPD, and its highest political authority, had said, 'even in his old age he would pick up a gun to fight the Russian Tsar'. So the end of Tsarism left an ideological vacuum in the minds of ordinary German soldiers. And with America's entry into the war, the balance of forces tipped in favour of the Allies.

WORKERS AND THE ARMY

Before the war, the German army had some 650,000 troops. As a conscript army, all young men had to serve in the army or the reserve for two years. With rapid industrialisation and the growth of the working class the SPD had grown over the previous 30 years to become the largest workers' party in the world. In 1882 there were about ten million workers in all industries (including agriculture and forestry). Thirty years later, in 1912, there were nearly 18 million, and 55.9 per cent of those were industrial workers. By 1914 two-thirds of all Germans lived in towns and the whole population had grown from 41 to 64 million between 1871 and 1912.[1] By 1914, the SPD had 1.1 million members. Its trade unions had a total membership of 2.6 million and 4.25 million men above the age of 25 (30 per cent of the electorate) had voted for it in the elections of 1912.

It would be reasonable to assume that the social composition of the army had changed as the population itself had changed. But this was not the case prior to the war. The elite of the German empire were very concerned about 'the enemy within', and there were in fact detailed plans to exclude the working class from the army and the middle class from the ranks of officers. Soldiers were not allowed to go to bars frequented by left-wing workers, and a decree of 1890 had said that any conscript who had had contact with the SPD should be reported to the district recruiting office. There was also a plan to abolish the conscript army in the event of civil war with the left and rebuild it as a small, well-paid professional force. So it was that in 1911, 64 per cent of all recruits came from rural villages with fewer than 2,000 inhabitants, even though this sector made up no more than 40 per cent of the population as a whole. By that time 23 per cent of the population lived in big cities, yet only 6 per cent of ordinary soldiers came from them. The officer corps was kept similarly free of middle-class members and was restricted largely to members of the old aristocracy.[2]

An exception, however, was the navy, where the proportion of workers was much higher than in the army. In 1929 the *Illustrated History of the German Labour Movement* explained that the operation of such a complicated machine as a modern warship needed qualified men. Thus sailors were mainly recruited from the industrial working class: 'It is no coincidence that just as in Russia, in Germany it was in the Navy in 1917 that the flag of rebellion was first raised.'[3]

The constant fear of the military and political elites of the penetration of socialist elements into the army conflicted increasingly with Germany's imperialist war plans. By 1887, the military expert Frederick Engels warned that

'the most likely war Prussia-Germany will be facing is a world war, and indeed a world war of unprecedented severity. Eight to ten million soldiers will kill each other, and the consequence would be the ravages of the Thirty Years' War compressed into three or four years and spread across the continent.'[4]

The coming war would be a world war which would consume huge amounts of material and people.

With the annexation of Alsace-Lorraine in the war of 1870–71 by Otto von Bismarck, war with France in the west became inevitable. Karl Marx predicted in a letter to the German socialists that, as a consequence of the exploitative peace of 1871, there would be a war on two fronts: with Russia in the east and France in the west. 'Let's take Alsace and Lorraine,' he wrote, 'then France and Germany will be at war with Russia.' And just as Marx had foreseen, the end would be the destruction of the German empire.[5]

The military planning for a European war, with Germany/Prussia and Austria-Hungary against Tsarist Russia in the east and against England and France in the west was completed in 1905. The Schlieffen Plan (named after its author, General Alfred von Schlieffen) assumed a surprise victory against France in the west, freeing enough troops to defeat the Tsarist empire. The surprise victory, however, depended on the substantial military superiority of German troops, which would have required a quadrupling of the size of the army, and that would only be possible with the involvement of young men from the urban industrial working class of the cities, regardless of their political loyalties. This conflicted with the concerns of the conservative military command, who feared the contamination of socialist forces and a dilution of the officer class. The social and political reliability of the army seemed to them to be more important than its numerical superiority. For example, in the spring of 1914 Germany possessed over 748,000 soldiers, while France had over 750,000 and Russia more than 1.4 million.

SOCIAL DEMOCRACY AND THE ARMY

When it came to war between Prussia and France in 1870–71, two socialist deputies, Wilhelm Liebknecht and August Bebel, voted in the North German Reichstag against the granting of war credits; under their influence there were protests by the fledgling labour movement against the annexation of Alsace-Lorraine. In 1872 both men were tried for treason and sentenced to two years' imprisonment.

In 1907, Karl Liebknecht (1871–1918), the son of Wilhelm Liebknecht, in a pamphlet titled *Militarism and Anti-militarism*, called on the Social Democratic Party to conduct a special campaign among the troops of the Imperial Army against imperialism, war and the abuse of soldiers. The state reaction was immediate and violent. The pamphlet was confiscated and Karl Liebknecht, like his father, was sentenced to 18 months in prison for high treason. In his speech to the first International Conference of Socialist Youth Organisations in Stuttgart, he had argued that 'capitalist expansion . . . will bring individual capitalist states into increasingly fierce competition with each other. The planet is already too small for them and they stand chest to chest, eye to eye, armed to the teeth.' The basic feature of capitalism, he said, is 'not you and me, but you *or* me.'[6]

His pamphlet ended with a challenge:

'The proletarian youth must be systematically inflamed with class consciousness and hate against militarism. Youthful enthusiasm will take hold of the hearts of the young workers inspired by such agitation. These young workers belong to Social-Democracy, to Social-Democratic anti-militarism. If everyone carries out his task, they must and will be won. *He who has the young people has the army.*'[7]

Liebknecht's conviction shows that the ruling elite of the empire took this challenge from the left wing of social democracy seriously. The presence of Gustav Noske (1868–1946) in the Reichstag, however, showed how far the defenders of the capitalist system had already penetrated the ranks of the workers' party. Liebknecht's assertion that 'He who has the young people has the army' needed an additional clause: 'He who has social democracy has the youth.' Liebknecht's application to the SPD party congress in Mannheim (1906) to establish a special 'committee on anti-militarist propaganda' by the party leadership did not win a majority. Not only the right wing but the party leader, August Bebel, opposed it.

A year later, at the Essen party congress, Karl Liebknecht grabbed his later co-executioner and the first Defence Minister of the Weimar Republic, Noske, who in his maiden speech in the Reichstag made a commitment to homeland defence and praised the courage of Germany. This was a reversal of the party's previous rejection of militarism and colonialism from the perspective of international working-class solidarity. Social democracy still held ostensibly to the principles of class struggle and internationalism. The representatives of the SPD had – albeit reluctantly – supported a statement by the International Socialist Congress of Stuttgart (in August 1907) in which the parties of the Second International undertook 'to exploit with all their might the economic and political crisis created by war to arouse the population and to hasten the overthrow of capitalist rule'. But in the discussion of the resolution Bebel, for the SPD leadership, prevented the inclusion of concrete actions such as the mass strike.[8] Noske's commitment to a 'strong defence of Germany' stood in absolute contradiction to the anti-war resolution of Stuttgart.

The impact of the Social Democrats as a mass party with almost one million members in the years before the outbreak of war is demonstrated in well-attended mass meetings by Rosa Luxemburg against the growing threat of war. In Frankfurt (1913), she had exclaimed: 'If we are expected to turn our murder weapons against our French and other brothers, then we say, We will not.' In February 1914 she was sentenced to one year's imprisonment for that speech. Her speech in her own defence against imperialism and warmongering reached millions of workers. In another speech, she had complained about the daily mistreatment of soldiers common in the German army. The Prussian Minister of War, speaking 'on behalf of the entire officer corps', complained that he had been slandered and brought charges against her. The socialist press called on its readers to corroborate Luxemburg's accusation of abuse. Within days thousands of reports were received from soldiers and former soldiers. When the trial opened, the defence flooded the court with evidence, the prosecutor then retreated and the trial was adjourned *sine die*. In fact, it never took place. The Social Democrats celebrated the withdrawal of the prosecution as a victory. And it showed how great was the influence of social democracy in the army and the navy at that time, despite the policy of active exclusion of social democratic youth from the ranks of the armed forces.

Conversely, however, the choice of Friedrich Ebert (1871–1925) as party leader in 1913 showed that the bourgeoisie's influence on social democracy over the years had grown. In the debate of 1907 he had emerged as a strong supporter of German colonial policy and he was used at the time to rein in the 'Young Guard' youth organisation, among whom Liebknecht's anti-war speeches and writings had been very well received.

The SPD had changed; in two decades it had moved from being the revolutionary workers' party to a bourgeois reformist workers' party. The historian Ulrich Wehler sees the explanation for this development in the steep economic recovery between 1895 and

1913. The GNP grew annually during this period by 3.3 per cent, three times the average during the previous era of the long depression (1874–94). The average hourly wage of industrial workers had increased rapidly in these years of rapid growth by 54 per cent and the working day fell from 16–17 hours in 1879 to 9–10 hours by 1913.

Wehler summarises the political consequences for the SPD thus: 'The continuing increase in real wages is the key feature of the period. Without it, we cannot understand the ascent of social democratic reformism and the failure of radical ideology and politics.' The number of trade unionists belonging to the Confederation of Social Democratic Trade Unions (General German Trade Union Confederation) increased during the same period by several hundred thousand to 2.6 million. The right wing of the party had its mass base in the trade unions. It was the trade union wing of the SPD that blocked Luxemburg's call for support for the mass political strike at the Mannheim congress in 1905. The separation of the trade unions from the political struggle for socialism was perhaps the most important feature of the new reformism.

1914: THE PROLETARIANISATION OF THE ARMY

Military needs rendered futile all attempts by the Supreme Command of the pre-war period to limit the recruitment of socialist-dominated industrial workers into the army. In agreeing to the war in August 1914, the leaders of the SPD and trade unions had also allayed the military command's fear of socialist troublemakers.

Within weeks of the outbreak of war, the peacetime strength of 761,000 German soldiers increased to an initial three million. In the end the army in the field numbered five million soldiers at the front, while a further 1–2 million remained in reserve. Of 15.6 million able-bodied German men aged between 17 and 50, around 85 per cent, or 13.2 million, served in the military. At the outbreak of war, the proportion of urban workers was already 57 per cent of the total and thus they made up a higher proportion of recruits than other classes, reaching more than two-thirds of the total recruitment.

The belligerent countries as a whole provided 74 million soldiers, 50 million fighting for the Allies and 24 million for the Central Powers. The German forces suffered 466,000 deaths per year, totalling more than two million overall. Each month nearly 3 per cent of the total were lost, 2.4 per cent of them wounded, 0.4 per cent dead or missing. 32 per cent of all soldiers were wounded in the course of the war and nearly nine million were taken prisoner.

There are no exact figures on how many of the dead and wounded were workers. In close cooperation with the military recruitment offices, the right-wing SPD leaders in the districts ensured that members of the party's left wing were recruited. That enabled the right wing of the party, especially in the early war years, to bring the party at all levels under their control. Control of the widely read party newspaper *Vorwärts* had been removed from the party's left wing by the military authorities and the SPD leadership acting together. The spokesman of the revolutionary shop stewards, Richard Müller, who in 1917–18 worked as a lathe operator in AEG, one of the largest metal factories in Berlin, was drafted into the army after the strikes of April 1917 and January 1918, while others, like Kostja and Maxim, the sons of Clara Zetkin, lost their lives at the front. Conversely, the spokesmen and officials of the 'social-patriotic' wing of the SPD were 'requested' by their employers, in other words exempted from military service, 'while every politically suspect worker was immediately dressed in the field grey'.[9]

Between the arms industry and the Supreme Army Command there was constant argument over the number of reserves. The staffing needs of the military and the economy could not be satisfied simultaneously from the limited numbers of men available. A crisis in the defence industry due to a lack of skilled workers led to the fact that in 1916 two million men were exempt from military service. The result was that a very large proportion of the workforce in certain highly skilled groups of workers with a key role in production did not go to the front. This was particularly important for the group of revolutionary shop stewards in the Berlin metal industry, most of whom were turners, an elite group of skilled workers.

By 1916 the membership of the Social Democrats was down by 64 per cent in comparison with 1914. With the split between the SPD and USPD in 1917, the SPD was left with only 170,000 members as opposed to 100,000 in the USPD. Equally dramatic was the decline of union membership, from almost 2.6 million in 1913 to 967,000 in the third year of the war. The major losses occurred at the beginning of the war and newly hired women workers and unskilled youth could not offset them. The dramatic loss of members also meant a serious decline in working-class consciousness. This was reflected in the simultaneous rise of new forms of organisation, such as the *Arbeiterrräten* (workers' councils). Their unconditional support for the war meant that they had no means of fighting the deepening poverty on the 'home front'.

But there are no precise data to tell us how many members withdrew out of disillusionment and how many were among the war dead. A report by the SPD Rödermark branch stated: 'Many branches have stopped functioning, because all their members were at the front.'[10] The fear of being drawn into the war was intimidating and paralysed many workplace activists. After each strike wave hundreds of thousands of activists were inducted into the army, while others were held in military prisons; in either case the likely outcome was death or injury.

THE DIALECTICS OF ECONOMIC AND POLITICAL CLASS STRUGGLE

The official policy of the SPD against the growing threat of war had been increasingly ambivalent since 1907. On the one hand, opposition to war was a consistent theme of Social Democratic foreign policy. The Basle Congress of the Socialist International in 1912 declared its opposition to the impending war and its support for proletarian internationalism. Fourteen days before the outbreak of war, on 3 August 1914, *Vorwärts*, the central organ of German social democracy, published a rousing anti-war statement that ended: 'We do not want war! Down with war! Long live international solidarity!'

With the first shot, however, the SPD abandoned this stance in favour of a policy of 'national defence'. The leadership of the SPD insisted that it had not wanted war, but now that it was an 'inescapable fact' the question had become 'not whether we are for or against the war, but whether today we provide the necessary funds for the defence of the country'.[11] The party of the working class could not 'leave the fatherland in the lurch at this hour of danger'. Subsequent statements by the SPD on the war ceased to emphasise the purely defensive character of the war. The cautious, guarded tone of the new policy showed the dilemma the party leadership were in. Yesterday they had organised mass protests against the war; today they were calling on the masses to achieve victory. Müller, who later became leader of the Berlin workers' councils, was at that time spokesman for 8,600 members of the German Metalworkers' Union. He wrote in 1924 about the mood in the working class as the war began: 'It wasn't nationalist euphoria that prevailed, on the contrary, workers and bosses were very reserved about it.'[12]

Ulrich Wehler described the mood of the working class at the time in similar terms: 'Instead of rejoicing, there was a prevailing anxiety and depression, fear and even despair. Police reports are clear as to the depressed mood in the Berlin working-class neighborhoods.' The prevailing mood in some parts of the farming and rural communities was more oppositional than in the cities, for the army undermined the livelihood of small peasant farmers who, especially in the south of the country, accounted for the vast majority of agriculture. They not only took away essential workers, but also horses as draft animals. It was no coincidence, wrote Fröhlich and other witnesses, 'that even in the rural areas of Bavaria, a strong dissatisfaction with the war developed relatively early'.

The mood in August 1914 was 'anything but irrational joy. Reactions varied according to class, from the frenzied cheers of the educated middle-class elites to the fearful anxiety felt by the majority . . .'[13] Of course, once war had been declared, the large majority of all classes hoped that the promises of the Emperor's military experts would prove correct and that the war in the west would end with a quick victory over France, as it had in 1870–71. On the railway carriages soldiers had written in chalk, 'See you at Christmas', and that was also the expectation of the Military High Command as set out in the Schlieffen Plan and the general expectation of how long the war would last. However, things did not go to plan. The military offensive through neutral Belgium was arrested 70 km outside Paris on the Marne. A bloody seven-day battle followed, which cost 300,000 lives and ended with the decisive defeat of Germany on the Western Front. The brilliant Schlieffen Plan had failed, and the war on two fronts would now become trench warfare. Germany's only chance of winning the war was lost by the end of the first month. The war followed a simple logic: the longer it lasted, the more significant was the economic and hence political superiority of the Allied Powers – Russia, France, England and Italy in 1915 and, from 1917, the United States.

Millions of soldiers were living in wastelands of mud, in trenches and dugouts which they shared with rats, fleas and lice, and where they vegetated like moles.

By Christmas 1914 the mood was already changing; the first fraternisation between German and French soldiers took place during the Christmas and New Year holidays. In April 1915 the German army command used mustard gas for the first time; but the poisonous clouds did not usher in a breakthrough. The great battles at Verdun and the Somme (1916) cost nearly two million lives. At the Somme, the German defenders lost 455,000 soldiers, while 400,000 British and 200,000 French soldiers on the attacker's side were killed. The front moved forward by about 2 km over a 50-km stretch.

Death, injury, trauma, barbarous cold in the east, a ceaseless struggle with mud in the west, sickness, hunger, mounds of dead and wounded, burying the remains of battered bodies, mass hysteria under enemy bombardment, panic at gas attacks, raids by night patrols – all led to the slow disintegration of morale, especially after the great battles of 1916. Open strikes and mutinies, which broke out first in the French army in 1917, only erupted in the German army in 1918, though they had occurred in the German navy as early as August 1917. Slowly, this huge army began to fragment into its class elements: 'The reality of life at the front destroyed the ideological illusion of the community of the trenches . . . in fact the social inequalities of peacetime were now penetrating life in the trenches.'[14] The military futility of the war was coupled with intensifying class antagonisms in the trenches.

As the war continued, the mass of soldiers suffered increasing shortages, but not so the officers. The number of complaints increased by leaps and bounds, so much so that the Minister of War addressed a letter to the army generals: 'There are endless lawsuits and complaints about the luxurious life of officers as opposed to the mass of soldiers in the field.' The minister then described the menus in the officers' messes, which had been sent to members of parliament, and compared them with what the men were eating on the same day. 'The longer the campaign lasts,' the minister complained, 'the worse becomes the immoderate drinking of many officers while for the ranks it is often impossible to obtain even the simplest drinks.'

The dramatic deterioration of provisions to the soldiers as opposed to what was available to the officer corps stood in stark contradiction to the prevailing ideology of the national community and the patriotism of the war effort in which the whole German people would sacrifice themselves for the common good. In their short home leaves, the soldiers were told the whole truth. They saw the poverty, hunger and wretchedness their own families were suffering.

HUNGER AND MISERY ON THE HOME FRONT

The war had exposed the proletarianisation of the army. The vast majority of the male working class was drafted in the first two years of the war. Their wives were also absorbed into the great arms factories. From 1913 to 1918 the proportion of women in the working class rose from 22 to 34 per cent. From 1917 onwards they were becoming a majority in many of the key wartime defence plants. Hardship and the struggle for survival drove working-class women into dangerous work for starvation wages. Women workers in Berlin who had earned 128 marks a month in 1913 were being paid just 30 marks for themselves and a child by 1916–17, an amount which just covered their rent.

The conversion of the entire economy to war production, the huge waste of raw materials and foodstuffs by the unproductive war machine, the successful naval blockade by the Allies and the use of the unskilled labour of women, youth and prisoners of war, together with a growing shortage of labour more generally, produced economic constraints not only in industry but also in transport and agriculture. Social production fell by 60 per cent during the war and personal real incomes declined by at least 30 per cent but more often by 40 per cent. The daily calorie intake, which had been 3,400 per capita before the war, was reduced by two-thirds and by 1917 had dropped to 1,000. Government rationing led to the development of a flourishing black market, which absorbed over the last two years of the war a third of all dairy products and half of all meat products. Black market prices were on average ten times official prices. This denied the entire working class access to such products. At the same time, company profits rose by 50 per cent, and in key defence sectors by 800 per cent, over the peacetime average. The growing poverty contrasted with the luxurious life enjoyed in high society circles. Rosa Luxemburg captured the glaring disparity in the memorable phrase: 'The dividends rise as the workers fall.'

The General Command meeting at Magdeburg in July 1918 described the political consequences of the situation: 'The great rift between rich and poor is growing wider. Among the poorer population there has grown up a malicious hatred of the rich and the so-called war profiteers. We can only hope that this will not lead again to a dreadful explosion.' It was not so much the ownership of wealth itself that produced this reaction as 'the fact that some sections of the population . . . surround themselves with every luxury while the majority of the population starve'.

FROM STRIKE TO MUTINY

The political elites of Imperial Germany before the war were not sure how the social democratic masses would react to the war. According to the original plans of the War Department, the new central executive authority under the state of siege, all socialist members of parliament were to be detained. On 31 July new instructions came from the War Department to the General Command, which read: 'According to reliable information, the Social Democratic Party's firm intention is to behave in a way as befits all Germans under the present circumstances, so there will be no arrests.'[15] No arrests were made.

A broad coalition of the military government with the informal participation of social democracy was formed. The military informed the SPD leadership about important decisions. The unions announced on 2 August the prohibition of all strikes and a general no-strike pledge for the duration of the war; the truce was described as 'social peace',[16] but it allowed a thinly veiled military dictatorship to be established. A state of siege was declared across the whole of Germany. The executive gave the commanding officer in each of the 24 military zones virtually dictatorial powers.[17] In 1916 the Social Democrats voted for the Law of National Service which abolished the free choice of employment and made it compulsory for all males between the ages of 17 and 60 to work. The Act provided for the establishment of national arbitration committees, which recognised the unions for the first time.

Despite this the relationship between the monarchist government and socialists was strained and marked by mutual distrust. The military mistrusted the vast army of workers with their mass organisations – trade unions, youth organisations, consumer cooperatives, sports clubs, etc. They were well aware that the leaders of the SPD and the free trade unions could not maintain absolute control the longer the war dragged on. After all, for decades these leaders had advocated something very different – ideas of class struggle and internationalism, though these had now been engulfed by a wave of nationalism and talk of a 'national community'. Yet they had not completely disappeared.

Unlike the middle classes, the workers' patriotism was wafer-thin from the beginning. After hopes for a quick victory had faded following the defeat on the Marne, scepticism rapidly spread. Karl Retzlaw, who worked in a shoe factory in 1914, wrote: 'Every day at my work colleagues are asking behind closed doors, what Liebknecht will do, as if it was obvious that you could expect something of him without showing solidarity with him.'[18] Liebknecht did not disappoint the hopes placed in him. On 3 December he was the only deputy in the Reichstag to vote against the war credits. Thus, the SPD leaders' 'truce' had been broken, even if only by a single vote, and millions of young workers knew about it. The ranks of the army and especially the navy, with its high proportion of technicians and skilled workers, were not only largely proletarian in social composition after the outbreak of war, they were also basically social democrats.[19]

The immediate effects of war were similar everywhere in Europe. Trotsky described it in his *History of the Russian Revolution*: 'At the first sound of the drum the revolutionary movement died down. The more active layers of the workers were mobilised . . .'[20] But the carnage on the battlefields and impoverishment on the home front ensured that the truce slowly but surely broke down. As Trotsky described it in Russia, so it was in Berlin, Paris and Glasgow: 'Their indignation finds expression first of all in food disturbances, sometimes rising to the height of local riots. Women, old men and boys, in the market or on the open square, feel bolder and more independent than the workers on military duty in the factories.'

A crisis in agriculture due to lack of fertilisers and labour, together with a failure to maintain machinery, meant that agricultural production in Germany fell by over a third. In 1915, famine led to the first demonstrations of women and young people, and looting of shops. 'The number of housewives who are openly expressing their discontent is growing all the time,' the Berlin police reported in early 1916, 'and in the lower classes there is serious anger.' The food riots during the winter of 1915–16 were the beginning of a chain of economic and political strikes and eventually mutinies in the army, which culminated in the revolution of 9 October.

WORKERS' STRIKES AND SOLDIERS' RIOTS

In the *Illustrated History of the German Revolution*, Paul Fröhlich and others vividly describe why the economic and then the political mass strikes prepared the soldiers for 1917–18:

> 'The class struggle of the proletariat passes through a whole series of stages until it culminates in armed rebellion. The revolutionary struggle of the soldiers and sailors of the imperial army did not have that much leeway. The preliminary stages – the demands for

better food and better treatment and food are soon surpassed; as the revolutionary movement in the army becomes more political it is immediately confronted with the question of insurrection. The worker may refuse to work and thereby slow production down. But if the soldier strikes and refuses to obey orders, he cannot just stand still. He will either be shot or he will shoot first.'

Two major political obstacles had to be overcome: first, the fear of repression by the military governments and – more importantly – the usual loyalty to party discipline of the social democratic workers and soldiers. The spontaneous demonstrations against hunger paved the way for the first major political (1916) and economic (1917) strikes.

Liebknecht's voice against the war in parliament on 3 December 1914 was to lead to the formation of the Spartacus League. A group of revolutionary Marxists, including Liebknecht, Luxemburg, Franz Mehring, Clara Zetkin, Kate Duncker, Ernst Meyer and others formed the 'International' group in 1915, which a year later became the Spartacus League. A second, much larger pacifist opposition movement coalesced around two members of the Reichstag, Hugo Haase and George Ledebour, and met for the first time on 29 December 1915 with 20 members, when it voted against further war credits. Finally, under the pressure of the growing discontent among the working class, a separate parliamentary group was formed in April 1916 with 18 of the 102 SPD members of parliament. A year later, in April 1917, the Independent Social Democratic Party of Germany (USPD) was proclaimed.

In addition to the spontaneous demonstrations of hunger and food riots the political opposition to the war began to transform; initially it met behind closed doors and later took to the streets. In 1915 there were several small political demonstrations against the war. On 1 May 1916 the revolutionary left organised a series of demonstrations against war – in Dresden, Jena, Hanau and especially in Berlin itself, where about 10,000 workers demonstrated on the Potsdamer Platz near the Parliament. It was headed by Karl Liebknecht, who was immediately arrested when he shouted: 'Down with war! Down with the government!'

In his defence speech in court, he cited Bonaparte – 'Better war than rebellion' – but called for the slogan to be turned around: 'Better rebellion than war.'[21] The presence of Liebknecht had a lasting effect. 'After this first of May,' wrote Karl Retzlaw, 'the discussions [in his company AEG] were now more openly about our disappointment and bitterness. During breaks we discussed and complained . . . and there was much more sympathy for Liebknecht and his claims.'[22]

The real breakthrough for the mass movement came when the shop stewards of the Berlin administrative office of the Metalworkers Union called for a political strike against the two and a half years prison sentence on Liebknecht (later increased to four years; he also lost his seat in the Reichstag). Their spokesman, Richard Müller, had already declared at the first meeting of the Metalworkers Union after the war began in 1914, in his capacity as spokesman for the Berlin turners, that they would not support the truce.[23] In fact, there was a series of smaller strikes over wages and working conditions in 1914–16. On 28 June 1916 there was a strike call from the stewards.

In Berlin alone, 55,000 workers went on strike in the munitions factories in Braunschweig and the workers in all the big companies in the Bremen shipyard also struck. The strike was brutally suppressed; many strikers were immediately arrested and sent to the front. While the Spartacus League was able to organise a demonstration of 10,000, its influence did not extend to being able to call a strike, so it depended on the support of the stewards. A call from the Spartacus League for mass strikes against the re-arrest of Rosa Luxemburg in August 1916 was unsuccessful; the stewards had not supported the call. Although Liebknecht's call for a second strike was unsuccessful, the 'Liebknecht strike' marked a turning point. Shop stewards now had to go beyond the terrain of labour disputes and enter with confidence the field of 'big politics'.

The large demonstrations increased the confidence of all opposition activists and intensified the factional struggles within the SPD, leading to the formation of the USPD. The Spartacus League and the Revolutionary Shop Stewards joined the new party of the masses; the Spartacus League, however, retained its organisational and political independence. The unconditional supporters of the war in the SPD had now lost their hegemony over the working class, and the elites of the empire could no longer be sure of their control of the soldiers and workers in the trenches and in the workplaces.

After the great famine of winter 1916–17 (the 'turnip winter'), following the outbreak of the Russian revolution in February 1917 and one week after the founding of the USPD, the Revolutionary Shop Stewards considered the time ripe to launch a new mass strike. On 15 April the daily bread ration was cut. Stewards again called for a strike, this time involving about 300,000 workers in several major cities (Berlin, Leipzig, Halle, Magdeburg, Brunswick, Bremen). At the founding congress of the USPD one week before the strike, representatives of the various centres had met and agreed. This time a 'bread strike', with purely economic aims, became political because of the arrest of Müller two days earlier. Now the demand was for his release and return to work.

The impact of the strike was such that the union leadership had to change tactics. For the first time they took on the demands of the strikers and negotiated with the Army High Command. The government then promised a full bread ration, the Supreme Command prohibited the arrest of strikers and Müller was released. Adolf Cohen, the chairman of the Berlin Metalworkers Union, was then able to meet with the stewards and win a slim majority to end the strike.

A significant minority, however (about 50,000), continued the strike and took over the political demands of striking workers in Leipzig: the release of political prisoners, 'peace without annexations', the end of martial law and censorship, suspension of the Auxiliary Service Law, as well as universal, equal and secret suffrage, and most importantly, for the election of a workers' council of strikers on the Russian model. Ballots received by the revolutionary shop stewards in the workplace gave the union an independent basis of legitimacy. But the successful breaking of the strike as a result of Cohen's intervention meant that the strike collapsed completely within a week. That was followed by a brutal wave of repression, many strike leaders were sacked, including the majority of the Revolutionary Shop Stewards, the armaments factories were placed under military command, the workers were to be subject from now on to the same disciplinary rules as the soldiers, and they had to continue working for soldiers' pay.

Cohen's success in the vote of the General Assembly of the Metalworkers Union showed that the SPD and the Free Trade Unions had suffered a severe blow, but they were by no means broken. In June and July there was a new wave of strikes, this time with their focus mainly outside Berlin.

The last great wave of strikes before the November revolution began on 28 February, directly influenced by the Russian revolution and Russia's withdrawal from the war. It began with a demonstration of 400,000 manual workers and 180,000 white-collar workers led by the Berlin armaments factories. This time the demands were both economic and political – for peace without annexations, a central USPD demand – an end to the militarisation of the factories, the release of all political prisoners and an improved food supply. The next day, the strike spread to all major industrial centres to become a virtual general strike.

On the same day 414 workers' representatives were elected to a central strike committee which would organise and conduct the strike. This time with a large majority in favour of the strike, the key was to ensure that it did not get out of hand and that people did not leave the union. This was the origin of the workers' councils, born of the need for democratic control of the strike by the strikers themselves. Its central action committee was composed almost exclusively of the Revolutionary Shop Stewards, and women joined the picket lines for the first time, this despite the fact that they had been in the majority in the mass strikes of 1917 and 1918.

The Assembly then called on the Independent Socialists to send three representatives to the committee and on Müller's insistence the SPD was also offered three seats; the USPD still retained a majority. Yet this gave the SPD a lever to bring the strike under their control. The new council then sent a joint delegation of workers and members of parliament to negotiate with the government. The government, however, declined to negotiate with workers and the workers refused to withdraw their representatives from the delegation. By the evening the strikes had been declared illegal and a new wave of arrests began. Müller was first to be arrested but released in September 1918, while USPD members of the negotiating team were arrested and given long prison sentences by military courts. Faced with the choice of armed insurrection or ending the strike, the committee chose the latter. Their assessment was that there were enough loyal troops in Berlin to put down the rebellion by military force. The former SPD chairman and later President, Friedrich Ebert, would say in 1924 that he and his party had only joined the strike in order to end it.

In the months that followed, the debate was about the right time for the uprising.

FROM MASS STRIKE TO SOLDIERS' REBELLION

In February 1917 mass strikes in Petrograd had confronted army units, which were supposed to suppress the strikes and demonstrations. Soldiers refused to fire. Trotsky wrote: 'This was a new stage, it was the result of the strike and the growing confrontation between the workers and the army. Such a step is inevitable in any revolution.'[24]

In Germany, the strikers were working in 1917 and in January 1918 the striking workers still did not have the confidence to move on to this stage. In Russia, the dissolution of the Imperial Army into its class components had progressed after the October revolution. German and Russian forces fraternised. In 1918, there were several instances of collective refusals to fight by German troops on the Eastern Front. Concern was growing among the military leadership about the influence of Bolshevik propaganda. German defectors to the Red Army – Otto Bauer, Ernst Reuter, Tito, Bela Kun – organised German prisoners of war and distributed leaflets calling for a revolution. Of the units that were moved from the Eastern to the Western Front, no less than 10 per cent of the soldiers disappeared en route. The Supreme Command tried to take the war in a new direction, turning west, but their 'spring offensive' failed, suffering huge losses within a few weeks. It was clear now to both officers and men that the war was lost. Fresh troops from the east and those who were recruited from the defence industry arrived in a critical and negative mood. In some units the 'Reds' were already unofficially in control, even if the formal chain of command still existed. In the late summer of 1918, an undercover soldiers' strike spread throughout the German front line. Ordered to attack, the troops remained in their shelters and refused to move.

Hundreds of thousands of wounded soldiers marched back. Many went willingly into captivity. About one million deserters and 'slackers' left secretly for home. But the decisive breakthrough in the mutiny came from the navy with its high proportion of skilled workers. In August 1917 there had already been a sailors' rebellion, which was defeated. It had been prepared by small groups of men on individual warships who had distributed propaganda systematically. They were connected and there were periodic secret meetings of delegates. The network was linked politically to the Independent Socialists who had a significant influence among the sailors. Their model was the Russian sailors' councils and their goal was a strike across the whole fleet which would force the government to negotiate a peace treaty without annexations. But the plan was betrayed and a wave of arrests followed; 5,000 sailors nevertheless demonstrated, but they were unarmed and were easily overwhelmed by loyal elite units. Ten sailors were sentenced to death, and two executions were carried out (on Albin and Max Köbis Reichpietsch); dozens of others were sentenced to long prison terms. The sailors had paid dearly; their next uprising (30 October 1918) would take a different course.

WORKERS AND SOLDIERS UNITED

Mutinies had also occurred among British, Italian and French units, the largest of which was the refusal of up to 40,000 French soldiers to obey orders in the summer of 1917. These mutinies were all brutally suppressed; 49 French soldiers were executed. In the German army, in all 48 soldiers were executed for mutiny and refusal of commands.

The abortive naval strike of August 1917 was intended to be a military strike, not a signal for a workers' uprising. And the mass political strike in January 1918 had failed because the workers had shied away from a clash with the army in an armed uprising. But when is the right time for such a showdown? Fröhlich and his colleagues conclude that, 'The armed insurrection is a weapon that can only be used in certain historical situations . . . The transformation of the imperialist war into a civil war can therefore be neither the work of the workers at home alone, nor the work of the sailors and soldiers on their own.'[25]

From the summer of 1918 the prospects for a successful armed uprising were improved given the mass strike movement in January 1918, which took over all major industrial centres, and the failure of the spring offensive on the Western Front. It had been the last hope of victory for German imperialism. Strikes, food riots and mutinies in the army continued throughout the summer months. The rulers could no longer continue as before, and the oppressed masses were no longer willing to continue with business as usual.

The revolution broke out in Kiel. The war was nearing its end and the German government was beginning to discuss the possibility of peace negotiations. When the fleet was ordered to sail on the morning of 29 October, with its 80,000 sailors, the crew on several ships refused to obey. This passive resistance spread rapidly and the plan had to be repeatedly postponed. At first, the officers managed to overpower the protesting sailors, and 1,000 were arrested. The memory of the death sentences imposed on the leaders of the mutiny the previous year led to a second wave of resistance, 1,000 prisoners were freed by force and the officers disarmed.

On 2 November the insurgency spread through the country. Kiel shipyard workers joined in, and the attempted crackdown by the military failed because the soldiers were in solidarity with the workers. The first workers' and soldiers' councils were formed. On 5 November the newly elected workers' council called a general strike and the sailors occupied the shipyards. They were all wearing red hat bands and the red flag flew from the masts of the ships. In Kiel the revolution had triumphed, then the first uprising spread to the northern German coastal cities and from there to the south. Everywhere there were groups of sailors leading the workers.

There were various armed clashes, the last in the capital, Berlin, where there had been violent conflicts between the shop stewards and Müller and the representative of the Spartacus League, Karl Liebknecht. Liebknecht wanted to strike immediately, Müller wanted to prepare everything well for 11 November. But Liebknecht and the Spartacus League, with its 3,000 members, were dependent on the chairmen and Müller, who criticised Liebknecht's 'wildcat' action, while he in turn criticised Müller's conservatism and excessive caution. Finally, the advisory group called the general strike for 9 November. Coordinators had procured weapons in the weeks beforehand, so that the huge demonstrations always had a unit of armed workers at their head.

The revolution had triumphed at that moment; the old power was broken, a new one not yet built. In Berlin, as in every town, a workers' and soldiers' council was formed. Next, the SPD and USPD took over the national government (as a 'Council of People's Representatives'), in consultation with the councils and the General Headquarters (GHQ). The old power, as it turned out, did not have a force of its own. Two attempts (made on 6 and 24 December) to crush the revolution using elite army units failed. It seemed that even the elite units were not immune to the 'red poison' of the capital. They formed their own breakaway council structures or simply drove home.

At this point the old order resorted to a pre-war plan, turning the army into a professional force. In collusion with Ebert, the Supreme Command moved directly to form a new force using professional officers and volunteers (the *Freikorps*). Finances were not a problem – there were generous donations from the bourgeoisie – they rapidly acquired sufficient weapons and good food, and were initially held outside Berlin and barracks in the major cities. By Christmas 1918, the *Freikorps* under General Groening possessed some 10,000 well-trained and heavily armed units; six months later it had swelled to 200,000. At the same time the SPD and the unions expanded their influence within the workers' and soldiers' councils so that, on 16 December, at the first Federal Congress of Soviets there were 490 delegates – 405 workers and 84 soldiers – nearly 300 of whom were members of the SPD, with just over 90 from the USPD (including ten from the Spartacus League). Just one third of delegates were factory workers. In the event, the assembly decided by a majority to dissolve in favour of parliament.

The aim of the counterrevolution, rallied behind the SPD and its 'People's Council', was to provoke the revolutionary forces and their political leadership in the Spartacus League into an early test of strength and drown them in a bloodbath. The revolutionary left of Luxemburg and Liebknecht was too weak and too inexperienced to influence events after the founding of the Communist Party on New Year's Day 1919. The revolutionary shop stewards maintained their influence over the masses, but remained under the political influence of the USPD until it split in 1920.

The congress twice voted down a motion that would have allowed the Spartacist leaders, Liebknecht and Luxemburg, to speak. In the end the congress called for a general election to a constituent assembly and liquidated itself. This gave the generals and their capitalist backers breathing space in which to crush the revolution. But defeat was not inevitable. Thousands of workers, led by Liebknecht and the Spartacus League, marched on the second day of the congress calling for 'all power to the workers' and soldiers' council'.

The political composition of the congress reflected the revolution's uneven development between the revolutionary mood of the Berlin workers and the very different mood elsewhere in the country. Furthermore, many of the most militant workers belonged to the USPD which could not agree to that demand. And the Spartacus League could lead tens of thousands of workers, but it did not have a disciplined organisation when the first wave of revolution hit. The Social Democratic Party (SPD) betrayed the ideas for which it had fought for over 50 years when it decided to support the slaughter of the First World War. After the outbreak of the revolution on 9 November 1918, the SPD leadership took control of the central government and built close ties with the Army High Command. Around 200,000 of its members left to join the new, more left-wing USPD. There was no other political force with over one million members and a major influence over the trade union leaders.

Officially, the SPD supported the revolution and promised socialism after a new parliament was elected. But its leaders desperately wanted to dismantle the workers' and soldiers' councils, so much so that they helped to reorganise the army. Gustav Noske, an SPD MP since 1906, became Minister for the Army and the Navy. He immediately began discussions with the Army High Command. 'Someone must become the bloodhound' that would put down the revolution, he said, and he was the one to do it.

The *Freikorps* moved into Berlin in the first days of January, with the object of provoking the revolutionary forces into an early test of strength and drown them in a bloodbath. When Ebert, the SPD leader of the government, sacked Emil Eichhorn, the popular police chief of Berlin, Eichhorn refused to stand down. The Berlin workers' and soldiers' council had given him their mandate. On 5 January, the Berlin USPD and the newly founded Communist Party called for a general strike. Hundreds of thousands of workers poured onto the streets. A revolutionary committee emerged out of this movement and issued a call for the toppling of the Ebert government – in effect a call for a second, socialist, revolution.

But the forces were not in place and after a day of demonstrations the masses went home. The *Freikorps* then moved in and expelled protesters from the SPD newspaper print shops, which they had occupied. Luxemburg understood that the SPD was too strong and the revolutionary socialists too weak for there to be a successful revolution at that moment. Even if the revolutionary forces had been victorious in Berlin, the majority of the working class in the rest of the country still had faith in the SPD and the trade union leaders. The *Freikorps* murdered Luxemburg and Liebknecht two weeks later.

NOTES

1. Hans Ulrich Wehler, *Deutsche Gesellschaftsgeschichte 1849–1914*, München: Becks, 1995, p. 772.
2. Ibid., p. 1121f.
3. Paul Fröhlich, *Illustrierte Geschichte*, Berlin: Internationalen Arbeiter Verlag, 1929, S. 157.
4. Wehler, *Deutsche Gesellschaftsgeschichte*, p. 1120.
5. Marx–Engels, *Complete Works*, Volume 17, Berlin: Dietz Verlag, 1964, pp. 268–9.
6. Karl Liebknecht, *Complete Works*, Volume II, Berlin: Dietz Verlag, 1960, p. 46.
7. Liebknecht, *Complete Works*, Volume I, p. 456.
8. Carl Schorske, *German Social Democracy: The Devolopment of the Great Schism 1905–1917*, New York: Harper, 1972, p. 85. The Stuttgart congress was a milestone in the evolution of German social democracy. The party had revealed itself as the leader of the conservative forces of the International. On the one hand, it had resisted the formulation of a more radical policy against militarism and war in the face of growing international tension; on the other – and this was a really significant change of policy – it had pressed for fuller acceptance of colonialism.
9. Fröhlich, *Illustrierte Geschichte*, p. 129.
10. SPD-Rödermark.de.
11. Fröhlich, *Illustrierte Geschichte*, p. 99.

12. Richard Müller, *Vom Kaiserreich zur Republik*, Vienna: Malik, 1924. Zitiert nach der 2. Neuauflage Berlin 1979, p. 70.
13. Wehler, *Deutsche Gesellschaftsgeschichte*, p. 16f.
14. Ibid., p. 104.
15. Fröhlich, *Illustrierte Geschichte*, p. 96.
16. In France and Britain workers' leaders were integrated into the government.
17. Wehler, *Deutsche Gesellschaftsgeschichte*, p. 40.
18. Karl Retzlaw, *Spartakus, Aufstieg und Niedergang, Erinnerungen eines Parteiarbeiter*, Frankfurt: Verlag Neue Kritik, 1971, p. 34.
19. By comparison, the French section of the International SFIO in 1914 had 91,000 members, not even a tenth of the members of the SPD; the gap between union membership and votes was similar. The SPD had achieved 33 per cent of the vote in the last general election before the war, the SFIO in 1914, however, got just 14 per cent of the vote. Similarly, the CGT had 250,000 members before the war of 1914, nearly one tenth of the membership of the free trade unions, though the French population was a third smaller.
20. Leon Trotsky, *History of the Russian Revolution*, www. marxists.org, accessed 20 March 2012.
21. Fröhlich, *Illustrierte Geschichte*, p. 142.
22. Retzlaw, *Spartakus, Aufstieg und Niedergang, Erinnerungen eines Parteiarbeiter*, p. 37.
23. The turners, Müller, wrote in *Empire*, p. 94, were crucial to production. They were well paid and enjoyed better working conditions. The group were against the war measures. And they did not only defend their own interests, but also more vulnerable groups, especially women workers, against employers.
24. Trotsky, *The Russian Revolution*, p. 97.
25. Fröhlich, *Illustrierte Geschichte*, p. 160.

BIBLIOGRAPHY/FURTHER READING

Pierre Broue, *The German Revolution*, Chicago: Haymarket Books, 2006.
Chris Harman, *The Lost Revolution*, London: Bookmarks, 1982.
David Morgan, *The Socialist Left and the German Revolution – A History of the German Independent Social Democratic Party*, Ithaca, NY and London: Cornell University Press, 1975.
Richard Müller, *Vom Kaiserreich zur Republik*, Vienna: Malik, 1924.
Karl Retzlaw, *Spartacus*, Frankfurt: Verlag Neue Kritik, 1971.
Carl Schorske, *German Social Democracy: The Development of the Great Schism 1905–1917*, New York: Harper, 1972.
Victor Serge, *Witness to the German Revolution*, Chicago: Haymarket Books, 2011.

3
Nation against Nation: Italy 1919–21

Megan Trudell

It is arguable that Italy, not Germany, was the country in which the relationship between the civil and the military was most transformed by the First World War.[1] Army morale was at a low point following defeats in Africa at the turn of the twentieth century; the war gave the military a new national role and prestige, which were shattered following the armistice by class conflict within both the army and society as a whole. The upheavals in the army played a central role in the post-war conflict.

The Mussolini regime stressed the importance of the war as the moment of the death of liberal Italy and the birth of fascism. Throughout its existence, the regime continued to foster the identification of veterans with fascism which the nascent fascist organisation had struggled to cultivate during the *biennio rosso* ('two red years') of 1919–20. As Giuseppe Bottai expressed it: 'If I had to draw a line between the *"arditismo"* [audacity] of the war . . . and the civil *"arditismo"* of the Fascist squads, I would not know where to put it.'[2]

The view that the war was central to creating the nation was shared by liberal anti-fascists like Benedetto Croce, who saw the war as overturning Italy's reputation as a cowardly nation and as an affirmation of the strength of the liberal political state.[3] During the late 1960s and early 1970s the work of Piero Melograni, Giorgio Rochat and Giovanni Sabbatucci attempted to reinsert into reflections on the war some consideration of socio-economic conditions and political choices in order 'to conserve the globalist approach to military problems in the debate about the very rich yet contradictory immediate post-war period'[4] – a period in which veterans emerged as autonomous political actors.

However, the discussion of soldiers, the violence of war and fascism has come full circle in recent years to embrace the conviction that fascism was the continuation of a 'surge in warring energy' unleashed by the war.[5] Niall Ferguson, for example, has written that combat experience heightened veterans' receptiveness to right-wing politics: 'For many men who had fought, violence had become addictive.'[6] Much existing literature on the *biennio rosso* has tended to elide the role of soldiers in Italy's revolutionary moment or to see them as homogeneously opposed to the industrial conflict which culminated in the factory occupations of September 1920.[7] Fascism as the outcome of soldiers' intoxication with or brutalisation by the war, depending on one's viewpoint, appears to have been predestined or was at least predictable.

However, while it is unquestionably true that the war was fundamental in shaping the nature of fascism in Italy, it is important to grasp a sense of the ideological flux at the end of the war. Many of those in the upper echelons of the army cleaved to the right from the beginning, but not all soldiers and veterans supported fascism, and among those who did the decision was not an automatic outcome of their experiences. In fact, 'veteran mentality' during the immediate post-war period was more likely to lean to the left than the right for the majority of soldiers. A rightward shift was not generally apparent even among the majority of the officer corps and ex-officers until the end of 1919, and took place considerably later – if at all – among ex-infantrymen.

The war transformed the people who fought in it and generated expectations of change. Between the armistice and the end of 1920 there was a generalised rebellion in the army which often connected with civilian revolt, especially in rural areas. The myriad forms of soldiers' protest led to attempts to create an independent political alternative to the mass parties, overlapped and at times connected with other forms of dissent, and posed a fundamental threat to the government and the integrity of the state.

This is not to dissolve the connections between the experience of war and fascism that did exist – the 'moment' of the First World War was the dramatic rupture that made fascism realisable – but rather to describe a more complex picture, characterised by a fragmentation of political impulses in different directions, in which the political allegiance and inclinations of soldiers fluctuated, and by a search for alternatives to the post-war world that failed to bear fruit. Only in the last instance – and then only for some – did post-war tensions resolve in adherence to far-right solutions to the crisis.

The Italy that entered the war in 1915 was a new nation, unified in 1860 but far from united. The Risorgimento process had not created a common national feeling among the majority of Italians and most of the country's mainly peasant inhabitants did not speak standard Italian. They were denied political representation in the new liberal state and were often further impoverished by economic policies which exacerbated the divide between the relative wealth of the north and the extreme poverty of the centre and south.

In the years before the war regional and class differentials widened. Industrialisation led to a growing urban middle and upper class in the north while workers faced poor working conditions and low wages; in 1911 more than half the southern population were illiterate and disease was rife. Strikes and protests were politicised by the state's identification with employers and landowners and its use of violent repression. The Liberal Prime Minister Giovanni Giolitti had maintained power through electoral alliances with parties to his left and right, but these alliances finally collapsed and he resigned in favour of the arch-conservative Antonio Salandra in March 1914.

AN INCREASINGLY INTERVENTIONIST STATE

The new government faced an ideological climate in which 'economic crisis strengthened the appeal of revolutionary socialism and syndicalism, on the one hand, and the worsening international situation provoked ever-more overt expressions of nationalism, on the other'.[8] In such circumstances, Salandra stood for authoritarian solutions, and the army was used heavily to police social protest – in June the 'Red Week' uprising in central Italy was suppressed with a force of 100,000 soldiers.[9] Nevertheless, during the winter, protests by workers and peasants against inflation and unemployment progressed into overt opposition to the war.

The Italian state increasingly looked to intervention to solve the deep problems it faced. In so doing, it was in step with an increasingly wide layer in Italian society. Since the outbreak of war in Europe, the influence of interventionist ideas had spread. Democratic interventionists, including many liberals in the upper and middle classes, represented by the *Corriere della Sera* newspaper, wanted Italy to enter the war to defend republicanism (embodied by France) against the autocratic monarchies of Germany and Austria-Hungary. They found unlikely allies in nationalist and revolutionary interventionists – the reactionary poet Gabriele D'Annunzio, the Futurist artists led by Marinetti, Mussolini, who had reversed his aggressive anti-war position and resigned from the PSI (Partito Socialista Italiano – Italian Socialist Party), and some revolutionary socialists and syndicalists – who saw war as an opportunity to forge a new Italy, a completion of the Risorgimento process which would win back from Austria the 'unredeemed lands' of Trieste and Trentino. On all sides, war was seen as the moment to free Italy from bureaucratic and unrepresentative Giolittian politics.[10]

Mussolini's newspaper, *Il Popolo d'Italia*, launched in November 1914, quickly became the 'organ of the interventionist left',[11] which identified war with a revolution that would sweep away the old order and proclaim a dynamic and modern society. For the Nationalist Corradini, war would create a 'proletarian nation', a synthesis of working-class syndicalism with imperial designs.[12] This combination of socialist language with the glorification of an idealised Italy sought to establish 'a direct relationship between the political forces supporting intervention and the popular masses, which in this way could be detached from socialist influence'.[13] The government wanted the same. Territorial ambition and a seat at the Allied peace table were the external elements of its calculation in entering the war; the internal element was an opportunity to resist apparent social disintegration. Salandra took advantage of interventionist demonstrations to suppress anti-war protests and wrest powers from parliament to take Italy into the war in spite of public and parliamentary opposition.

The interventionists were ecstatic in the 'radiant May' of 1915. A short, victorious war would reorganise a fractured Italian society around national values that had been weakened, as they saw it, by Giolitti's liberal rule and leniency towards social protest. Initially, they appeared vindicated; those in the industrial and political classes who had been neutralist before the war now supported the war effort. The Vatican remained opposed to the war, but kept quiet. The PSI still opposed the war but passively, adopting the slogan of 'neither support nor sabotage', and the unions agreed to abide by wartime industrial legislation.

Yet the national project was not won. The war had broken down barriers between the interventionists and many neutralists, but national identification among workers and peasants – and therefore most soldiers – had not been strengthened. For many, the notion of fighting for a country that had not existed for their grandparents, where most did not speak the national language and were alienated from the political apparatus, was one they faced with resignation, not enthusiasm. The war widened, rather than healed, divisions in Italian society. It was being fought for areas which meant little to peasants from southern Italy where many soldiers came from; it was fought for the rich, while the poor suffered food price inflation and shortages. Peasant soldiers resented skilled workers who were exempt from conscription. Workers who stayed in the factories faced legislation which banned strikes, forced up productivity and imposed military discipline.[14] Vatican and socialist opposition to the war meant religious and political affiliation ran counter to calls for national unity for Catholic and socialist workers and peasants. The period of 'social peace' at the outbreak of war owed as much to disorientation at the shock of wartime conditions and the passivity of their leaders as to increased national identification.

From mid-1916 social protest began to rise again. War weariness translated rapidly into renewed political opposition to the state. The demands of wartime had accelerated the growth of industry and there was a corresponding explosion in the size of the working class, qualitatively altering the scale and nature of social conflict. Most new workers were women and peasants drafted in to fill the factories. The demands of wartime production gave them increased leverage and confidence, which expressed itself in increasingly militant political activity against the war. The interventionists' social base of intellectuals and officers was progressively undercut by the social weight of the anti-war movement among 'the masses'.[15] National identification with the Italy of interventionism, in other words, was often outweighed by class identification. Giolitti understood the class resentment that was fuelling anti-war feeling:

'I could not help but note the deplorable greed and avarice of many who had made contacts with the State, and the ostentation and luxury of the war profiteers, which made a sinister impression on the soldiers who came from the trenches for their brief leaves with their families.'[16]

Frequent demonstrations in the countryside against the lack of food, conscription, requisitioning and other injustices often led to violence against the police and wealthy citizens. Many of the protests joined forces with strikes in towns, which were often led by women who could not be punished by being sent to the front.[17] Strikes were often encouraged or even provoked by soldiers, who wrote letters urging their families to protest at the low wages and inadequate food supplies and to demonstrate against the war.[18] Whatever the immediate cause – food shortages, harsh factory discipline, new waves of conscription – 'it was always against the war and for peace'.[19]

1917: THE MOMENTUM GATHERS PACE

Anti-war sentiment gained massive momentum after February 1917. The revolution in Russia had overthrown the Tsar and established a provisional government, alongside workers' and soldiers' councils (soviets). Despite continued prosecution of the war, many Russian soldiers were deserting and the soviets were calling for peace.[20] The Russian revolution had a tremendous effect in Italy. It was a beacon for those who wanted an end to the war and a fearful warning to the government and the wealthy. The reformist socialist Claudio Treves declared that Italian troops would be 'out of the trenches before next winter' and the Pope called for an end to the 'useless carnage' of war. In Turin, a 40,000-strong public meeting to greet delegates from the Petrograd soviet turned into an anti-war demonstration, 'with cheers for Lenin and revolution'.[21]

A general strike, which began in Turin in August, quickly became insurrectionary – the most powerful expression so far of a potentially revolutionary anti-war movement. According to Marc Ferro, 'the strikes . . . were reminiscent in many ways of those in Petrograd in February. Women and youth had a vital part in them, trying to fraternise with the *carabinieri* [armed police] and shouting, "Don't fire at your brothers".'[22] The British ambassador described the revolt as 'a spontaneous movement of popular discontent'. He subsequently blamed the strikes on socialist propaganda put about 'mainly by women' and inspired by the events in Russia.[23]

The Turin events were brutally repressed: troops armed with machine guns killed more than 50 people and wounded 800; over 1,000, mainly Fiat, workers were arrested and sent to the front.[24] However, a spontaneous movement revealed the depth of anger and had become identified with the socialists, which made revolution appear a more credible proposition. In response, the government extended the war zone in north-eastern Italy to include Alessandria, Genoa and Turin, and as far south as Reggio Calabria and Sicily, thereby extending the militarisation of Italian society as a form of social control. This strategy was to become a double-edged sword – military rule encouraged the belief among officers that *they* should run Italy after the war, an impulse that would threaten the liberal state from the left and eventually bring it down from the right.

The retreat at Caporetto in October, the same month as the Bolshevik revolution, was regarded by the interventionists as the direct result of socialist propaganda, but beneath that lay an understanding of the weakness of national identification among the masses in Italy. Their rhetoric of a 'proletarian nation' mutated into attacks on those who had 'stabbed the nation in the back'.[25] If a new nation was to be created, the existing one had to be preserved. It would therefore have to be imposed on those who opposed the war and threatened revolution.

Many of those, including volunteer officers, whose social position led them to rush to the defence of the nation held an extreme form of nationalism, identified with opposition to social revolution. With many in this group, their conflicted self-identification would eventually be resolved by supporting fascism, yet material and social factors influenced their expressions of nationalism, and for many, the progression was not straightforward.

Emilio Lussu described the ambiguous nature of national feeling among the officer class. In his novel based on his experiences at the front, a group of officers debate a mutiny in 1917. One is supportive of the action and argues 'the slaughter is not worth the sacrifice'. 'And what of Italy's interest?' asks another. 'What of us? Aren't we Italy?' rejoins the first, reminding his audience of the new boots they received with 'Long live Italy' in the colours of the Italian flag printed on the soles, only to discover the soles were paper varnished to resemble leather. 'The boots don't matter. What is terrible is that they have varnished our very lives, stamped the name of our country on us and driven us like sheep to the slaughter.'[26]

Lussu was not a socialist when war broke out. He was an interventionist student who volunteered early on and as such was representative of many young men in Italy who welcomed the war as a dramatic escape from mediocrity of politics and in life and hoped for freedom and democracy, or revolution and rebirth. The vision of a purifying war articulated by the extreme interventionists captured and nurtured these feelings: 'Only war knows how to rejuvenate, accelerate and sharpen human intelligence, to make more joyful and air the nerves, to liberate us from the weight of daily burdens, to give savour to life, and talent to imbeciles,' wrote Marinetti in 1914.[27]

The fervour of interventionist language was most successful among middle- and upper-class young men, who formed the core of the officer class. For these the stripping away of conventional life was exhilarating, the 'nation' for whose glory they fought was concretely expressed in the community of the trenches and the intense experiences of comradeship and collective expression, which were entirely new.

The First World War differed radically from the European wars in which many of the young officers' fathers and grandfathers had fought. The war crystallised technological changes which had been developing since the industrial revolution.[28] The machine gun was used in combat causing slaughter on a vast scale; artillery barrages hurled tons of metal at armies of millions. This military replication of the factory system reduced soldiers to the level of industrial workers and mixed men of all classes together in the miserable conditions of battle. The disillusionment many officers felt, which contributed to their bitterness after the war, was a function of this industrialisation of war and their own 'proletarianisation'.[29] Conflicting social messages of 'community' and the abolition of social status were internalised within a context of a rigid class and military hierarchy and the general brutalisation of the war.

Despite the promises of interventionists and governments, war did not usher in a 'proletarian nation'. The stubbornness of class relationships in the army alienated ordinary conscripts and dashed the hopes of idealistic young officers that the war would create a natural community. The more the idea of the war as a classless enterprise was raised, the more bitter the disappointment when officers faced inept generals and soldiers more keen on desertion than on defending the nation. Many were left spiritually and socially bereft. Italy mobilised 5.25 million men; at least 615,000 were killed, 500,000 disabled, 1 million wounded and 600,000 taken prisoner.[30] At the end of the war prisoners poured back into Italy from Austria, 'more than half a million desperate men let loose without provision of any kind', coming down from the mountains often without boots, greeted not with food or clothing but with fear and suspicion.[31]

They returned without 100,000 of their comrades. One-sixth of the Italian prisoners of war died in enemy camps due to the Italian government's refusal to supply food and medicine (in contravention of the articles of the Geneva Convention) in an attempt to dissuade soldiers from deserting to the enemy.[32] The treatment of prisoners provided a gruesome counterweight to the proclamations of impending national glory and the synthetic national culture it was attempting to create. The reality was that discipline, repression and murder were often the preferred tools of the state in welding its citizens to the idea of the nation. The Italian army 'mounted a violent campaign of repression in which a largely petit bourgeois officer corps subjugated southern peasant soldiers'.[33] It is no surprise, therefore, that adherence to the national idea among combatants was experienced in a contradictory fashion. The anger that ordinary soldiers felt at having fought and died in the name of freedom and democracy for a state that did not seem to care about the quality of either within its own borders was matched by the authorities' concern that battle-hardened men would turn their fire on the state. The government feared that potentially revolutionary soldiers might unite with the widespread urban and rural protests as they had in Russia.

In the last few months of 1918 the level of protest had risen sharply. Discontent was exacerbated by the continued escalation in food and fuel prices and the influenza epidemic. Yet to those who had sacrificed, Treasury Minister Francesco Nitti spoke in parliament of the need to continue to do so. Strikes were 'widespread and numerous'.[34] The British ambassador telegraphed that in Naples, 'Immediately on announcement of enemy armistice proposals workmen in munitions factories went on strike'.[35] Similar strikes took place in Milan, Turin and Venice where, 'If these new overtures are rejected it is to be feared that considerable trouble, if not actually open rebellion, will be rife amongst the soldiery and the lower classes'.[36]

Under such circumstances, the social and political weight of returning soldiers was crucial. Mussolini realised this and sought to ensure that veterans, especially those of the *arditi* (the elite assault brigades) adopted extreme nationalism rather than revolutionary socialism. He changed the description of *Il Popolo d'Italia* from a 'socialist daily' to 'daily of combatants and producers', a blend of nationalism and revolutionary politics specifically aimed at the 'trenchocracy' (*trincerocrazia*) of young officers.

DEMOBILISING THE WARTIME CULTURE

In March 1919 demobilisation halted as a combined result of the pressures of the Peace Conference, social tensions and transport difficulties, so that at the beginning of July there were still 1.5 million men under arms. Of these, 630,000 were stationed in Italy – half employed in public order and territorial duties.[37] The new Prime Minister Orlando's massive internal force indicated that a vital concern for the state was domestic rather than foreign tension – Italy's 'internal enemies' (a wide category that included socialists, the new Catholic Popular Party, strikers and parliament) were gaining ground.

The government, as much as the army, was bound to the militarisation of Italian society and the politicisation of officers and *arditi* to protect the liberal state from the possibility of revolution threatened by the politicisation of the mass of conscripts and veterans. These measures played an important part in Italy's 'failure to demobilise wartime culture'.[38] The government's reliance on the army to keep order – at times amounting to calling on one class in the army to suppress another – was a key ingredient in the eventual backing that generals and officers gave to Mussolini. The Liberal state's willingness to strengthen the army hierarchy against social revolt, and in the process to bind together government and military, was more centrally culpable in the rise of fascism than the 'veteran mentality'.

The initial post-war months were therefore marked by the return to political life of many officers who supported the extreme interventionists, and many soldiers suspicious of the nationalists' class motivations. The rising level of social conflict posed sharply the choice between nationalism and international revolution; soldiers were attracted to both. National identification was complicated by a confused desire for change and for peace. Most former soldiers were not, according to the socialist Angelo Tasca, either extreme nationalists or revolutionary socialists, but 'for the most part Wilsonian and democratic, with a vague but sincere desire for reconstruction mixed with distrust for the old political cliques'.[39]

It was not automatic that national identification prevailed over other forms of identification. Individuals' self-identification in the different spheres of their lives, whether political, economic or cultural, fluctuated, often dramatically, during this short period of intense social and political crisis. The great economic transformations of the war brought profound social changes which reverberated through the armed forces. For the traditional nobility in privileged positions in the army the war 'seriously eroded the material foundations of the old aristocratic way of life [and] at the same time . . . undermined the prestige and glamour associated with the officers' corps and military service'.[40] This invoked insecurity and – among some generals – the defence of their positions was an important aspect of their adherence to a nationalism that clamoured for continued war.

The new world of liberal capitalism hailed by the Wilsonian interventionists as the prize for victory against autocratic imperial powers was a place of uncertainty for this group, and social revolt in the countryside threatened further disorder and the decline of large-scale landownership. An aggressive assertion of the integrity of the nation that was a refutation of such democratic values and impulses led some generals into active support of D'Annunzio's illegal military seizure of Fiume (now Rijeka in Croatia) in September. Lower down the social scale, of the 186,000 officers remaining at the end of the war, most were from what Luigi Salvatorelli referred to as the 'humanist' petty bourgeoisie. These semi-rural lower-middle-class officers from central and southern Italy were often educated and drawn from positions as teachers or provincial lawyers. Salvatorelli viewed fascism as the result of the autonomous action of this group, arguing that within it class struggle had been replaced by nationalism:

'the myth of the nation was for the petty bourgeoisie the banner of its revolt; its class struggle against capitalism and the proletariat consisted in the negation of the very concept of class, and in its substitution with that of the nation. It could not have been otherwise; since the petty bourgeoisie was too weak and inconsistent as an organic class – that is, as a holder of power with an economic function – to be able to fight on a class basis against the other two, or to pull them to its ideology.'[41]

In the period under discussion here, the substitution of 'class' with 'nation' as the language of revolt was not fully realised but was *in process*, a critical point in understanding the volatility of consciousness among these men. The shared conditions of war had generated some measure of solidarity between officers and soldiers, even if the former were implicated in repression: they shared a desire for a new politics without the corruption of the pre-war era. Piero Melograni has described the impact of this development:

'These soldiers who . . . returned home with the desire to see the rise of a new society, did not constitute a 'class', but they were numerous enough to produce anxiety in all classes. They failed in their attempt to remain united to conduct political work in a direct and permanent way . . . but they continued to express, in whatever confused and disorganised forms, their aspirations for the transformation of the established order.'[42]

The majority of veterans had, of course, not been officers but ordinary soldiers for whom the end of the war also brought high expectations. For these working-class and peasant soldiers, uninspired by bellicose patriotism and suffering the hardship of the trenches and the terror of repeated, fruitless assaults on the enemy, a combination of collective experience and propaganda had transformed their relationships with one another. Antonio Gramsci observed the changes in the mentalities of peasants who went to fight:

> 'Four years in the trenches radically changed the peasant psychology…selfish, individual instincts were blunted; a common, united spirit was fashioned; feelings were universalized . . . Links of solidarity were forged which would have taken decades of historical experience and intermittent struggles to form.'[43]

Lussu asserted that 'the ex-servicemen were in short embryo socialists, less through a knowledge of socialist doctrine than through a deep international feeling acquired through the experience of war'.[44]

The great hopes of '1919-ism' (*diciannovismo*) were stimulated by voices across the political spectrum. Government, nationalists and socialists sought to reflect powerful antipathy to war among soldiers and turn it into political support. Politicians keen to undermine social and industrial protest and support for the socialists promised that the war would remake society and that soldiers' sacrifices would earn the reward of land. Orlando described the war as 'the greatest politico-social revolution recorded by history, surpassing even the French Revolution' and Salandra marked his return to politics by proclaiming the transformative nature of the war: 'Let no one think that a peaceful return to the past will be possible after this storm.'[45]

This revolutionary hope for a transformation in social conditions and a collective political role inspired ex-servicemen, but clashed strongly with the realities of post-war Italy. In place of new lives they found unemployment and reluctance by elites to demobilise society or to grant them their due. Veterans' social interests and economic necessity sent some into factories as workers, swelling the ranks of the union federations: 'Energetic and enthusiastic, and full of the illusions of *diciannovismo*, they intended to squeeze the maximum out of their employers – the 'profiteers' whom they had learned to hate in the trenches – in the shortest possible time.'[46]

The involvement of ex-combatants in the social crisis of 1919 – especially that of the middle-class reserve officers – stemmed from their return from the front full of illusions and prospects of renewal, convinced of their duty to play a primary role in political life. Yet, 'petty bourgeois officers suffered a searing disappointment in the spring of 1919 when the failure of the Italian delegation at the peace conference loomed and, at the same time, hopes for the rapid establishment of the "new international order" based on Wilsonian principles fell.'[47]

Officers' difficulty in reinserting themselves into the productive structure, aggravated by the psychological problems of those used to command and unhappy to resign themselves to work with modest pay and little prestige and rising inflation, was added to this 'ideological and moral trauma'.[48] The politicisation of the army did not, therefore, take place in a single direction. A broad spectrum of veterans' groups proliferated in Italy following the armistice. A minority of officers cleaved to anti-Bolshevik, right-wing and monarchist groups with an emphasis on order; the Unione nazionale ufficiali e soldati (UNUS) was one of these. However, these right-wing groups were numerically puny by comparison with the Associazione Nazionale dei Combattenti (ANC).

'A significant number of veteran officers (mainly professionals, white collar workers and teachers) made up much of the upper and middle sections of . . . [the ANC]: a movement that, at a time when fascism numbered a few thousand members, already had assumed the dimensions of a genuine mass organism.'[49]

Clearly influenced by developments in Russia, the democratic programme of the ANC called for a Constituent Assembly, the replacement of the Senate with a council system, the reduction of military service to three months and for the distribution of unused land to veterans.[50] Ideologically, the organisation expressed a permutation of Wilsonianism and nationalism which often propelled it into the leadership of local struggles for land seizures and pensions, most militantly in the south. It represented an explicit attempt by veterans to play an independent role in the movements reshaping Italian society.

The ANC was an organisation of 'petty-bourgeois radicalism';[51] its membership was overwhelmingly made up of the lower classes, with a middle-class leadership:

'The history of the ex-combatant movement consisted, in the first years, in the attempt by petty-bourgeois officialdom to propose itself as a new ruling class – as an alternative to the old conservative and liberal-democratic personnel as well as to the socialists – relying for support especially on the peasant masses that until then had been excluded from political life.'[52]

ANC sections mushroomed around the country in the months after the armistice. In Udine and provinces, the ANC made up 23 of the 33 veterans' sections, with over 8,000 members. In comparison, the right-wing officers' group UNUS had 200 members and the socialist Proletarian League 250. A thousand veterans gathered at Tradate in Como province in June to establish a section, addressed by the secretary of the metalworkers' section and a junior officer.[53]

The organisation was divided politically: it was constitution-alist in Turin, republican-reformist in Liguria, democratic in Milan and Brescia, nationalist in Cremona, republican in Treviso, pro-government and strongly Catholic in the Veneto and Trentino, and radical-republican in Emilia-Romagna.[54] It tended to be strong in the cities of the north, where the professional middle class which constituted its leadership were predominant, and in parts of the south – where socialist forces were weaker – among the rural masses in Calabria, Sicily, Puglia, Basilicata, Irpinia, Abruzzo and Sardinia.

In June 1919 Vittorio Orlando was replaced by Francesco Nitti, an appointment reviled by the right as a return to Giolittian politics. Food riots broke out, often with veteran involvement. Land seizures began in the Spring in Puglia, around Rome and the Marche. Reports on the seizure of land in 200 localities in the countryside around Rome in the Summer noted the 'Leagues of Fighting Soldiers who have been the initiators'.[55] The ANC tried to keep rural protest within legal limits, but land seizures and protests for public works grew in both number and militancy. Anti-government protest became *in practice* a democratic revolt for equal distribution of food and land, which was difficult to contain.

Much smaller than the ANC, the Proletarian League sought to organise veterans on a class basis. The League organised around 500,000 veterans, mainly in smaller centres in Tuscany, Umbria and the Marche. Its programme was anti-militarist, against renewed war and the occupation of Fiume. The League attempted to tie the spontaneous socialist impulses involved in veteran action to socialist ideas, and succeeded in organising a significant number of ex-soldiers on this basis. However, it was dependent on the PSI and the CGL union federation and was, therefore, riven by the same divisions between maximalist revolutionaries and parliamentar-ian reformists who fought for control over its various sections, neither of which was able to relate to the rising soldier and veteran movement organised by the ANC.[56]

The contradiction within the veteran movement was its 'dual character': on the one hand, these organisations were established to defend veterans' economic interests, but on the other, they inevitably represented the expectations of *diciannovismo*, and therefore 'posed with extreme clarity the question of power, the question, that is, of their progressive insertion into national political and economic life, no longer in a subordinate position, as in the past, but in the position of an alternative power to the ruling elites'.[57]

The contradiction was exposed in the November elections. The ANC stood as part of a veterans' coalition. The PSI gained 1.8 million votes and the Catholic Popular Party 1.6 million, while the ANC won only 200,000. The nationalists and fascists also did very badly. As Nitti wrote to General Badoglio: 'Combatants have voted nearly everywhere for the socialists and the Catholics.'[58] The elections were decisive in formalising Italy's polarisation and forcing the subsequent reorientation of the right.

MUTINY, PROTEST AND DISILLUSIONMENT

1920 saw progressively generalised social unrest and wide-ranging forms of revolt among the armed forces, from small-scale subversion to mutiny. The divisions within the ANC leadership made it incapable of keeping land protests under control, and these became significantly more extensive and militant. Mutiny and protests by soldiers increasingly became connected with other forces in the general population and among anarchist and communist groups. In Milan in July, the prefect recommended that while he would 'intensify vigilance of soldiers when they are outside the barracks', military command ought to do so *inside*, 'where affiliates of subversive parties are more numerous than would have been believed'.[59]

In Ancona, a battalion of riflemen mutinied on receiving orders to leave for Albania. Around 100 anarchists fought alongside the soldiers and, armed with machine guns and rifles, held the barracks against the police. A general strike was launched to coincide with the action, showing the planned nature of the mutiny and the interlocking of forms of struggle in the region. It took a field-gun bombardment to force surrender and the 'people of the town appear to have been in general sympathy with mutineers'.[60]

Class revolt among serving soldiers within the army reflected increasing class polarisation in the country as a whole. In April 1920, the British ambassador wrote:

'A general strike has been proclaimed in Venice, the reason given being that an officer lost his temper with a soldier, drew his revolver and shot the latter. That such a cause should have such an effect is one of the most interesting events of recent months in Italy. The newspapers today report that the strike, which has an entirely political colour, has taken the form of chasing officers, many of whom have been thrown into canals and otherwise molested.'[61]

There were counter-currents which cut across joint action between veterans and the working and agrarian populations. One was competition for land, another the troops' public order role, with the massive 'national guard' often used to break strikes or suppress agrarian protests. In Lecce province, striking peasants resisted the occupation of their town by troops. 'On hearing . . . that reinforcements were on their way from the neighbouring garrison of Gallipoli, the mob proceeded to disarm the *carabinieri* and surround the station where the troops were expected to arrive.' In the fighting which followed, a policeman and three strikers were killed and 'quiet was only restored when the authorities promised that the troops should not be allowed to enter the town but should be encamped outside'.[62]

The most serious battle took place in April in Turin where half a million workers joined a general strike. The state backed the employers and, fearing insurrection, turned Turin into what Gramsci called an 'armed fortress'. Fifty thousand troops were stationed there:

'gun batteries stand ready on the hills . . . armoured cars are roaming the streets; in the suburbs reputed to be particularly rebellious, machine guns are trained on the houses, on all bridges and crossroads, and on the factory gates.'[63]

These were significant signals that the government could still rely on the army against socialists and striking workers, but they did not render the potential for combined action impossible as much as indicate an absence of forces to connect separate struggles. In the case of Turin, the PSI did not even support the April strike, which was influenced as it was by Gramsci's minority *L'Ordine Nuovo* group, so allowing it to be isolated and defeated.[64] More generally, the maximalist leadership of the PSI held to a rigid anti-militarism which led the party to alienate and abuse veterans moving tentatively into action or towards socialism and a formal opposition to individual ownership of land that in practice was a sectarian barrier to relating to veteran land seizures.

Also, and not dimmed by socialist attitudes, many soldiers resented industrial workers who had been paid well and exempted from military service. Nonetheless, many workers did serve – those less crucial to the war effort and those sent to the front as punishment for organising strikes – and therefore came into contact with soldiers from rural backgrounds, and many veterans took factory work following the armistice. Socially, therefore, those barriers were porous. Significant numbers instinctively responded to socialist propaganda and 500,000 joined the Proletarian League. Crucially, the economic situation meant that the government continued to unite opposition to itself. There were, therefore, very real opportunities for the battles in the factories and on the land to be connected and for the momentum for change among ordinary peasant soldiers to be pulled leftwards.

Gramsci understood the need for unity between workers and the peasantry, including soldiers, and stressed the importance of factory councils carrying out propaganda in the countryside to try to forge links between the various struggles. Tragically, the PSI's inability to relate to the peasantry, to soldiers and to sections of the middle classes, all of whom were moving into struggle – often with confused ideological motivation that spanned political Catholicism, democratic reformism, and nationalism – meant that it underestimated the genuine, albeit sometimes contradictory and confused, potential to forge revolutionary unity.

During 1920, the ANC's fear of the mass movement within its ranks and an inability to control it led the moderate 'centre' to accommodate to the government around a patriotic defence of order and militarism. This in turn provided oxygen for the nationalists and the right in the veterans' movement. Fascism was able to regroup after the debacle of the elections through the new tactic of *squadrismo* in rural northern Italy. The squads first emerged during 1920 in the 'nationalist cauldron' of Trieste, which was under military rule. The anti-working-class actions of the fascists became braided into the anti-Slavism of the military state. The defeat of the factory occupations at the end of 1920 removed the possibility of revolutionary solutions to the crisis of Italian society, and the fright the social movements had given the wealthy classes tipped the latter towards support for the violence of fascist suppression of working-class action in the interests of a conservative maintenance of 'order'.

Disillusionment with the failure of their attempts at autonomous political action propelled many officers and veterans towards support for the fascists during the months between the end of 1920 and the March on Rome, but soldiers' adherence to fascism remained uneven. Many among those who had joined D'Annunzio at Fiume regarded Mussolini and the fascists as counter-revolutionary, and many ex-*arditi* joined the anarchist *ardito* Argo Secondari's anti-fascist Arditi del Popolo. The fractures in the 'veteran mentality' – and that of serving soldiers – that had come about as a result of the war and the vast expectations of change in 1919 were in time largely integrated into fascism, but that outcome does not erase the profound turmoil among those under arms and the (unrealised) potential that existed for a relationship with the people transformed by revolutionary impulse and collective action.

NOTES

1. John Gillis, *The Militarisation of the Western World*, New Brunswick, NJ and London: Rutgers University Press, 1989.
2. Giuseppe Bottai, quoted in Michael Ledeen, 'Italy: war as a style of life', in Stephen R. Ward, ed., *The War Generation: Veterans of the First World War*, New York and London: Kennicatt Press, 1975, p. 104.
3. See Marco Mondini, *La politica delle armi: Il ruolo dell'esercito nell'avvento del fascismo*, Rome–Bari: Laterza, 2006, p. 5.
4. Giorgio Rochat, *L'Esercito Italiano da Vittorio Veneto a Mussolini 1919–1925* (1967), Bari: Laterza, 2006, p. vi.
5. Stephane Audoin-Rouzeau and Annette Becker, *Understanding the Great War*, New York: Knopf, 2002, p. 236.
6. Niall Ferguson, *The Pity of War*, London: Penguin, 1998, p. 391.
7. See, for example, Martin Clark, *The Failure of Revolution in Italy, 1919–1920*, Reading: University of Reading, 1973. Clark refers to the hostility felt by troops for the industrial strikers during the war, but does not discuss how this changed during 1919 and 1920.
8. Paul Corner, 'State and society, 1901–1922', in Adrian Lyttelton, ed., *Liberal and Fascist Italy: 1900–1945*, New York: Oxford University Press, 2002, p. 27.
9. Giuliano Procacci, *History of the Italian People*, London: Penguin, 1991, p. 400.
10. James Burgwyn, *The Legend of the Mutilated Victory*, New York: Praeger, 1993, p. 27.
11. Christopher Seton-Watson, *Italy from Liberalism to Fascism 1870–1925*, London: Methuen, 1967, p. 423.
12. Ibid., p. 359.

13. Giovanna Procacci, 'Italy: from interventionism to fascism 1917–1919', *Journal of Contemporary History*, 3(4), October 1968, p. 158.

14. Giovanna Procacci, 'Popular protest and labour conflict in Italy, 1915–18', *Social History*, 14(1), January 1989, p. 37. See also Paul Corner and Giovanna Procacci, 'The Italian experience of "total" mobilisation', in John Horne, ed., *State, Society and Mobilisation in Europe during the First World War*, Cambridge: Cambridge University Press, 1997, p. 229.

15. Procacci, 'Italy: from interventionism to fascism', p. 161.

16. Giovanni Giolitti, *Memoirs of My Life*, London and Sydney: Chapman and Dodd, 1923, pp. 403–4.

17. Procacci, 'Popular protest and labour conflict', pp. 42–3. Women were 21.9 per cent of the workforce by 1918, 64.2 per cent of strikers in 1917 and 45.6 per cent in 1918, Procacci, 'Popular protest and labour conflict', p. 46.

18. Ibid., p. 46.

19. Ibid., p. 43.

20. See, for example, Christopher Read, *From Tsar to Soviets: The Russian People and Their Revolution, 1917–21*, London: UCL Press, 1996.

21. Seton-Watson, *Italy from Liberalism to Fascism*, p. 471.

22. Marc Ferro, The *Great War 1914–1918*, London and New York: Routledge, 2002, p. 201.

23. Ambassador Rodd to Balfour, 19 September 1917 (dated 15 September 1917), TNA. FO 371/2945/182469.

24. Florence Speranza, ed., *The Diary of Gino Speranza: Italy 1915–1919*, Volume II, New York: AMS Press, 1966, p. 95.

25. MacGregor Knox, 'Fascism: ideology, foreign policy, and war', in Adrian Lyttleton, ed., *Liberal and Fascist Italy*, Oxford: Oxford University Press, 2002, p. 109.

26. Lussu, *Sardinian Brigade*, pp. 180–2.

27. Filippo Tommaso Marinetti, *Futurismo e fascism*, Foligno, 1924, pp. 96–7, quoted in Robert Wohl, *The Generation of 1914*, London: Weidenfeld & Nicolson, 1980, p. 169.

28. Enzo Traverso, *The Origins of Nazi Violence*, New York: The New Press, 2003, p. 79.

29. Eric Leed, *No Man's Land: Combat and Identity in World War I*, New York: Cambridge University Press, 1979, p. 75.

30. Ferro, *Great War*, p. 227; Martin Gilbert, *The First World War*, London: Weidenfeld & Nicolson, 1994, p. 541; Agenlo Tasca Rossi, *The Rise of Italian Fascism 1918–1922*, New York: Gordon Press, 1976, p. 9; Ferguson, *Pity of War*, p. 369.

31. Ambassador Rodd to Balfour, 25 November 1918, TNA. FO 371/3228/194529.

32. Corner and Procacci, 'The Italian experience of "total" mobilisation', p. 231.

33. Procacci, 'Popular protest and labour conflict', p. 51.

34. Ambassador Rodd to Balfour, 8 October 1918, TNA. FO 371/3228/168785.

35. Ambassador Rodd to Balfour, 10 October 1918, TNA. FO 371/3228/169727.

36. Rochat, *L'Esercito Italiano*, p. 26.

37. Marco Mondini, 'Between subversion and coup d'état: military power and politics after the Great War (1919–1922)', *Journal of Modern Italian Studies*, 11(4), 2006, p. 445.

38. Rossi, *Rise of Italian Fascism*, p. 11.

39. Anthony Cardoza, *Aristocrats in Bourgeois Italy: The Piedmontese Nobility 1861–1930*, Cambridge: Cambridge University Press, 2002, pp. 11–12.
40. Luigi Salvatorelli, *Nazionalfascismo*, Turin: Einaudi, 1977, p. 13.
41. Piero Melograni, *Storia politica di grande guerra*, Bari: Laterza, 1969, pp. 558–9.
42. Antonio Gramsci, *Selections from Political Writings 1910–1920*, London: Lawrence & Wishart, 1977, pp. 84–7.
43. Quotes in this paragraph are from Rossi, *Rise of Italian Fascism*, p. 12.
44. Both quoted ibid., p.10
45. Seton-Watson, *Liberalism to Fascism*, p. 521.
46. Sabbatucci, *I combattenti*, p. 46.
47. Ibid.
48. Ibid., p. 47.
49. Michael Ledeen, 'Italy: war as a style of life', in James Diehl and Stephen Ward, *The War Generation: Veterans of the First World War*, Port Washington: Kennikat Press, 1975, pp. 109–10.
50. Sabbatucci, *I combattenti*, p. 47.
51. Ibid., p. 9.
52. Interestingly, for all *Il Popolo*'s advocacy of veterans as the vanguard, the motion to form an ANC section at this meeting was opposed by the fascists, who argued instead for an association under their control.
53. Gianni Isola, *Guerra al regno della guerra!: Storia della Lega proletaria mutilati invalidi reduci orfani e vedove di guerra (1918–1924)*, Florence: Le Lettere, 1990, p. 37.
54. TNA: TNA, FO 371/3810/125486, 30 August 1919 and 128837, 13 September 1919.
55. Isola, *Guerra al regno della guerra! Storia della Lega proletaria*, p. 5.
56. Ibid.
57. ACS, Carte Nitti, b.38, f.107, sf.5, no.33564, 20 November 1919.
58. ACS, PS, Aff. Gen, 1920, b.85, f.18, no.10172, 27 July 1920.
59. TNA: TNA, FO 371/3813, 206094, 28 June 1920 and 206495, 29 June 1920.
60. TNA: TNA, FO 371/3812, 195086, 30 April 1920.
61. TNA: TNA, FO 371/3812/191717, 14 April 1920.
62. TNA: TNA, FO 371/3812/191717, 14 April 1920.
63. Quoted in Giuseppe Fiori, *Antonio Gramsci: Life of a Revolutionary*, London: Verso, 1990, p. 128.
64. John M. Cammett, *Antonio Gramsci and the Origins of Italian Communism*, Stanford, CA: Stanford University Press, 1967; Fiori, *Life of a Revolutionary*.

BIBLIOGRAPHY/FURTHER READING

English

Paul Corner and Giovanna Procacci, 'The Italian experience of "total" mobilisation', in John Horne, ed., *State, Society and Mobilisation in Europe during the First World War*, Cambridge: Cambridge University Press, 1997.

Adrian Lyttleton, ed., *Liberal and Fascist Italy*, Oxford: Oxford University Press, 2002.

Marco Mondini, 'Between subversion and coup d'état: military power and politics after the Great War (1919–1922)', *Journal of Modern Italian Studies*, 11(4), 2006.

Giovanna Procacci, 'Popular protest and labour conflict in Italy, 1915–18', *Social History*, 14(1), January 1989.

Agenlo Tasca Rossi, *The Rise of Italian Fascism 1918–1922*, New York: Gordon Press, 1976.

Christopher Seton-Watson, *Italy from Liberalism to Fascism 1870–1925*, London: Methuen, 1967.

Robert Wohl, *The Generation of 1914*, London: Weidenfeld & Nicolson, 1980.

Italian

Bianchi Bruna, *La follia e la fuga: nevrosi di guerra, diserzione e disobbedienza nell'esercito italiano, 1915–1918* Roma: Bulzoni, 2001.

Piero Melograni, *Storia politica di grande guerra* Bari: Laterza, 1969.

Marco Mondini, *La politica delle armi: Il ruolo dell'esercito nell'avvento del fascismo*, Rome–Bari: Laterza, 2006.

Giovanni Sabbatucci, *I combattenti nel primo dopoguerra*, Bari: Laterza, 1974.

4
Soldiers on the Side of the People: Portugal 1974–75

Peter Robinson

THE ARMED FORCES MOVEMENT AND THE APRIL COUP

It is hard to believe that General Antonio de Spinola, with his monocle and swagger stick, was seen by rebellious officers in the Portuguese armed forces as the lynchpin in the overthrow of a fascist dictatorship. Spinola fought for Franco in the Spanish civil war and had been the military governor of Guinea, one of Portugal's African colonies. He was also a director of the Champalimaud group, one of two huge native conglomerates (the other was CUF) which had enjoyed state protection against foreign competition; even Coca-Cola was prohibited. Yet the attention of Portuguese business was beginning to turn away from Portugal's African empire and towards Europe. And the political strategies favoured in ruling-class circles increasingly reflected this shift.

In search of cheap labour and a friendly regime, multinationals like Timex, Ford and ITT set up large modern plants, mostly in the Lisbon industrial belt. New developments, such as the gigantic shipyard complexes of Lisnave and Setenave, were financed with the help of foreign capital. The urban working class grew, along with shanty towns. By 1968, foreign capital accounted for 52.2 per cent of Portugal's total manufacturing investment. Portugal in 1974 was the least developed country in Western Europe. It had a large peasantry in the north, landed estates in the south and relatively small, concentrated industrial centres around Lisbon and along the north coast. Social provisions were archaic and the population actually declined in the late 1960s.

Spinola's *Portugal and the Future* (1974) expressed the growing discontent within the establishment. When the Portuguese Prime Minister Marcelo Caetano read it he understood 'that the military coup, which I could sense had been coming, was now inevitable'.[1] But Caetano only saw Spinola and his associates as a threat, not the junior officers. He did not understand how deeply Portugal's interminable colonial wars had undermined the confidence and political loyalty of the army's middle ranks.

The number of Portuguese dead – 13,000 – was greater than in any conflict since the Napoleonic Wars. And it was the army that was blamed for these failures. The last straw was a government decision in July 1973 to allow conscripted officers with short service records to be promoted alongside regular officers, like those in the Armed Forces Movement (MFA). The coup of 23 April 1974 was not planned by Spinola, but by people too subordinate to register on the radar. On Sunday, 9 September 1973, 136 officers, none more senior than captain, met deep in the countryside, ostensibly for a 'special farmhouse barbecue'. This was the first meeting of the MFA. They built a network of 300 supporting officers from all three services and published their *Democracy, Development and De-colonialisation* manifesto. At this point there was little to choose between Spinola's views and those of the MFA.

All this made a clash with the regime inevitable. On 25 April 1974, at 25 minutes past midnight, the Catholic *Rádio Renascença* played a song which was the signal to launch the coup. Under Otelo de Carvalho, the engineering regiment Pontinha, on the northern outskirts of Lisbon, revolted and occupied its barracks. Carvalho hoped to re-establish the prestige of the armed forces; photographs showed him weeping at the funeral of the dictator Antonio Salazar, yet he would be radicalised by events and play an important role in the development of the revolution.

The coup succeeded with remarkable ease. A dozen military units were mobilised. Only four people were killed, shot by terrified PIDE (secret police) agents. After 50 years, the regime Salazar had built collapsed in less than a day.

THE CARNIVAL

Public reaction at first was cautious. Many rushed to stock up with petrol and groceries. Parents kept their children indoors. But soon people began to move tentatively into the cafés, streets and squares to see what was happening.

The MFA itself was equally tentative in approaching the population. Its first concern was the organisation of the coup, but it had mutinied and now needed mass social support to legitimise its position. Red carnations were famously adopted as the symbol of the revolution, and soldiers stuck them in their rifle barrels.

'The soldiers were on the side of the people', the walls announced. By the end of the day the tanks were swarming with joyriders. Demonstrators attacked the hated PIDE, who had to be saved from lynching by bemused soldiers. Walls blossomed with graffiti, slogans and posters, and, later, with brilliant murals. May Day was declared a national holiday. Even the prostitutes of Lisbon organised. They campaigned to sack their pimps and offered their services half-price to all ranks below lieutenant.

In its first ten days it was only the personal intervention of MFA officers which persuaded the workers at places like Lisnave and ITT to return to work. Although the MFA later claimed that it was the motor of the revolution, Melo Antunes of the MFA saw things differently: 'A few hours after the start of the coup the mass movements began. This immediately transformed it into a revolution. It showed that the military were in tune with the Portuguese people.'[2] The coup released a multitude of popular energies and aspirations. On 29 April more than 100 families living in the shanty towns occupied a new government housing project on the outskirts of Lisbon. In the next two weeks more than 2,000 houses were occupied around the country, launching a movement that would grow dramatically over the next 18 months.

On the day of the coup only one workplace, the Mague metallurgical factory, with 2,000 workers, was actually on strike, for a minimum monthly wage of 6,000 escudos. This was immediately conceded by the management. The MFA leaders, however, warned that the new pay deal was an example which should *not* be followed.[3]

Workplaces erupted, but these eruptions were not coordinated and their demands, both political and economic, varied enormously. Some strikes lasted a few hours; others continued for months. The disputes were mainly in the newer industries (electronics, shipyards) and newly expanded parts of older industries (textiles, construction). Wage claims sprouted haphazardly. The predominantly female workforce at the Timex watch factory, for example, went on strike for wage increases and the purging of six PIDE informers. They sold the watches in the streets to boost their strike funds. On 13 May 1,600 miners at Panasqueira struck for a minimum wage of 6,000 escudos, free medical care, an annual bonus of a month's wage, one month's holiday and the purging of fascists. Within a week they had won all their demands. On 15 May, Lisnave's 8,400 workers occupied their shipyard and struck for a 40-hour week and a 7,800 escudo minimum monthly wage. In May at least 158 workforces were involved in fierce confrontations, including

35 occupations.[4] By the end of May 1974 workers' commissions, councils and committees, usually called *Comissões de Trabalhadores* (CTs), had been formed in almost every workplace in the Lisbon region. It has been estimated that between May and October 4,000 workers' CTs were established, almost always following mass meetings (*plenários*).

In the big companies, especially the multinationals, the demand that all members of the management with fascist connections be purged usually accompanied wage claims. This ousting of fascists was known as *saneamento* (cleansing). It happened in more than half the firms which employed more than 500 people.

MFA set up a 20-member coordinating commission but did not intend to govern the country. An elaborate governing structure, headed by General Spinola, was established, which was supposed to last only until the forthcoming Constituent Assembly elections. The first 'civilian' provisional government was formed on 15 May. Nominally a coalition, it included the Communist Party (which was given the Ministry of Labour) and two of the newly founded parties – the Socialist Party (PS) and the Popular Democratic Party (the PPD which emerged out of Caetano's short-lived 'liberal wing') – both of which supported the Western European social democracy model.

In the absence of a parliament the Prime Minister and cabinet had the power to decree laws, but in practice its main functions were administrative. The military laid down the policies which the government enacted into law. Over the course of the next 18 months there were to be five more provisional governments.

THE COMMUNIST PARTY AND THE FAR LEFT

What forces were active in the workers' movement?

The Portuguese Communist Party (PCP) had a respected tradition of opposition to fascism; by 25 April 1974 the party had some 5,000 members, a substantial social base and some influence in the working class. It had no tradition of social democracy (or Euro-communism) and this may explain in part its hard line, pro-Soviet position. As a member of the provisional government, the PCP immediately played its main card – its influence over the workers' movement. It distanced itself from the wildcat strikes and the workers' commissions, and within a fortnight organised a demonstration against strikes, accusing the workers' commissions of being 'ultra-left' and 'playing the game of the right and the bosses'.

While working with the MFA, the PCP was putting its resources not into the workplaces but into the Intersindical. This had emerged in 1970 as a loose conglomeration of relatively independent unions. Within weeks of the coup the number of affiliated unions rose from 22 to 200, transforming Intersindical almost overnight into the national trade union umbrella organisation. (Over the next 18 months a smaller national rival emerged, led by the Socialist Party.)

In some cases, however, the unions were mere façades, a creation from above. Workers related to each other through their commissions rather than unions.

Many leading activists in the workers' commissions were members of the PCP and were dismayed by its attacks on the commissions. These activists often left or were expelled. As a result a great many 'Maoist' sects emerged, the largest and most strident being the Movement to Reorganise the Party of the Proletariat (MRPP). Revolutionaries from other traditions were also active at the time, albeit in small numbers. The PRP/BR (Revolutionary Proletarian Party/Revolutionary Brigades), for example, had carried out various attacks on military installations before 25 April 1974; the Movement of Left Socialists (MES) originated around 1970 as a network of socialist forums, including trade unionists, Catholics and students.

The first major industrial confrontation involving the army took place in mid-June. On 19 June the government gave the order to call in the army against 1,000 postal workers employed by CTT who had gone on strike. Faced with this threat, the strike committee called off the strike and secured desultory gains. A number of PCP members tore up their party cards in disgust and joined the rapidly expanding revolutionary left. The Socialist Party, by contrast, conspicuously supported the strike, stressing its democratic (i.e. non-PCP) nature, enhancing the party's 'democratic' and 'left-wing' credentials. And when two army cadets who had refused to participate in the mobilisation against the striking postal workers were imprisoned, far-left groups organised a demonstration in their support. This was the first of many occasions when the rank and file came into conflict with military orders. The dispute was an isolated victory for the first provisional government, but the MFA had discovered that the tap of revolution, once turned on, was difficult to turn off.

The issue of decolonisation was also tearing the government apart. Its instability was reflected in the growing flight of domestic and foreign capital from Portugal. It fell on 9 July 1974.

One of the priorities of the new second provisional government was to create a 'reliable' internal state security force, which incorporated most of the armed regiments in Lisbon, called COPCON (Continental Operations Command). COPCON had to appear to be independent of the old structures and also untainted by the soldiers 'who were on the side of the people'. It was commanded by the avuncular Otelo de Carvalho, the architect of the 25 April coup. He was still not considered to be left-wing and COPCON at first had none of the left-wing character it was later to assume.

COPCON was soon called into action. On 28 August workers at TAP (the national airline) went on strike. Lisbon airport was placed under military control and one workers' leader, Santos Junor, was arrested by COPCON, which on the same day sent troops to break up the occupations in two other workplaces. On 29 August, the government, backed by the PCP but not the Socialist Party, passed a series of strike laws. They officially legalised strikes for the first time, but banned political stoppages and sympathy strikes. A 37-day cooling-off period was introduced.

A handful of revolutionaries, mainly Maoists, from the Lisnave shipyard called an 'illegal' one-day strike and a demonstration against the legislation. It was denounced by the PCP and banned by the government, which made preparations to use COPCON troops to prevent the demonstration. On the day, 12 September, more than 5,000 helmeted Lisnave workers marched in close formation to the Ministry of Labour in Lisbon. The shipyards were brought to a standstill. A soldier recalled:

'Before lunch the rumour circulated that we were going out and we soon guessed it was to Lisnave . . . the commander told us that he'd received a telephone call about a demonstration at Lisnave, led by a minority of leftist agitators and that our job was to prevent it from taking place. We were armed as we had never been before with G3s and 4 magazines . . . The demo began and a human torrent advanced with shouts of "the soldiers are the sons of the workers", "tomorrow the soldiers will be workers" and "the arms of soldiers must not be turned against the workers". The commander soon saw that we weren't going to follow his orders, so he shut up. Our arms hung down by our side and some comrades were crying . . . The following day in the barracks, things were livelier. Before morning assembly many comrades were up and shouting the slogans of the demo, "the soldiers are sons of the workers", "down with capitalist exploitation".'[5]

One of the key characteristics of the Portuguese revolutionary process was how the workers persuaded the soldiers to break ranks.

On 7 February, Inter-Empresas, a joint workers' council representing 38 factories in the Lisbon region, called a demonstration against redundancies and unemployment. Many small and medium enterprises were being bankrupted or simply abandoned by their owners. At the last minute, the Inter-Empresas decided on another slogan: 'NATO out, national independence', in response to the presence of the US fleet in Lisbon harbour during NATO exercises.

All the political parties in the coalition government opposed the demonstration and it was banned by the Civil Governor of Lisbon, a PCP fellow-traveller. The PCP raised doubts as to the 'true intentions' of the demonstrators, but the MFA still had to consider its position. It was expected to support the ban. But on the Friday morning members of Inter-Empressas went to see COPCON. At the end of this meeting the MFA announced that it did not object to the demonstration. Effectively, the MFA turned against the parties in the coalition government.

Eighty thousand people took part.[6] Artur Palacio, a well-known member of its workers' Lisnave commission, described the soldiers' response on the day:

'The army had blocked the streets leading to the American Embassy. I asked the people through the megaphone whether or not we should keep marching, but they wouldn't let anyone stand in their way. We carried on. As the demonstrators passed, the commandos turned their backs, pointed their weapons at the building and joined in with the chanting.'[7]

Libération reported that 'people were crying with joy'.[8] Actions like these eroded the bond between the PCP and the MFA, the majority of the MFA preferring to side with autonomous grassroots organisations.

TWO ATTEMPTED COUPS

The dates of 28 September 1974 and 11 March 1975 have been etched into the history of those times; on both occasions coup attempts from the right were thwarted by the military, with the help of the 'people'.

By September 1974, many factory owners and foreign investors were withdrawing entirely from Portugal. Industrialists and sections of the traditional military elite had little faith in the government, which was generally regarded as favourably disposed towards 'communists' and drew the conclusion that the use of armed force was becoming necessary and urgent. They were worried that the troops could no longer be trusted. Leading industrialists met President Spinola and a few of the generals and called for a mobilisation of the 'silent majority' on 28 September. The coup was defeated by the military, coupled with barricades manned by the population, blocking the threatened march of the 'silent majority', orchestrated by the President.

From January 1975 the situation began to move in a more radical direction. Factory and land occupations increased in number, school students struck and soldiers went to the countryside to 'educate' the rural population. By March 1975, sections of the ruling class were becoming convinced that a military coup was the necessary response to radicalisation. Military resistance to the attempted March coup was led by COPCON, which had some forewarning and was on the alert. Working people responded magnificently. Within hours of the attack, barricades were set up along the main roads, sometimes using expropriated bulldozers, lorries and cement mixers. Soldiers fraternised openly with workers manning the barricades and handed over arms. Armed workers searched cars, and strikers at Rádio Renascença went back to work and occupied the radio station in order to 'defend the revolution'.

After the failure, some right-wing generals and company directors were arrested. Spinola and others were whisked off to Spain 'by the helicopters of reaction'. The MFA emerged considerably stronger, and the PCP was strengthened within the reorganised provisional government. Marx once said the revolution needs the whip of counter-revolution. The successful resistance on the ground gave a considerable boost to the whole of the left. Workers and soldiers were hungry for new ideas: pornography vied with political pamphlets on the street-stalls; Lenin's *State and Revolution* headed the booksellers' lists; arguments were purchased wholesale. Workers were prepared to tolerate vitriolic language and seemingly obscure arguments in their search for new explanations and solutions.

One conscript from the Caldas da Rainha barracks (consisting of 690 soldiers and officers) remarked how easy it was to build on that resistance:

'I joined the PRP after March 11th. When I joined there were five militants in the barracks. After three months there were twenty, two of whom were officers . . . The PRP demanded, in response to March 11th, that one platoon of armed volunteers be assembled and if necessary, mobilised, to help the local population, and, if necessary, attack the fascists. The commander of the regiment, who probably had Socialist Party sympathies, succumbed.'[9]

Carvalho became increasingly sympathetic to the ideas of the PRP.

THE ELECTIONS

After 11 March the MFA was able to consolidate the power of its assembly of 240 delegates, who in theory could hold any rank and represent any of the three wings of the armed forces, and they elected the 'Supreme' Council of Revolution responsible to the assembly and nobody else. Reluctantly, the MFA decided to honour its commitment to hold free elections.

For the right, the failure of the coups had made it clear that the strategy of military intervention and paternalist modernisation could not prevail. The alternative was to build a Western European-type social democracy within a parliamentary framework. The key to this was the Socialist Party, which had been receiving support for some time from the United States and Europe.

The anniversary of the overthrow of the old regime, 25 April, was chosen for Portugal's first elections based on universal suffrage. Three weeks were allocated for electioneering, which was subject to complex rules, including equal TV time for all parties, regardless of their size; hence parties to the left of the PCP, which eventually won less than 8 per cent of the vote, had more than 50 per cent of the TV air time. As parties were not allowed to fly-post over one another's posters it became necessary to carry longer and longer ladders to reach blank wall space. Interest was immense. Of the 6,176,559 enrolled electors, 5,666, 696 went to the polls – 91.73 per cent of the electorate.

'Socialism' was obviously extremely popular, for the Socialist Party won 37.87 per cent of the vote, whereas the PCP polled a meagre 12.53 per cent plus the 4.12 per cent of its close ally, the MDP. From 200 members in April 1974 the Socialist Party had become the leading *parliamentary* party in Portugal under the banner of freedom of speech, democracy and a managed, modern economy. The very vagueness of its slogans for 'progress', 'democracy' and 'socialism' enabled it to appeal to broad sectors of the population, including the less organised workers who fell outside the influence of the Intersindical and the PCP. The Socialist Party often appeared more left-wing than the PCP. It had attacked the government's new labour laws in 1974 and tolerated the left within the party. Portugal had had no experience of the betrayals of reformism in power.

The newly elected constituent assembly was not a supreme body, but merely an advisory body to the MFA, which continued to appoint the President. The subordination of the victors of the elections to the armed forces was to be a source of increasing tension. Within 24 hours there was chanting at a Socialist Party victory demonstration of 'down with the MFA'. For the first time there was open conflict between a major political party and the MFA. Over the next six months the Socialist Party relentlessly pursued the interrelated themes of 'power to those elected', 'democracy' and 'freedom of speech'.

POPULAR POWER

The election results were a humiliation for many within the MFA. They regarded themselves, and not Mario Soares and the Socialist Party, as the 'saviours of the people'. Some within the MFA were asking whether the Socialist Party was just another face of the bourgeoisie and whether it would continue the revolution.

The left within the MFA had to develop its alternative. In the months after the election, it was the slogan *poder popular* (people's power) that emerged as the ideology of the MFA. It spanned classes, uniting the military with workers, peasants and tenants.

The first act of the Council of Revolution after 11 March was to nationalise the Portuguese-owned banks and insurance companies. Land occupations increased dramatically. Over the next six months land workers in the Alentejo region occupied 200,000 hectares. For the first time in living memory the drift from the land by workers was reversed. Workers were taking over their factories on an unprecedented scale. In the case of the larger enterprises the action of workers often forced the nationalisation of the firm or the industry.

The workers at *República* took over their newspaper. The takeover of *Rádio Renascença*, the former Catholic station, in Lisbon was particularly well publicised. The broadcasters hung a live microphone in the street so that whenever there was a demonstration passing by, or a deputation outside, there would be a live broadcast of street politics.

When COPCON refused to remove occupying workers from the broadcasting station *Rádio Renascença*, and when it allowed the newspaper *República*, previously closed down by the government, to reopen under workers' control, it became increasingly clear that the PCP no longer had the means at its disposal to discipline and control the working class. (In this respect it is perhaps not without significance that the government was most heavily criticised by the Socialist and PPD parties not for those situations in which the PCP was firmly in control of the workers' movement, but for disputes like *Radio Renascença* and *República* in which the PCP was marginal.)

The cases of *República* and *Rádio Renascença* became internationally famous, polarising opinion between the supporters of 'freedom of speech' and those who sided with 'control by the workers'.

Discussions in the MFA increasingly oscillated between the claims of discipline and those of *poder popular*. There was talk of refusing to hand over power, of turning the MFA into a party, and even mention of creating a benevolent dictatorship. The options that presented themselves made the game of balancing, of making concessions to both sides, more and more risky.

On the weekend before the elections, 660 people attended the founding conference of the CRTSMs (Revolutionary Councils of Workers, Soldiers, and Sailors). It included representatives (not delegates) from 161 workplaces, among them Lisnave, Setenave, TAP and, most significantly, 21 military units. A number of the soldiers in uniform were present. This was the first attempt to unite workers with soldiers in a 'non-party' organisation, but despite this most people saw it as a PRP creation.

The CRTSMs superficially were very political, but in practice were remote from the day-to-day economic struggles. There was no equivalent of 'Land, Peace and Bread'; instead, they called for 'a revolutionary government without political parties'. This disdain for party politics fitted with the military tradition of the MFA and its role of reflecting and mediating the different classes. Carvalho was linked to the proposal; his hope was that a national network of councils would provide a support base.

The CRTSMs were soon to be forgotten, overridden on 8 July when the General Assembly of the MFA narrowly approved the 'guidelines for an alliance between the people and the MFA', known as the Povo–MFA Pact. Its aim was to set up a parallel authority to the state and parliamentary system. The organisations of *poder popular* – residents' commissions, soldiers' committees (ADUs), workers' commissions and other local organisations – would be integrated under the protection of the MFA.

The Pontinha regiment of engineers, the command headquarters for the 25 April coup, was a source of inspiration. The regiment established direct links with the local population, building roads and bridges with military equipment. The first joint assembly was held just before the MFA–Povo Pact was announced, with 17 factories and about 30 local tenants' commissions present. At its peak the Pontinha assembly had some 200 delegates from its constituent associations. The adoption of the MFA–Povo Pact, together with the government's continued failure to ensure the return of *República* and *Radio Renascença*, led Soares and the Socialist Party to resign from the government on 10 July, the day *República* reopened.

The next five months were to witness a proliferation of local popular assemblies – *República* mentions at least 38. These assemblies spent hundreds of hours planning and sometimes implementing actions, but they were dominated by representatives from residents' commissions, swamping those from workplaces. When soldiers did attend, the impact was electrifying. In reality, few of these assemblies really got off the ground, and the more stable of them in effect assumed the functions of local government. But they inspired the popular movement.

A demonstration in support of the COPCON document on *poder popular* (which opened with the words: 'The working class and the MFA are the driving force on the road to socialism') was held on 20 August and attended by 100,000 people, including a large number of soldiers. It had the support of more than 200 workers' and neighbourhood committees. A new revolutionary front, FUR, was set up and the PCP only backed it at the last moment.

REACTION

Within 24 hours of the demonstration the PCP withdrew from the front and called for reconciliation with the Socialist Party and the formation of a coalition government. We have to step back slightly in time and outside Lisbon to understand why the communists preferred to throw in their lot with the Social Democrats, and the moderates. Western capitalist governments were insisting more and more urgently that Portugal 'put its house in order'. The retreat from the colonies meant that half a million bitterly disillusioned and destitute *retornados* had to be resettled and reintegrated into a population of nine million. Many settled in the centre and the north, traditionally conservative areas.

Land reform had far less impact in the north, where most farms were owned by smallholders or were farmed by individual tenants, than in the south, where much of the land was worked by wage labourers on large estates. Extensive areas of the north were still extremely underdeveloped; some of the remote mountain villages in the Tras os Montes had only recently started using money as a medium of exchange. The proposed land reform, which limited holdings to 500 hectares, or 50 hectares of irrigated land, scarcely touched those in the north where the majority of holdings were below 5 hectares. The minimum wage law did not apply to agricultural workers.

The failure of agricultural policy played into the hands of the Catholic Church. The Archbishop of Braga likened the communists to Satan: 'We are called upon to fight for God or against Him.'[10] He regularly supplied funds and premises to far-right organisations, which in the 'hot summer of 1975' were responsible for burning down more than 50 offices of the PCP and the revolutionary left.[11] The growing confidence of the right was fuelled by the virulent anti-communist campaign launched by the Socialist Party after its resignation from government. Splits too were beginning to appear within the MFA's Revolutionary Council.

On 7 August nine members of the Supreme Revolutionary Council, led by Major Melo Antunes, issued an open letter known as the *Document of the Nine*. They were immediately suspended from the Revolutionary Council. But the *Document* represented the opinions of a significant bloc of moderate officers – all but two were authors of the original MFA platform – who were growing weary of the revolution and it became a rallying call for moderates everywhere. It would contribute to the collapse of the fifth provisional government.

SOLDIERS DISOBEY ORDERS

At the beginning of September the Military Police regiment refused orders to go to Angola. Others followed suit. The authors of the *Document of the Nine* complained of what they saw as 'a progressive decomposition of state structures. Everywhere wildcat and anarchistic forms of the exercise of power have gradually taken over even reaching as far as the armed forces'.[12]

These fears were confirmed in a totally unpredicted quarter, a new movement of rank-and-file soldiers in the north. A few militants met secretly in a forest and drew up a leaflet protesting against the poor conditions of the soldiers. Thus began SUV (*Soldados Unidos Vencerao* – Soldiers United Will Win), the first autonomous rank-and-file soldiers' organisation in Portugal.

SUV called a demonstration in Porto on 10 September. An estimated 30,000 workers marched behind a contingent of 1,500 soldiers. Jorge, who was involved in SUV from the outset, said: 'As soldiers weren't allowed to sing in public we started whistling. However, by the end everybody ends up singing the *Internationale*. The number of people on the demonstration grew in front of our very own eyes.'[13]

SUV began to expose to the soldiers the conservatism of their officers, which had been masked by the prestige of the MFA. The soldiers started to make demands concerning the inequalities between them and the officers. They began to agitate for pay increases and free transport. For many soldiers a single trip to see their family cost them almost a month's pay. As a member of secretariat of SUV said:

'In the general headquarters of Porto there were three separate mess halls, one for soldiers, one for noncoms, and one for officers. Three days after the Porto demonstration, some soldiers calmly walked in and sat down to eat in the officers' mess. The next day all the soldiers occupied the officers' mess. Since that day there has been a struggle to eliminate the separate mess halls and unify them.'[14]

On 25 September SUV held an unusually large demonstration in Lisbon calling for the release of two soldiers who had been arrested for distributing SUV literature. Hammond tells us that

'when a speaker at what was supposed to be the concluding rally announced that there would be a protest at Trafaria the next day, the crowd shouted "Let's go today!" Leaving the park close to midnight, marchers boarded city buses and announced to drivers and passengers they would be taking a detour. The buses took the huge crowd to Trafaria, and before morning the authorities announced that the two soldiers would be freed.'[15]

SUV was the first organisation within the armed forces to take up rank-and-file, bread-and-butter demands.

THE CRISIS INTENSIFIES

The resurgence of the right in the summer of 1975 led to renewed fears of a coup. Carvalho commented: 'What worries me is the possible *Chileanisation* of Portugal . . . they are building machines to kill. With them they can set off a new Chile. I am haunted by that fear.'[16] He was referring to the overthrow of President Salvador Allende on 11 September 1973. The vast majority of the left thought 'that there would be sharp armed clashes between the classes . . . within a few months (at most)'. This view was shared by much of the far left internationally, which stressed that there was 'Only One Solution: Socialist Revolution'; the alternative was barbarism.

The sixth provisional government took office on 19 September and would remain in power until April 1976. All the major parties were represented, but the Socialist Party and the officers around the 'Group of Nine' had gained at the expense of the PCP. The mass movement, however, was still strong. Land occupations were accelerating and whole sections of society were beyond government control. The unresolved struggle over *Rádio Renascença* epitomised the powerlessness of the government. On 29 September Prime Minister Pinheiro de Azevedo ordered COPCON to occupy it. After a demonstration by workers, Carvalho, in tears, ordered his troops to withdraw. Within six hours the radio was re-occupied by the commandos under Colonel Jaime Neves. An enormous demonstration two weeks later forced the commandos to withdraw and the radio started transmissions again.

The government was almost powerless. What emerged was what Tony Cliff called 'dual powerlessness'. At the time he wrote: 'Up to now the capitalists have not managed to get a clear grip on state power in Portugal, while the proletariat has not been able to challenge them for it. The result has been an unstable balance whose centre of gravity has been the MFA.'[17] On 7 November government saboteurs blew up the station's transmitters. The paratroopers who carried it out thought they were providing protection and that 'the orders came from the left'. This betrayal so shocked them that they were to revolt within weeks.

The mass movement involved huge numbers of people and there was still enormous potential support for *poder popular*; but weaknesses were becoming apparent. Controlling their own workplaces did not always lead workers to greater militancy. Cliff and Peterson wrote: 'The fight for workers' control without workers' power tends to become control over the workers by the capitalist system and a loss of confidence among workers in their ability to manage the economy.'[18]

Meanwhile, rumours of impending coups from both left and right became an endemic feature of political life. There was much talk about the involvement of the CIA.[19] Many workplace and community meetings went on until the early hours of the morning. Some workers, especially those who were not inspired by a revolutionary vision, dropped out. In the factories, decisions were increasingly left to the technicians, experts and 'politicos' and, elsewhere, to the PCP and the Socialist Party. Stability became an increasingly persuasive objective. Financial crisis and withdrawal of investment had also taken their toll. How could such a poor country have a socialist revolution and survive? Where was the money to come from?

In Lisbon militants in the factories were turning to a network of workers' committees built up by the PCP. The PCP had founded the *Cintura Industrial de Lisboa* (CIL – the Workers' Committees of Lisbon), which launched what was to be a massive demonstration (some said of more than half a million) on 16 November against the threat from the right within and beyond the sixth provisional government.

In contrast, only 48 km to the south, the Setubal Comité de Luta (Committee of Struggle) showed how differently things could be done. Here the revolutionary left set the pace and the PCP were sufficiently flexible (and isolated) to feel it had to be involved. The Comité de Luta was almost certainly the closest thing to a soviet in Western Europe since the Second World War.

The struggle within the workers' movement was by no means exhausted. But in mid-October workers from 32 workers' councils in the construction industry met to formulate a demand for a national wage structure and a single union. A national strike and march to Sao Bento, the home of the constituent assembly, was organised. The streets around the assembly, many of them narrow, were blocked with tractors, cement mixers and trucks. Construction workers armed themselves with pickaxes, clubs and the like, and held hostage the members of the Constituent Assembly. Prime Minister Azevedo asked the commandos to rescue them. They refused. He then requested a helicopter. The Military Police overheard the request, alerted the construction workers and the helicopter was prevented from landing. After 36 hours the Prime Minister conceded all the workers' demands with effect from 27 November.[20]

The paralysis of formal government was so complete that on 20 November it declared it was not going to do anything 'political' but would merely act in an administrative capacity until the resolution of the power conflict.

THE TURNING POINT: 25 NOVEMBER 1975

By late November it was obvious that 'something' had to happen. The government threatened to withdraw to Porto while peasants and farmers in the north threatened to cut off food supplies to the 'red commune' of Lisbon.

The moderates in the army had been consolidating their position since October and preparations were being made for a decisive move against the radicals.

COPCON knew, even in September, that the Group of Nine was preparing a coup. They provided the political dimension, while another group, the 'Operationals', which had the support of many non-committed and right-wing army officers, added the military weight. They were led by Lieutenant Colonel Ramalho Eanes, who was later elected President.[21] It happened that those officers who had not been 'contaminated' by political considerations also commanded the best-disciplined troops, able to move at short notice.

Events in the army were coming to a head: 1,600 previously loyal paratroopers from Tancos, some of whom had been used in the demolition of *Rádio Renascença* on 7 November, had been harshly criticised by workers and soldiers from other units. They now rebelled and forced out 123 of their 150 officers.

When, on 24 November, the Council of the Revolution confirmed the appointment of Vasco Lourenco to replace Carvalho as commander of the Lisbon military region, which included the paratroopers, a showdown was inevitable. By the next morning paratroopers at five bases had occupied their barracks, demanding the dismissal of their commanders and to be placed under the overall command of Carvalho and COPCON. Carvalho went to see his fellow officers and the President, and was forcibly detained.

By this time a state of emergency had been declared, and the 'Operationals' under Colonel Eanes had set up their headquarters at the commando barracks at Amadora. It included the commandos led by the notorious Colonel Neves and some officers who had been sacked by their underlings. They moved into action, hoping to avoid a bloody confrontation. But even they must have been surprised at how easily they succeeded. One by one, all the rebel units collapsed. It seems that the most radical units were the most chaotic. The officers 'on the side of the people' failed to act, which caused confusion and disorientation.

All the revolutionary groupings were taken completely unawares by the speed of the events. None was involved in instigating the military response. The government, with the backing of the PCP, spread stories claiming that the attempt to prevent the sacking of Carvalho represented a bid for state power. The radical soldiers and their friends on the revolutionary left were isolated. In the preceding weeks the PCP had once again turned left in order to retain its political support and buttress its position within the government. On 24 November it called a two-hour general strike against the threat from the right, but with limited success.

The sergeants in the paratroopers and some of the officers who planned the resistance to the removal of Carvalho were encouraged by the PCP. But on the afternoon of 25 November the PCP sharply altered tack, using its main agencies, the Intersindical and the Cintura Industrial de Lisboa, to do so.[22] Officials and activists in the engineering union offices who were organising overnight occupations and strikes changed their tune at 6 o'clock on the Tuesday evening when the message from headquarters got through.[23]

Costa Gomes, the President, made it quite clear:

'We have to thank the PCP for not letting 25 November end up in civil war. On that day, the PCP supporters were intending to block the barracks of the commandos with bulldozers and excavators. They invaded and surrounded the naval unit at Almada and the Alfeite arsenal. These communists withdrew when I asked [Intersindical] to do so. The communist supporters were armed and, if they had not withdrawn, there would have been a civil war.'[24]

Vasco Lourenco explains the reasons for the about-turn:

'The PCP was always trapped between two attitudes: one was its desire to control large sections of Portuguese society, such as local government, the media, etc., with its own methods; the other was that it had to deal with the ultra-left and not appear reactionary, and this sometimes made the PCP act in a cavalier-like way.'[25]

On 26 November, Melo Antunes announced on television that the participation of the PCP was essential for the construction of socialism. He made it clear that there would be no wholesale repression, certainly no return to fascism, and so it proved. There was little physical repression. Some 200 soldiers and officers, plus a handful of construction workers, were jailed briefly. COPCON and the principal left-wing military units were disbanded. The following day all collective bargaining and strikes were suspended. Most of the firms which had been taken over by the state, and many of those under workers' control, were returned to their former owners in 1977 and 1978. The events of 25 November had been the turning point.

REFLECTIONS

The focus on fascism was to be one of the reasons for the collapse of the MFA–Popular Power axis. The MFA were the saviours, and time and time again it could rely on the people, and vice versa. There was a tendency to label anything authoritarian as fascist, in the loosest sense. Yet the neo-fascists were not real contenders for power and both the NATO powers and the Portuguese ruling class preferred to build a stable bourgeois parliamentary system. One reason the outcome of Chile 1973 was rather different from that of Portugal was in part because of the very strength of the popular movement in Portugal.

Fifty years of fascism, however, had left a vacuum. It meant that social democratic ideas were hardly developed and there was little experience or understanding of them. It also meant that sections of the revolutionary movement were characterised by voluntarism and an emphasis on shortcuts in alliance with the more politicised sections of the military. They had seen how a relatively small group of people could seize power on behalf of the majority.

Looking back it is clear that the focus of the PCP, and indeed most of the left, was on the military and not the working class. There were illusions in COPCON and the MFA. Admittedly, some sections of the left shifted the emphasis away from the officers towards the soldiers and talked about distributing weapons to the masses. But the emphasis was still militaristic. For example, it was noted with regret that Lisnave had only 60 guns. On 25 November 'Some went to the barracks asking for machine guns; there were assemblies in factories, but no-one knew what to do. People stopped working – but there was no organised strike.'[26]

The reliance did much to retard the development of an active class consciousness. Even in the Setubal *Comité de Luta*,

'When the soldiers spoke it was like God speaking. It was the soldiers' moment. They knew lots of things which nobody else knew. What was going on, in the army, in the government. It took up a lot of time . . . and left very little for discussing our own problems.'[27]

There was a vast gap between the economic and so-called political (i.e. military) dimensions.[28] The stress on the organisations of the workers and the popular power movement, although inspiring, in practice was abstract, largely rhetorical. On 25 November neither the officers 'on the side of the people' nor the left groups called for strikes, occupations or barricades. Although some sections were exhausted, the movement was still enormous. Construction workers, using walkie-talkies, commandeered enormous earth-movers and concrete mixers in order to block the advance of the commandos. In Setubal they contacted the *Comité de Luta* and asked them to set up blockades around the city. A strike and occupation by a powerful group of workers such as Lisnave could have given a lead to those waverers in the armed forces and to other sections of workers. Or perhaps it was too late.

The popular power movement was, if anything, dispersed and localised. It was not confident in its own strength. It had not flexed and developed muscles acting independently of the militants in the armed forces. In short, there was no alternative strategy. Kenneth Maxwell argues convincingly that the social ferment was central to the transition to democracy – 'the strength flows from the fact that it was a democracy born of struggle'. Maxwell suggests that 'the Portuguese upheaval was more like the European revolutions of the 1820s and 1848 than the great revolutions of 1789 in France or 1917 in Russia'. But this is not to suggest, and Maxwell does not, that the movement for change was superficial.[29]

At the time, Western capitalism was anxious about what was happening in Portugal. The Spanish regime was still fascist, but looked as if it might collapse. The conservative figures put out by the Spanish government showed that 1,196 industrial disputes were registered there in 1974, involving 669,861 workers.[30] Troops in other European countries were becoming restless. In Italy more than 1,000 soldiers, in uniforms but wearing handkerchief masks, took part in a demonstration in support of Portuguese workers and soldiers. Many argued that the Portuguese experience could have sparked an international revolution. With hindsight such a conflagration now appears improbable. However, it has to be remembered that events in Portugal did not occur in isolation. They occurred because Portugal could not continue to exist in isolation!

The fact remains that during those 18 months hundreds of thousands of workers took over their workplaces, the land and houses, and tens of thousands of soldiers rebelled. Nobody predicted that soldiers, along with civilians, would try quickly to learn and put into practice the ideas that explode from those who are exploited when they seek to take control of their own destiny. Portugal 1974–75 was an extraordinary period, one that still needs to be studied and celebrated.[31]

NOTES

1. Antonio Figueiredo, *Portugal – Fifty Years of Dictatorship*, London: Penguin, 1975, pp. 231–2.
2. Interview in Hugo Ferreira and Michael Marshall, *Portugal's Revolution: Ten Years On*, Cambridge: Cambridge University Press, 2011, p. 163.
3. *Sunday Times* Insight Team, *Portugal: The Year of the Captains*, London: Sunday Times, 1975, p. 120.
4. Details are provided in Maria de Lurdes Lima Santos, Marinús Pires de Lima and Vitor Matias Ferreira, *O 25 de Abril e as lutas sociais nas empresas*, 3 volumes, Porto: Afromento, 1976.
5. Published in the first issue of *Causa Operario*, a Marxist-Leninist paper, September 1974.
6. Despite the support from Lisnave for the demonstration of 7 February, the support from that shipyard was by no means unanimous. *Diario Popular* (6 February 1975) reported: 'The workers of Lisnave, meeting in general assembly in the Margueira yards, published a communiqué against the demo and refused to allow their CT to form part of the *Inter-Empresas* commission.'
7. Interview, 2 August 1982. Artur Palacio was a veteran militant who worked at Lisnave for many years. He first became involved with the Communist Party in the early 1950s when he was in his teens. At the time of 25 April he was a militant in one of the Marxist-Leninist sects which later was to help to found the UDP and was very involved in the very first *Inter-Empresas* meetings.
8. The article from the French weekly *Libération* was republished in the pamphlet 'Portugal, a Blaze of Freedom' by Big Flame, June 1975.
9. Interview with Jorge, 2 August 1980. He joined the PRP after 11 March, having attended the first CRTSMs conference. Subsequently, after 25 November, he became a full-time organiser for the PRP.
10. Richard Robinson, *Contemporary Portugal*, London: George Allen & Unwin, 1979, p. 242.
11. Gunter Wallraff, *The Undesirable Journalist*, London: Pluto Press, 1978, pp. 13–14. The author of this chapter was given a copy, via the IS, of a telexed arms order, which included mortars and bazookas. This was sent from Porto, in the north. This telex was passed on to the PRP, and thence to the COPCON.
12. Expresso, 9 August 1975, quoted in Tony Cliff, 'Portugal at the crossroads', *International Socialism*, 1(81–82), 1975, p. 29.

13. Interview with Jorge, 13 August 1980. In August and September 1975 he was based in the north in the RTM (regional transport barracks) and was very active in SUV.

14. Interview, 23 September 1975, included in Os SUV em Luta, translation in Imprecor 35.

15. John Hammond, *Building Popular Power: Workers' and Neighborhood Movements in the Portuguese Revolution*, New York: Monthly Review Press, 1988, p. 233.

16. Jean Pierre Faye, *Portugal: The Revolution in the Labyrinth*, Nottingham: Spokesman Books, 1976, pp. 49–50.

17. Cliff, 'Portugal at the crossroads', p. 41.

18. Tony Cliff and Robin Peterson, 'Portugal: the last 3 months', *International Socialism*. This article quotes from several interviews with workers about the problem of workers' control in their own workplaces.

19. In early November I called on a leading rank-and-file soldier in a Lisbon barracks, out of the blue, and told him that Philip Agee (a CIA defector who had been stationed in Portugal) was eager to warn the movement of the role of the CIA. My contact said he could, within days, organise a meeting with delegates from all the barracks in Portugal to hear Philip and left me to arrange the date. It had to be abandoned because of 25 November. At times I was accused of being a CIA agent (a not uncommon allegation) and subsequently I found a letter, dated 1977, from the PRP to all other political groups on the left, specifically warning them about my CIA involvement!

20. Refer to a marvellous eye witness account by Ben Pimlott, in *Labour Leader*, February, 1976.

21. Eanes became army chief of staff after 25 November and was elected President in June 1976. He was accepted by the moderate left in the armed forces as he was not a conservative.

22. The first issue of *República* following 25 November contains similar examples.

23. Conversation on 26 November 1975 with Jan Birkett-Smith, a Danish comrade who was in the union offices the day before.

24. Interview in Ferreira and Marshall, *Portugal's Revolution*, p. 181.

25. Ibid., p. 136.

26. Interview with Mauricio Levy, December 1975.

27. Interview with Isabel Guerra, 4 June 1984.

28. I well remember when the building workers came and spoke to the Comite, days before barricading the Prime Minister into the Parliament. They were listened to civilly, but there was no engagement.

29. Kenneth Maxwell, *The Making of Portuguese Democracy*, Cambridge: Cambridge University Press, 1995, p. 1.

30. Cited by Cliff, 'Portugal at the Crossroads', p. 48.

31. My studies would have been impossible without help from many people. Special mention must be made to Bill Lomax, who among other things made available all the materials he and others accumulated while working on a project financed by the Ford Foundation; Jorge Freire who worked at the Ministry of Social Communications in 1975. He helped me tremendously then and has encouraged me to revisit Portugal. Jorge served in the army in Guinea under General Spinola; Mauricio Levy, who was the international organiser for MES, when I first got to know him. He left the army shortly before 25 November 1975 and had been one of the people responsible for the takeover of the state radio and using this to broadcast news about the 11 March coup attempt.

BIBLIOGRAPHY/FURTHER READING

Colin Barker, ed., *Revolutionary Rehearsals*, London: Bookmarks, 1979.

Ronald H. Chilcote, *The Portuguese Revolution of 25 April 1974*, Coimbra: Universidade Coimbra, 1987.

Tony Cliff, 'Portugal at the crossroads', *International Socialism*, 1(81–82), 1975.

Lawrence S. Graham and Douglas L. Wheeler, *In Search of Modern Portugal*, Madison, WI: University of Wisconsin Press, 1983. See especially the chapter by Bill Lomax, 'Ideology and illusion in the Portuguese revolution: the role of the left'.

John Hammond, *Building Popular Power: Workers' and Neighborhood Movements in the Portuguese Revolution*, New York: Monthly Review Press, 1988.

Phil Mailer, *Portugal: The Impossible Revolution?* London: Solidarity, 1977.

Kenneth Maxwell, *The Making of Portuguese Democracy*, Cambridge: Cambridge University Press, 1995.

Immanuel Ness and Dario Azzellini, *Ours to Master and to Own: Workers' Control from the Commune to the Present*, Chicago: Haymarket Books, 2011.

Douglas Porch, *The Portuguese Armed Forces and the Revolution*, London: Croom Helm, 1977.

Peter Robinson, *Workers' Councils in Portugal 1974–1975*. M Phil thesis, Centre for Sociology and Social University, Open University, 1999.

Peter Robinson, *Portugal 1974–1975: The Forgotten Dream*, London: Socialist History Society, 1989.

Maria de Lourdes Lima Santos, Marinús Pires de Lima, and Vitor Matias Ferreira, *O 25 de Abril e as lutas sociais nas empresas*, 3 volumes, Porto: Afromento, 1976.

Sunday Times Insight Team, *Portugal: The Year of the Captains*, London: Sunday Times, 1975.

The Popular Forces Mobilise

5
Militia and Workers' State: Paris 1871

Donny Gluckstein

A NEW TYPE OF ARMY

According to conventional political thinking armies and civil affairs are entirely separate. There is, however, a reverse approach to the relationship between military force and society which can be traced back to Carl von Clausewitz's famous axiom that 'war is the continuation of politics by other means'. Marxism develops this more fully by arguing that conventional armies are not separate from but intimately linked to maintaining capitalism as a whole. If the system's ideological hegemony falters, the coercive power of armies will act as guarantor of last resort. Indeed, 'armed bodies of men' (as Lenin called them) are integral to the state because its primary function is to secure the system of exploitation. The intervention of an army in domestic affairs is therefore not a deviation from the 'normal' pattern or an aberration, but expresses the inability of a system to obtain sufficient compliance or stability.

France, in the period between the Great Revolution of 1789 and the Paris Commune of 1871, was a test of this thesis. It not only highlighted the interrelationship between arms and the people under capitalism, it also covered the transition from feudalism and offered unparalleled insights into the revolutionary transformation of that relationship in a post-capitalist society. During the eighteenth century the country was under the *ancien régime,* a society dominated by a tiny layer of landowners with the monarch at its head. The political structure excluded not only the poor (peasants and urban artisans, known as *sans-culottes*), but significant sections of the rising bourgeoisie. The *ancien régime* relied on a standing army of professional soldiers which was relatively small and commanded by aristocrats, or those who bought their commissions. The soldiers were essentially mercenaries without links to the local population, even if they were drawn from it. A symptom of this isolation was that once the revolution began in 1789 the only force the old ruling class could depend on were foreign – the Swiss Guards. Although they were soon overcome, the revolution faced a more formidable opposition; the international establishment was determined to eradicate the contagion before it could develop. In 1793 a number of states decided to intervene and sent their professional armies against Paris.

To defend the revolution it required an army of a new type. Initially, this was formed by combining a mass of volunteers with the remnants of the professional army. The *levée en masse* – wholesale conscription of the population – followed soon after. Thus the revolutionary army was fundamentally different from its predecessor. The latter was consciously distinct from and hostile to the population because its role was to defend the ruling class from the population. The new national body under Jacobin leadership melded armed force and the people. Its role was to defeat reaction and protect the people from any restoration of the *ancien régime*. And it was spectacularly successful, propelling France to a dominant position on the continent.

This new structure was built in a particular constellation of circumstances which gave birth to the assumption that the interest of *all* the French was embodied in defence of a 'nation' founded on the principles of 'Liberty, Equality and Fraternity'. The victories of the French revolutionary army against Prussia and the other European monarchies occurred because it was a mass army, inspired by these progressive nationalist ideas and with a command structure organised according to talent rather than the accident of birth. The foremost example of this was Napoleon Bonaparte. Paradoxically, however, the feeling of shared interests that characterised the revolution's struggle against the *ancien régime* disappeared at the very moment when the army was victorious and a society based on modern capitalism was made possible. The conflict between the aristocracy on the one hand and the peasantry and *sans-culottes* on the other may have been abolished by the elimination of feudalism, but now it was replaced by an antagonism between the working class and a newly dominant, rich bourgeoisie.

The latter now wanted protection from the masses. A popular army which afforded large numbers of workers military training was therefore seen as a risk. The close relationship between the army and people gave way to one in which, once again, soldiers were to be used as part of the coercive apparatus of the state against the people. And for this to happen they had to be separated from the masses. Ironically, this began under Bonaparte, who installed the

'First Empire', introduced a ruthless dictatorship and abolished the *levée en masse*. The butcher of the Paris Commune in 1871, Adolphe Thiers, explained why the size of the army must be restricted to a smaller but more reliable disciplined force: 'It was not safe to place a gun on the shoulder of every [potential] Socialist.'[1]

So the French revolutionary army was necessarily shortlived, but such was its effectiveness that many of its features were adopted elsewhere. The Prussians, for example, founded their highly effective military machine using nationalist rhetoric (shorn of its progressive aspects) and an officer class where promotion depended on talent. Half a century later France was under the Second Empire of Napoleon III, great nephew of 'Napoleon the Great' (but nicknamed 'Napoleon the Little'). In 1870, the Prussians invaded and quickly defeated its imperial army. The reversal of fortunes was explained by Jaroslaw Dombrowski, a Pole who would become the Commune's greatest general:

'The Prussian army is nothing other than the nation-in-arms . . . animated by a great idea, the idea of German unification. The German army's enthusiasm and popular organisation gives it a great moral force and massive numerical strength . . . France opposes this army with a much smaller force, without reserves and under the command of generals and senior officers who are as arrogant as they are stupid. It fights not in the name of the country, liberty or humanity, but in the name of the emperor and conquest.'[2]

At Sedan a large segment of the army became prisoners of war along with the Emperor himself. On 4 September 1870 an uprising in Paris formally brought the imperial system to an end. It was replaced by a Government of National Defence composed of upper-class representatives, which publicly announced: 'We will not give up one inch of territory or one stone of our fortresses.'[3] However, the sort of France the government was committed to defending was socially no different from the regime that had just been ousted. This was underlined by Louis Trochu, the new President, who stated he would only take office 'if nothing will be done against God, the family and property'.[4] The problem for this new state was how was it to deal with the enemy. How could the second largest city in the world, the French capital, be defended from a long Prussian siege?

With the conventional army in captivity the answer seemed to be through a popular militia – the National Guard. This had been a middle-class bulwark of property in earlier times, such as the 1848 revolution, when it had been used to massacre the workers of the capital. However, dramatic shifts were occurring among the 1.7 million-strong Parisian population.

Ahead of the enemy's arrival 100,000 wealthy people fled the city. As they went, they passed 230,000 impoverished refugees fleeing in the opposite direction from Prussian advances in northern France. A few months later, a further 150,000 rich people would abandon Paris to avoid civil war. The Prussian siege immediately paralysed the urban economy and generated mass unemployment. Vast numbers of mainly working-class men became desperate to join the National Guard, both to fight the enemy and to earn the small allowance: 1.50 fr, 0.75 fr for a wife and 0.25 fr per child. Eventually, its ranks swelled to 340,000. This was effectively the male working-class population of Paris under arms.

As yet there was nothing to indicate that the militia would be anything but a docile tool in the hands of the government. Several factors conspired to transform it, however. The first concerned democracy. Due to its origins as a middle-class volunteer force defending property, the Parisian National Guard of 1870 inherited a tradition of electing its officers. This had given it cohesion because democratic procedures and debate had encouraged a collective *esprit de corps*. However, when the Guard became the embodiment of the working class in 1871, this unusual feature endowed it with a quite different potential, both from the former middle-class Guard and a conventional army. The militia was now unlikely to turn against the working class as it had done in 1848 because that was the grouping from which its officers were drawn and to whom they were accountable. The Federation's constitution, as one historian put it:

'provided an elective body, at once rigid and flexible, completely democratic, and, most important, completely in opposition to the official organisation with its officers appointed by the government and responsible not to their men, but to the Minister for Internal Affairs.'[5]

A conventional army is mostly recruited from the same or similar social groups as the National Guard. But it is utterly undemocratic. Housed in its own barracks, it is consciously separated from the working class and rigorously trained to accept discipline from above. Hierarchical command structures, staffed by the upper class and backed by the threat of court martial, convey orders down to the lower ranks, who are required to act unthinkingly. This means they can be used against the people – either at home or abroad. Unless it mutinies, a conventional army expresses the will of officers drawn from and imbued with the values of the ruling elite, whereas the Parisian National Guard was structured to express the will of the working people through its democracy.

Secondly, and paradoxically, although the collapse of industry might have been expected to atomise the working class by destroying the bonds forged by collaborating in production, the Parisian masses attained a still higher level of unity in the militia. The reason for this lay in the peculiarity of Paris's industrial development. Before 1871, large-scale factories had been excluded from the city. Napoleon III had hoped to ward off revolution by counteracting the tendency towards increasing industrial concentration. So prior to the siege, fully 62 per cent of workplaces consisted of just two employees, and only 7 per cent exceeded ten. When these tiny workshops shut down as a result of the siege and workers joined the militia, they entered Guard companies averaging around 250 men.

Thirdly, six months of siege radicalised the Parisian population. The Government of National Defence was packed with ardent disciples of the market economy and it resisted food rationing despite horrendous shortages and rocketing prices. By the time the siege ended the death rate in Paris had tripled due to malnutrition and disease, though the few wealthy people who remained enjoyed spectacular levels of food consumption, even if what was on offer tended to consist of dogs, cats and rats, and notoriously exotic zoo animals. On the political plane, the French ruling class quickly tired of fighting Prussia, because it interfered with profit-making. However, the Parisian militia rejected any compromise. Entrenched behind city walls which Engels described as 'the hugest complex of military engineering works ever constructed', the National Guard's intransigence stood in the way of the government's peace overtures.[6]

BREAKING THE SIEGE

So Trochu came up with perhaps the most grotesque plan ever concocted by a military high command – to instil demoralisation by having his own side killed in large numbers. As one account explains:

'If 20,000 or 25,000 men are left on the ground after a major battle under the walls of Paris it will give in.' Voices of protest were raised. He returned to the theme: 'The National Guard will only accept peace it if loses 10,000 men.'[7]

Ignorant of their commander's intentions the militia were despatched on several futile breakouts and many were indeed killed. But instead of demoralisation, working-class rage grew stronger.

Despite all of these factors the militia did not automatically gravitate to the far left. This was proved when two attempts by revolutionaries to seize power (31 October 1870 and 22 January 1871) proved to be fiascos because only a minority of Guards were ready to lend support. When a peace deal was finally concluded and a general election held in February 1871, revolutionaries could only win one in five of Parisian votes. But this result looked positively radical compared to the rest of France, where the peasantry voted for right-wingers who had promised an end to the war. The highest proportion of hereditary nobles ever elected to a popular assembly was picked and, headed by the veteran monarchist Adolphe Thiers, they took their seats at Louis XVI's Palace of Versailles.

This location, outside the capital, was chosen as a deliberate snub to Paris and to the obduracy of its Guards. That decision and the flood of reactionary economic and political policies that accompanied it were hotly debated within the ranks of the militia. Their duties brought them together for around six hours each day and, with little to do but drill and patrol the walls, they had ample time to reflect on the character of society. As one contemporary put it: 'every National Guard company [was] a permanent public meeting.'[8]

The fruit of these discussions was already becoming visible during the February 1871 election campaign. Some National Guardsmen supported left candidates and described themselves as 'the party of the disinherited' committed to 'a new world'.[9] On 15 February a meeting of 7,200 delegates, representing 215 of the 260 battalions, decided to form a National Guard Federation. The constitution they adopted enshrined the election of officers and the 'absolute right . . . to recall them as soon as they lose the confidence of those who elected them'.[10] A Central Committee of 38 delegates was chosen soon after.

Now the militia embarked on a collision course with the capitalist state. On 24 February it decided that 'The entire National Guard must obey the orders of the Central Committee. If the [Government's] military leaders issue a contrary order, the High Command must be arrested.'[11] Furthermore, it would brook no competition from any other military formation. On the same day it effectively declared political war on the coercive foundations of the old state by passing an extraordinary resolution:

> 'The National Guard must henceforth replace permanent armies, which have only ever been instruments of despotism and which inevitably bring the fatal ruin of the country . . . The national citizen militia is the only national force, to the exclusion of any other . . .'[12]

For the first time in history there was a body which, through its internal direct democracy, was channelling working-class aspirations and at the same time had the power to be an alternative source of authority to the capitalist state.

The militia's procedures differed in key ways from capitalist democracy. Parliaments are only accountable to a geographical constituency where ballots take place once every few years. The Guard officers were answerable to daily assemblies and their continuous debates. So a constantly regenerated body of people subjected their representatives to direct control and could, if necessary, recall them instantly should they act against majority wishes. Furthermore, the Federation delegates were not paid a special salary for carrying out their functions. Instead they received the standard rate for their position and thus did not become a class apart. They could make no decisions affecting others without themselves being affected too.

To summarise thus far, the National Guard Federation was remarkable in being at one and the same time an army, a state, a class and an organ of democracy. This was a complete inversion of the 'common-sense' view, which assumes a complete compartmentalisation of all of these factors. The army is seen as peripheral to domestic politics, since its job is to act as a defence against external threats. Direct interaction between the army and society at home is therefore portrayed as an aberration, the result of a temporary emergency or a reflection of incomplete social development. The state is supposed to be neutral, above both class and army. While it may finance the military, its true purpose is portrayed as providing services, such as education and health. Class interests too are supposed to be subsumed in the higher concept of the 'common good' or 'national interest' and not reflected in the armed forces.

Yet all recent experience, from unpopular imperialist wars to the bailing out of bankers and industrialists at the expense of the vast majority of the population, points to the speciousness of this picture. In 1871 the National Guard was both a living negation of that ideology and a revelation that the common-sense understanding is a product of ruling-class ideology. Capitalists have to mystify the real situation because they are a minority exploiting the working-class majority; the Parisian militia being the working class itself could openly declare the truth.

The situation of dual power that now prevailed in Paris was inherently unstable since the ruling class would not tolerate a challenge to its monopoly of violence for long, and the Central Committee soon faced an important test. As part of its peace agreement with the Prussians, the French government had ceded 1.6 million citizens in Alsace and Lorraine, and colossal reparations of 500 million francs (which would be paid by the poor). From the Guards' point of view the most galling feature was that the Prussian army was to be allowed a victory parade through Paris. The militia felt, rightly, that it had not been defeated but betrayed. So it turned what was supposed to be a humiliation in the face of Prussian arms into a triumphant demonstration of its independent power, ordering that 'barricades will be established all round the quarters to be occupied by the enemy, so he will parade in a camp shut out from our town'.[13] This was a spectacular display of discipline and included removing the Guards' artillery pieces to Montmartre Hill, far out of reach of the enemy.

The Guards' act of defiance convinced Thiers' government that he had no choice but to confront the capital. It ordered the execution of Louis Auguste Blanqui and Gustave Flourens, two popular revolutionaries. For a city where the economy had collapsed and only the pittance earned by military service ensured survival, it announced the dissolution of the National Guard along with compulsory repayment of all debts and back-rents. Finally, Thiers ordered the seizure of the cannon stored in Montmartre. This would not be easy, as all that remained of the French army was 25,000 soldiers. Hoping to remove the guns surreptitiously under cover of darkness, an operation under the command of General Vinoy began during the night of 18 March 1871. It went disastrously wrong because the horses needed to haul away the cannon failed to arrive. When the working-class women of the district woke up and discovered what was happening they threw themselves between the army and the guns. The soldiers were ordered to shoot, but instead they mutinied. As a result a terrified Thiers decamped with his entire government to Versailles that very day.

The events in Montmartre destroyed the last vestige of governmental power in Paris. A diarist recorded the consequence:

'we had no more government: no police force or policemen; no magistrates or trials; no top officials or prefects; the landlords had run away in a panic abandoning their buildings to the tenants; no soldiers or generals; no letters or telegrams; no customs officials, tax collectors or teachers. No more Academy or Institute; the great professors, doctors and surgeons had left . . . Paris, immense Paris, was abandoned to the "orgies of the vile multitude".'[14]

With dual power at an end there was now just a single militia–state–class authority, a fact expressed by one contemporary in these terms: 'The Central Committee, which took power after 18 March, was composed solely of workers, of proletarians.'[15] The sense of a world turned upside down was described by an eye-witness who observed an aged Guardsman:

'This fighter had dreamed for perhaps 50 years of the triumph of the people and here, one fine day, all of a sudden, he was living his dream! He saw workers there like him, his workshop companions, his favourite club orators commanding, being obeyed! He saw the bourgeois, the big businessmen, the great industrialists, the bosses, begging for an audience, humble, submissive, and polite, coming to ask for permits for their merchandise or for their families to pass! "At last!" said his look.'[16]

There is no space here to describe in detail the remarkable social progress made in all areas of social life after 18 March, from women's rights, to education, the arts, justice, workers' control, and so on. But one aspect requires expansion – the evolving relationship between the National Guard and the population as a whole. As explained earlier, siege conditions had brought a considerable proportion of the adult male working-class population into its ranks, which is why one can talk about the militia substantially embodying the class.

Yet not all adult male workers were in the militia; nor were any women, the young or the old. However, this deficit was more than made up by the 'Red Club' movement. During the siege there were around 30 of these bodies in session. They met in theatres rendered inactive because their middle- and upper-class clientele had run away, and many thousands of people outside the ranks of the

National Guard found their voice in the debates. Vinoy's memoirs contain what was intended to be a hostile description of the clubs, but it is unwitting testimony to their powerful democratic effect:

> Public expression was now fully liberated so that the most exaggerated and often the most criminal opinions were aired. The clubs met in permanent session and there were even discussions in the street, with numerous meetings of citizens [in] a perilous and unwarranted growth of public opinion.[17]

Versailles ordered that the clubs be shut down, but the victory of the 18 March revolution and the Guards' assumption of power within Paris ensured that they were revived with redoubled vigour. The clubs expanded from the theatres into churches, and a constant stream of mass meetings, sometimes several thousand-strong, kept a vigilant watch over all city institutions. On one day in May, for example, the Club de la Révolution called for the abolition of magistrates, the ending of religious ceremonies and arrest of priests, changes to pawnshops, banning of brothels and the nationalisation of industry. If the National Guard Federation was indeed an incomplete reflection of the population, through its protection of the Red Clubs Paris attained full expression of all democratic forces.

All the measures adopted ultimately relied on the ability of the National Guard to defend the capital from hostile forces massing outside. How it carried out this task depended on the politics of its elected leadership. Three key groupings were involved: Jacobins, Blanquists and Proudhonists. Unfortunately, the events that propelled the Guards into power were so exceptional that none of these groupings could easily make sense of them or the militia-state that had now sprung up. The pre-existing theoretical frameworks simply could not cope. This lack of understanding of the people–arms relationship would also prove to be a serious handicap.

The Jacobins were the most influential current. They stood in the tradition of the Great Revolution of 1789 and their principal goal was the establishment of a republic. Jacobin leaders came from the middle class and although many demanded a 'social republic' which would provide 'justice and bread' for the workers, they were not aiming to abolish capitalist society *per se* but to radically reform it. Obssessed by the old debate of monarchy versus republic, the Jacobins did not grasp the potential of the National Guard as an alternative state. For them it was simply a military formation, a means to an end which was essentially defensive. They wanted a lever to convince Versailles that it should grant full local government rights to Paris and prevent the return of the monarchy.

The followers of Blanqui stood for 'Atheism, Communism and Revolution'.[18] As author of the concepts of 'class war' and 'dictatorship of the proletariat', Blanqui certainly could not be accused of wanting compromise or half-measures. However, his method of achieving social transformation was thoroughly elitist. Communism would be given to the working class by a small minority of educated individuals. Blanqui took this path because he had no faith in the ability of the masses to shake off capitalist ideology or liberate themselves. A narrow conspiratorial grouping of like-minded middle-class individuals must seize power and construct a new society 'on behalf of the general interest and human progress'.[19] For the Blanquists, the armed, democratically organised people was, as with the Jacobins, also a means rather than an end, although in their case that end was a military offensive. The Guard should destroy the Versailles government and replace it with an enlightened revolutionary dictatorship.

Pierre-Joseph Proudhon developed a variant of anarchism which was dominant in the organised Parisian working class. He emphasised workers' self-activity and self-liberation, but denied any role for politics or any focus on the issue of the state. Proudhon told workers that 'the social question can only be resolved by you, by you alone, without the assistance of power . . . maintain strict neutrality vis-à-vis power'.[20] So, while the Proudhonists, as active worker militants, took full part in the National Guard Federation, they opposed the notion that it should play any political role or even challenge the state machine of Versailles.

These three viewpoints framed the Central Committee debates immediately following the 18 March revolution. The Blanquists were absolutely correct to point out that at this time the forces of Versailles were at their weakest. For example, in response to a plea from within Paris by Vice-Admiral Saisset for a supply of soldiers to destroy the workers' government, Thiers replied: 'Neither 5,000, nor 500, nor five; I need the few troops still available – and in whom I don't yet have full confidence . . .'[21] This advantageous situation would not last because Otto von Bismarck, the Chancellor of the newly formed Germany, feared that the popular radicalism of Paris could spread internationally. So he began releasing French prisoners of war to the Versailles government. By this means Thiers would eventually amass an army of 200,000. In the hours following the 18 March uprising the Blanquists urged the National Guard Central

Committee to pre-empt this, set aside all reforms and march on Versailles without delay:

> 'the accomplishment of the political and social revolution still lay in the future . . . It would not be by striking it with decrees and proclamations that a breach in the Versailles Assembly would be achieved, but by striking it with cannonballs.'[22]

The Proudhonists countered by suggesting that social liberation had been the driving force of the movement thus far, and therefore the victory of Paris was dependent on inspiring the mass of the French people by example: 'We need to formulate briefly the straightforward and well-defined programme of communal autonomy, to explain to the population the simple mechanism of direct government by means of natural groupings.'[23] They concluded that the issue of state power was therefore irrelevant: 'Externally it is important to declare that Paris did not want to impose its will or supremacy on the rest of the nation in any way . . .'[24] Even though there were many Proudhonists in leading militia positions, their stance gave the Guard no political role at all.

The solution the Central Committee eventually adopted was a middle position along Jacobin lines. The militia would act defensively while a compromise with Versailles was sought. Within Paris it would cede power to a regular local government body – the Commune, which met at the Hotel de Ville. This body was elected on 26 March and formally constituted on 28 March, at which point the Federation Central Committee declared, 'Our mission is completed'. Ever since that time historians have labelled the period from 18 March to May 1871 under a single heading: 'the Paris Commune'. Unfortunately, this underestimates the significance of the militia in several important ways, and it is important to understand why.

THE PARIS MILITIA: AN ARMED FORCE OR A REVOLUTIONARY MOVEMENT?

In France, the word 'commune' referred to a standard unit of local government. The country was covered by a dense network of such bodies, as it is today. Indeed, Paris was exceptional in *not* having its own commune. This was due to its turbulent political tradition. Only Lyons, with a similar revolutionary history, shared that honour. For the same reasons that he had blocked large factories locating in Paris, Napoleon III had denied the capital any elected central administration which might provide a focal point for radicalism. Instead, a government-appointed Prefect was in charge of the city, although each of the 20 districts (*arrondissements*) had its own elected mayor.

When the National Guard Central Committee agreed to hand over power to a Paris Commune, it was ceding control to a parliamentary-style system that had none of the exceptional features of direct democracy which characterised the Federation. This is not to deny that the Paris Commune was far more responsive to the popular movement than a conventional parliament. That was due to the extraordinarily high level of mobilisation of the population which exerted strong pressure on its members through the clubs and other forms of mass expression. Nevertheless, once the geographical ballot had closed on 26 March 1871, no immediate control could be exerted over representatives by electors. The organic links that ran directly from the working class up through the National Guard Federation to its summit were missing. One sign of these structural differences was the social composition of the respective bodies. In the Central Committee the ratio of manual workers to non-manual professions was 13 to 2. At the Hotel de Ville meetings manual workers constituted only one third, with middle class professionals such as journalists and lawyers making up the rest.

Thus, the election of the Commune marked the end of the militia's ascendancy. It also was the beginning of a civil war during which growing Versailles forces subjected the Parisian Guard to ceaseless attacks and ultimately a horrific massacre – the 'Bloody Week' of May 1871. It would be fruitless, condescending and beyond the scope of this chapter to speculate on what 'correct policy' might have been pursued to avoid defeat. In any case, the lack of effective support outside Paris made victory highly unlikely. It is possible, however, to point out some of the difficulties in the relationship between the military and civilian aspects that followed from the abdication of power.

When the Federation was assigned the passive defence of Paris and shorn of its political function, it concentrated on a role as 'the great family council of the National Guard', a sort of militia trade union. However, the Versailles offensive gave little room for such work, but tended instead to exacerbate conflicts with the Communal Council. Part of the strain was because within the Hotel de Ville the delegates proved unable to formulate a clear or effective strategy. Arguments between Blanquists, Jacobins and Proudhonists escalated into threats of coups and counter-coups by one faction against the other. As disorganisation spread and the death toll in the civil war mounted, the Central Committee declared, in exasperation, that it was 'taking back the revolution that we made'. In truth, the Central Committee had no better idea of how to deal with Versailles than the Council, and the result of the clash between Guards and Commune was a deadlock.

Growing despondency undermined the class unity previously achieved in the ranks of the militia. A narrow defence of sectional interests now emerged. This was seen in very practical ways. The various Guard units began refusing to obey orders issued by the commander appointed by the Hotel de Ville. However, as the situation deteriorated this refusal even extended to orders issued by the Central Committee. Units became depleted as many volunteers began to absent themselves, while those that remained increasingly focused on their local areas at the expense of overall city defence. Rival authorities tried to exert some control, but this only made the situation worse. By May 1871 Federal forces were receiving commands from seven different and conflicting sources, including the Commune, the Delegate for War, individual generals and the Central Committee.

The fundamental problem was not new. Blanqui, writing in the 1860s after a lifetime of studying the numerous insurrections that had occurred in Paris (and 36 years in prison for his involvement in them), summarised his experience to date:

'[T]he vice of the popular tactics is responsible for some of its disasters . . . no point of leadership or overall command, not even consultation between the fighters. Each barricade has its particular group, more or less numerous but always isolated . . . Often there is not even a leader to direct the defence . . . The soldiers just do what they like. They remain, they leave, they return, as they see fit... [T]he majority of insurgents fight in their own quarter, a capital fault that has disastrous consequences . . .'

The situation in 1871 therefore reflected a wider problem – the tension between a popular militia's role as both an armed force and a mass insurrection. At one level it required absolute unity and obedience in battle, through maximum centralisation of command. At another level, to inspire the working class to join its ranks and fight perhaps to the death meant the militia had to faithfully embody the wishes of the base through maximum democracy.

The Guard had been immensely powerful when, in the period up to the 18 March revolution, centralisation and democracy were complementary. For that to continue it required a leadership which could offer a unifying vision embodying the aspiration for liberation *and* a sense of military purpose that instilled self-confidence in attaining that goal.

In 1871 only the Blanquists might have fulfilled this need. They were unique in combining a clear revolutionary goal with an understanding of military tactics. Tragically, Blanqui himself was arrested on the very eve of the March 1871 revolution. Furthermore, due to its elitist attitude towards workers, the Blanquist party remained tiny, a few hundred at most. As such it was neither able to convince the majority of the Central Committee to seize Versailles at the opportune moment, nor to shape strategy later. Instead, responsibility for the National Guard fell to successive Delegates for War, each appointed by the Communal Council. None found a strategy that could combine political inspiration and organisational cohesion. Charles Lullier, the first Delegate, made some disastrous decisions and was removed. His successor, Gustave Paul Cluseret, tried to persuade the Guard to become a conventional army but failed and he too was sacked. The Communal Council then turned to a former army officer, Louis-Nathaniel Rossel. He well understood the need for a strong central command: 'Success was impossible as long as the troops were not obedient and could sneak out of their military duties . . . All that was left to try was repression and it had to be real and swift.'[25]

Rossel planned to refashion the Guard by housing the troops in barracks, abolishing the election of officers and putting determined critics before a firing squad. But this proved impossible. It took no account of the essential character of a popular militia which depended on voluntary participation inspired by the idea of freedom and democracy. Rossel was jailed.

A NEW TERROR

The next Delegate, Charles Delescluze, was the very opposite of Rossel. He was a civilian and veteran Jacobin who, as the civil war reached a critical stage, appealed to 'the power of revolutionary feeling in the Commune to save the country'. He told the Guards, 'you are fighting for your liberty, and for social equality'.[26] But the call came too late and was not supplemented by a clear military strategy that could enable enthusiasm to find effective and organised channels. A sign of the problems was that, on 21 May 1871, the most important element in the defence of Paris – the impregnable city walls – was thrown away. Versailles soldiers simply walked through the Saint Cloud gate which had been left unguarded. Despite this fatal breach an heroic but desperate defence was mounted. With central leadership entirely broken down it relied on each company defending its own local area. Nevertheless, the fight the Guards put up was so ferocious and received so much active support from the rest of the population that it considerably slowed the reactionaries' advance. Nonetheless, the French ruling class exacted a bloody price for the humiliation it had suffered at the hands of the workers.

The government understood the close connection between the cause of the military and that of the people and showed this in the days after the Guard was defeated and fighting had stopped. Versailles then proceeded to massacre about five times as many civilians as fallen Federals. Although precise figures are uncertain, it is likely that in the seven days of Bloody Week some 30,000 were killed. This was more than died in the 18 months of the Revolutionary Terror (March 1793–July 1794).

1871 saw a social formation unprecedented in history: the Parisian National Guard was simultaneously an army, class and state. The steps leading to this unique situation – the Prussian capture of the conventional army, the dissolution of the working class through siege conditions, its reconstitution through service in a militia and its sudden rise to undisputed state power (at least within the confines of a major city) – is unlikely ever to recur. It would be wrong, however, to conclude that nothing can be learnt that is of general relevance to the relationship between arms and the people.

The Parisian militia encapsulated several institutions that would reappear in a rather more separate, but still overlapping and complementary form in subsequent social upheavals. It encompassed and united a significant proportion of the working class in a revolutionary movement, setting a pattern of proletarian action seen throughout the century that followed. With its elements of direct democracy through mechanisms such as instant recall and mass involvement it was a prototype of the soviet or council form which appeared in Russia (1917) and Hungary (1956) and formed the basis of a workers' state. Yet it remained throughout an alternative to conventional military formations, foreshadowing the Red Army of the Russian civil war (1918–21) and the resistance to Nazism mounted in several countries during the Second World War. Indeed, the experience of the National Guard and Paris Commune contributed directly to these later events because of its heroic example and the works of revolutionaries that took inspiration from these events.

Foremost among these was Marx, whose *Civil War in France* was published just weeks after the movement was crushed. Building on this foundation, Lenin argued that Marx had drawn on the model of the Parisian revolution to restore the idea of the state as a coercive class apparatus. This was central to his 1917 pamphlet *State and Revolution*, which took the concept to new heights in the form of the workers' and soldiers' soviets.

If the National Guard fought but was ultimately unable during Bloody Week to protect the gains ordinary people had made, the problem lay not so much with the Guard itself as in the isolation of Paris and the political weakness of its leadership. Yet it did not fight in vain. In the decades that followed the left learnt important lessons from the events in Paris and even today many continue to be inspired by the *Internationale*, the song composed by an active Communard who, in a lesser known verse, gives military advice appropriate to our age of imperialism: 'No more deluded by reaction, on tyrants only we'll make war.'

NOTES

1. Quoted in Donny Gluckstein, *The Paris Commune: A Revolution in Democracy*, London: Bookmarks, 2006, p. 65.
2. Jaroslaw Dombrowski, *Trochu comme organisateur et comme général en chef*, December 1870, p. 2.
3. Quoted in Gluckstein, *The Paris Commune*, p. 99.
4. Quoted ibid., p. 89.
5. Frank Jellinek, *The Paris Commune of 1871*, London: Gollancz, 1937, p. 92.
6. Friedrich Engels, 'Notes on the war', *Marx–Engels Collected Works*, Volume 22, p. 87.
7. Maxim du Camp, *Les convulsions de Paris*, Volume 2, Paris: Hachette, 1881, pp. 11–12.
8. Quoted in Gluckstein, *The Paris Commune*, p. 113.
9. 'Assemblée Nationale. Candidats socialistes révolutionaires proposés par l'Association Internationale des Travailleurs', in *Les révolutions du XIX siècle, 1852–1872*, Paris: EDHIS, 1866.
10. 'Fédération républicaine de la Garde Nationale.Comité Centrale, Statuts, Déclaration préalable', in *Les révolutions du XIX siècle, 1852–1872*.
11. Quoted in Gluckstein, *The Paris Commune*, p. 114.
12. Quoted in Jacques Rougerie, *Paris Libre*, Paris: Editions du Seuil, 1971, p. 89.
13. Quoted in Prosper Olivier Lissagaray, *History of the Paris Commune*, London: New Park, 1976, p. 55.
14. Elie Reclus, *La Commune de Paris*, Paris: Schleicher, 1908, p. 14.

15. Vermorel, quoted in Eugene Schulkind, ed., *The Paris Commune of 1871: The View from the Left*, London: Jonathan Cape, 1972, p. 144.
16. Arthur Arnould, *Histoire populaire et parlementaire de la Commune de Paris*, Lyon: J. M. Laffont, 1981, p. 130.
17. Quoted in Gluckstein, *The Paris Commune*, p. 102.
18. Quoted in E. S. Mason, 'Blanqui and communism', *Political Science Quarterly*, 44, 1929, p. 516.
19. Quoted in Gluckstein, *The Paris Commune*, p. 78.
20. *Le Représentant du Peuple*, 16 May 1848.
21. Quoted in Gordon Wright, 'The Anti-Commune, Paris 1871', *French Historical Studies*, 10(1), Spring 1977, p. 156.
22. G. da Costa, *La Commune vécue*, Volume 1, Paris, 1903, p. 312.
23. Arnould, *Histoire Populaire*, p. 149.
24. Ibid.
25. Louis Nathaniel Rossel, *Papiers posthumes*, Paris: E. Lachaud, 1871, pp. 137–8.
26. *Journal officiel de la Commune*, 11 May 1871.

BIBLIOGRAPHY/FURTHER READING

Stewart Edwards, ed., *The Paris Commune*, Ithaca, NY: Cornell University Press, 1976.
Donny Gluckstein, *The Paris Commune: A Revolution in Democracy*, London: Bookmarks, 2006.
Prosper Olivier Lissagaray, *History of the Paris Commune*, London: New Park, 1976.
Karl Marx, *The Civil War in France*, New York: International Publishers, 1988.
Eugene Schulkind, ed., *The Paris Commune of 1871: The View from the Left*, London: Jonathan Cape, 1972.

6
The People in Arms: Spain 1936

Andrew Durgan

The Spanish civil war (1936–39) provides one of the clearest examples of popular military mobilisation, as the disintegration of the army and the state in over half of Spain in July 1936 led to social revolution. During the first months of the war, real power in the loyalist (Republican) zone lay in the hands of diverse committees and workers' militias. The authority of the Republican government was only re-established with the elimination of these committees and the transformation of the militia into a new regular army, marking the end of the nascent revolution.

Heralded at the time as the *el pueblo en armas* (the people in arms), this great democratic military experiment rapidly faced apparently insurmountable logistical and political problems. Military and political strategy, the options available to this 'people in arms', were at the centre of the Spanish conflict. Despite being faced with a far better-equipped enemy, the revolutionary methods that had proved so successful in the defence of Madrid in November 1936 were abandoned to placate both the Western democracies and Soviet foreign policy. Whether there was an alternative path for the Spanish masses that would have led to both the defeat of fascism and the triumph of the revolution remains a central question for those who seek to change the world we live in.

THE ARMY OF COUNTER-REVOLUTION

By the early nineteenth century the army was one of the main components of Spain's ruling oligarchy, along with the landowners and the Church. The failure of the Spanish bourgeoisie to establish strong institutions meant that the army had a disproportionate influence. It had become the arbitrator of the country's political life, intervening frequently to change governments. Although by the end of the century the army played a less direct role in politics, it still saw itself as the defender of national unity. Defeat in 1898 and the end of the colonial war in North Africa in 1927 only served to reinforce the army's conservative nationalism.[1] The end of its interventions overseas meant the army was now only really active in maintaining public order, a role reinforced by its backing of the dictatorship of Primo de Rivera (1923–30).

While rank-and-file soldiers were mainly conscripts from a poor background unable to buy themselves out of military service, the lower ranks of the officer corps came from a relatively impoverished section of the middle classes. One of several sons would go to a military academy when they were very young; this led to a lack of reserve officers and a correspondingly large and permanent officer corps. By 1930, there were 20,556 officers to command 109,588 troops stationed in the peninsula.[2] Promotion was not based on merit but on a strict application of seniority, frustrating the more ambitious and capable officers. Commanders thus tended to be old; in 1936 only 26 of 217 colonels were under 55. This top-heavy command structure was combined with the absence of modern equipment, training and strategy.[3]

A lack of general education compounded the social isolation of the officer corps. Officers were 'like trainee priests in a seminary' and out of step with modern trends; they were 'not only an estate but a caste'. Moreover, they tended to marry the daughters of other officers, thus reinforcing the closed world they lived in.[4] The role of the army as defenders of the established order, combined with the inherent conservatism of the officer corps, meant it was likely to oppose any attempt at social or political reform.

When the Republic was established in 1931, the new government, elected after the abdication of Alfonso XIII and the fall of Primo de Rivera, promised both to modernise the army and to end its political role. The structure of the army was rationalised and all its judicial functions, whereby it could try civilians when national security was at stake, were removed. In order to reduce the over-manned officer corps, officers were offered retirement on full pay and 8,000 accepted the offer. The General Military Academy was closed and the number of entrants into the corps was drastically reduced. Henceforth, 60 per cent of officer training places were to be reserved for non-commissioned officers and promotion was to be on the basis of serious professional examinations.

Most accounts suggest that the military reform contributed to the army's willingness to rebel. But it was the ideological orientation of many officers, rather than reform as such, which made them susceptible to the same issues that inflamed right-wing opinion in general during the Republic. In conservative military circles the Republic was seen as impermanent and most officers did not feel any loyalty to the new democracy, but only to the army itself and the territorial integrity of Spain. Even prior to the introduction of the new government's reforms, sections of the army, in close contact with the monarchist right, were committed to the violent overthrow of the Republic. In 1932, an attempted coup, headed in Seville by the commander of the customs and border police, the Carabineros, had been thwarted by a general strike. Right-wing officers continued to plot the Republic's downfall and in 1934 a group of them formed the Unión Militar Española (UME – Spanish Military Union).

Opposition to the right inside the army was limited. A few officers, some promoted as a result of the reform, were committed to defending the Republic and in 1935 organised the Unión de Militares Republicanos y Antifascistas (UMRA – Union of Republican and Antifascist Soldiers) to counter the UME. Although it made little impact inside the army, the UMRA did organise a minority of officers, many of whom would later command the loyalist forces in the war.

With the victory of the Popular Front[5] in the elections of February 1936, and the abandonment by the mainstream right of even the pretence of supporting legality, plans to overthrow democracy intensified. In parliament, José Calvo Sotelo, head of the crypto-fascist Alphonsine monarchists, now the most influential voice on the right, called on the army to 'deal furiously' with the 'enemies of Spain'.[6] Being more concerned with the threat posed by a militant workers' movement, the Republican authorities were reluctant to take action against the military conspirators. Moving suspect generals to other destinations, in particular sending General Francisco Franco to the Canary Islands and Emilio Mola to Pamplona, far from putting an end to the plotting, placed Franco closer to the Army of Africa and Mola in contact with the Carlist militia, the *Requetés*. In March, the Republican Prime Minister, Manuel Azaña, denied that there was unrest in the army and insisted that the army was the 'Republic's strongest supporter'. Two months later, his successor as Prime Minister, Santiago Casares Quiroga, also dismissed the notion that there was any problem with the army. Even days before the uprising, Quiroga opposed a proposal by the UMRA to eliminate plotters, as there was 'not even the minimum possibility of an insurrection'.[7]

Meanwhile the return of the left to government encouraged workers and peasants to press home their demands for improvements at work and social reform. The right responded by organising armed gangs to spread terror on the streets. Among the victims was José Castillo, a left-wing lieutenant of the Republican Assault Guards.[8] Revenge was exacted by his comrades with the assassination of Calvo Sotelo on 12 July. This provided an opportune justification for the launching of the military rebellion five days later.

WORKERS' SELF-DEFENCE

The workers' militias that combated the fascist uprising of July 1936 had their precedent in paramilitary groups organised in the pre-war period. Strikes were frequently met with state repression and employer-backed violence and this had initially given rise to such groups. By the mid-1930s the threat of fascism would encourage their further organisation.

The anarcho-syndicalist union, the CNT,[9] was more disposed to use violence than its socialist rivals. Historically, rural anarchism had defended and practised insurrectionary tactics. In the cities individual terrorism had given way to 'direct action' and armed defence groups during the agitated post-First World War years. These groups were reorganised in the 1930s. They involved few militants, often unemployed workers, who received a wage from the union and were rotated to avoid 'professionalisation'. The defence groups were coordinated by local and regional committees, which in turn were in contact with the National Defence Committee. According to a report in 1934 each defence group should have an information service to identify presumed enemies: 'army officer, police, priests, state functionaries, bourgeois and Marxist politicians, gunmen, fascists' and study methods for attacking official buildings and communications infrastructures.[10] The inclusion of 'Marxist politicians' in the list of enemies reflected the deep distrust of anarchists towards their socialist and communist rivals, 'politics' being seen as subterfuge orchestrated by the workers' enemies to divert them from the revolution.

The CNT's defence structures tended to be dominated by members of anarchist affinity groups, especially the FAI.[11] Arguing that direct conflict with the state would open the way to revolution, a strategy known as 'revolutionary gymnastics', the National Defence Committee instigated armed insurrections under different pretexts in January 1932, January 1933 and December 1933. Called without consulting the CNT membership, the result of these abortive uprisings was hundreds of causalities and arrests, the closing down of many union centres, a steep decline in dues-paying membership and the exacerbation of existing divisions in the workers' movement. Recognition of the failure of the uprisings led a meeting of Barcelona anarchist groups in early 1935 to declare that 'a civil war will require . . . a combat apparatus that cannot be improvised on the basis of mere enthusiasm but [committees] that are structured with more preparation and forces'.[12]

Meanwhile the rise of fascism internationally had also led the Socialist Party (PSOE) to see the need to organise militarily. With the centre-right victory in the elections of November 1933 it was widely believed in the workers' movement that the reactionary Catholic CEDA[13] would soon join the government and introduce an authoritarian regime through parliament, as had happened in Germany and Austria. The socialists, already radicalised by right-wing obstruction to reform, threatened insurrection and set up a revolutionary committee to prepare for this eventuality. The anarcho-syndicalist defence groups launched a poorly prepared uprising only days after the elections, with the result that hundreds of CNT members were killed or wounded and thousands more jailed. This latest putsch only served to reinforce the division between the CNT and the other workers' organisations, as well as seriously weakening its unions.

Responsibility for organising militias as the basis of a future people's army was given to the Socialist Youth.[14] But the socialists were neither politically nor technically prepared to carry through their plans for insurrection. Their leaders' conversion to revolutionary politics was due to their need to keep control of an increasingly radicalised rank and file. As for the logistics involved, the first problem was that the socialists lacked arms or even the money to get them. Attempts to obtain weapons from Portuguese revolution-aries, by stealing them from arms factories or by smuggling them in by boat had very limited success.

When the CEDA entered government on 4 October 1934, the socialist leadership's bluff was called and its revolutionary committee reluctantly called a general strike. In Madrid, unprepared and poorly organised, the socialist militias failed to take any of the strategic points allocated to them and could only engage in sporadic exchanges with the police and army before the movement collapsed.

Only in the mining region of Asturias were the socialists involved in serious armed activity. A united workers' movement, combined with very specific local conditions, led to the establishment of a revolutionary commune where workers organised both the economy and military defence of the region. Pre-empting what would become generalised in July 1936, militias were formed that went beyond the rudimentary socialist formations or the CNT defence groups. After two weeks' fighting, faced with the overwhelming superiority of government forces, the lack of arms and ammunition and the movement's debacle elsewhere, the workers surrendered. Despite assurances that there would be no reprisals, the occupying troops, many from the Army of Africa under General Franco, launched a campaign of terror in the mining villages.

In the aftermath of October 1934, the socialist militias effectively ceased to exist until the spring of 1936. With the growing threat of military rebellion and the increasing activities of fascist hit squads, demands for some form of armed organisation became commonplace in the workers' movement. The socialists and other youth organisations responded by organising paramilitary-style parades.

Only the communists attempted to organise inside the army itself. By 1935 the Communist Party (PCE) published rank-and-file soldiers' newspapers and claimed to have 'contact with hundreds of soldiers . . . who it politically influenced and in many cases organised in committees that fought in defence of soldiers' rights and against fascist commanders', albeit the evidence for this is flimsy.[15] Parallel to this activity the communists had set up in 1933 the Workers and Peasants' Antifascist Militias (MAOC), but these were largely inactive until the Comintern called for the formation of 'antifascist defence groups' two years later. After the left's electoral victory in February 1936, with the increase in fascist violence in the streets, the MAOC became more active, especially in Madrid. The UMRA provided officers to train both the MAOC and the newly unified communist-socialist youth organisation.[16] According to the PCE, in May 1936 the MAOC had 1,500 members on the eve of the war, albeit they were 'barely armed'.[17]

The communists' military activity was limited politically by its support for the Popular Front government, which refused to act decisively against either the military plotters or the armed rightist groups. In contrast, the dissident communist POUM[18] argued that the workers had to rely on their own organisation and not the government to deal with the right. Dismissing as 'demagogy' the socialist and PCE propaganda in favour of militias, the POUM had organised its own 'action groups', which were active in supporting strikes and attacking rightist meetings.[19]

THE MILITIAS

The repression in October 1934 in Asturias had shown the workers' movement what to expect from the military right and the uprising of 18 July was met with fierce resistance in many areas of the country. Where the workers' organisations hesitated, waiting for support from the Republican authorities, the rebels triumphed. Where the masses took the initiative, the uprising was generally defeated. The presence of thousands of albeit poorly armed workers in the streets ensured that most of the police forces remained loyal and took part in the suppression of the rebellion.

Informed of the army's intentions, the CNT defence groups in Barcelona had drawn up an elaborate counter-plan. When the rebels left their barracks they were confronted by barricades manned by armed workers. Having obtained arms through the rapid capture of the Sant Andreu Artillery Barracks, the anarcho-syndicalists' hand was strengthened further.[20]

In Madrid hastily organised groups of armed civilians fought alongside the Assault Guards to take the Montana barracks and other rebel strongholds. In Valencia the workers' organisations also took the initiative, soon isolating the rebels in the Albereda barracks, which would be finally stormed at the end of the month. Far from the swift victory the military plotters had expected, they were now faced with the beginnings of an all-out war.

About 60 per cent of the population and most of the main industrial areas remained in the hands of the Republic. The rebels controlled some of the more important agricultural areas and had managed to divide the loyalist zone, the north being isolated from the centre and east. This geographical division – with the notable exceptions of Seville and Saragossa – reflected the political division of Spain: the conservative centre and north-west largely in insurgent hands and the liberal and revolutionary east, south and industrial north controlled by loyalists.

The army was divided, with 46,188 troops in the Republican zone compared with 43,926 in the rebel zone.[21] However, these figures meant little given that in the areas under loyalist control the army had disintegrated under the impact of revolution and mass mobilisation. Given the chance, the majority of officers sided with the rebels. This was particularly the case for middle-ranking and junior officers. Of 8,851 officers, 4,660 supported the rebels but only 2,000 initially backed the Republican government. Officers remained loyal for diverse reasons. Two hundred or so were members of the UMRA, but others felt there was no choice given the defeat of the uprising where they were based, and they served with minimum enthusiasm. While some would desert to the fascist side when they could or even sabotage the war effort, others, while not active Republicans, would loyally serve the government to the end. Many paid for this loyalty with their lives.[22]

One exception to the Republic's relative military weakness was that most of the navy remained in its hands thanks to crews swiftly taking over their ships. But fearful of the adverse reaction of the imperial powers, the navy was never deployed effectively, allowing the rebels to ferry much needed troops across the Straits of Gibraltar.

Soon thousands of volunteers were flooding into the militias being rapidly organised throughout the loyalist zone. Over the coming weeks, the unions and workers' parties organised militia columns amounting to some 150,000 volunteers; of these around 90,000 were in the central and southern zone.[23] There were few strictly Republican units, reflecting the lack of resolve of the lower middle-class parties in combating fascism. Most of the militiamen were workers or peasants. Recruitment was easy and there were far more volunteers than arms to equip them. Regular army officers and former NCOs served as advisers to the militia columns.

Since Catalonia was the centre of the social revolution that had erupted in the Republican zone, the most radical militia units were concentrated on the nearby Aragon front. Over 25,000 militia, most of them from the CNT, were organised by the Central Militia Committee, based in Barcelona.[24] They were joined on the Aragon front by another 15,000 volunteers from Valencia who occupied the Teruel sector. Other columns from Valencia were active in the first weeks of the war near Madrid and in Extremadura and Andalusia. Around Madrid, makeshift volunteer units were soon sent to hold up the enemy in the Guadarrama mountains. The CNT alone recruited 23,000 volunteers in the capital over the next four months.

The only area where the workers' organisations did not dominate both the rearguard and the militias was the Basque Country. The Basque militias were set up by decree on 8 August by the regional Defence Junta. Over the coming months, of the 70 units under its auspices, 32 were organised by the Basque Nationalist Party.

Rudimentary forms of democracy existed in many militia columns and political discussion was common. Most columns had a similar structure. The basic unit was the *centuria* of around 100 men, subdivided into sections (the equivalent of companies) of around ten. Both the *centurias* and sections were organised on the basis of volunteers from the same town or neighbourhood (often referred to as 'tribes'). The leaders of the *centurias* and sections were elected by the militiamen; the heads of columns, in contrast, were usually appointed by the union or party leaderships. Privileges of rank associated with traditional armies were absent. In the anarchist Iron Column, for example, each section nominated a delegate. All the sections' delegates in turn elected a *centuria* delegate who was in direct contact with the War Committee, which directed military operations as well as dealing with any other question that affected the Column.[25]

Columns were often headed by well-known militants, usually leaders of the different pre-war paramilitary formations. Rather than the CNT leadership, let alone the rank and file, in Barcelona the *Nosotros* affinity group decided alone who should lead the unions' columns.[26] This group had been the foremost advocate of the insurrectionist line in the pre-war years and included in its ranks Benaventura Durruti and other well-known 'men of action'.

Women's participation in the militia in the first days of the war reflected the depth of the revolutionary process. Armed women, dressed in the militia uniform of workers' overalls and marching alongside their male comrades, were one of the most potent images of the revolution. During the summer of 1936 the figure of the heroic militiawoman became a symbol of mobilisation against fascism despite women making up a very small percentage of frontline fighters. Used to encourage mass mobilisation, this image was, however, primarily aimed at a male audience. Propaganda directed at women tended to highlight their heroic role in the rear.[27]

Women's presence at the front was generally not accepted by the workers' organisations, which soon advocated they should be sent to the rear – a decision that not even the anarchist women's organisation *Mujeres Libres* resisted. Few had fought; most had cooked or washed clothes. By December 1936 even the posters depicting militiawomen had largely disappeared, itself a reflection that the revolution was on the defensive. In fact, most working-class women seem to have rejected the militiawomen as being out of place or even as morally suspect. Soon the militiawomen would be presented as 'contemptible figures' who had 'obstructed the war effort'.[28]

Yet despite the somewhat romantic portrayal of these women fighters, even this limited participation represented a massive rupture with the past and has to be seen within the context of 1930s Spain. Women's collective role both at the front and in the rear was a liberating experience which contrasted dramatically with their previous lives, let alone the years of clerical-fascist reaction that would follow the Republic's defeat.[29]

THE MILITIA AT WAR

A series of problems undermined the effectiveness of the militia, in particular a lack of arms, training, discipline and coordination, which led to the loss of fighters, positions and equipment. Reports by professional military personnel were critical of the militia, speaking of sudden and large-scale retreats, panic when subjected to artillery or air bombardment, low resistance to the cold and other discomforts, a lack of cohesion and discipline, enemy infiltrators spreading defeatism and poor communication with other units. Trenches needed to be dug, leave better organised to avoid exhaustion and training had to be improved.[30]

Although many of the problems referred to were real enough, such criticism often reflected army officers' prejudices towards irregular and revolutionary forces. Not only were reports of the collapse of the militias exaggerated, but regular officers, with no combat experience, often fled first.[31] On the Aragon front, deficient advice from professional officers meant the militias were less effective as the forces available did not concentrate on one objective but were dispersed.

Given both the traditional anti-militarism of the workers' organisations and the historically conservative nature of the Spanish army, distrust of regular officers was widespread among the militia. Some were even killed trying to prevent retreats. In the Iron Column it was believed that professional officers who had not risen up against the Republic were either cowards or just had not had the opportunity, so in general their advice was ignored. Even common soldiers were not considered trustworthy as volunteers and were often not sent to occupy frontline positions.[32]

Only a minority of militiamen had completed military service, so most had never handled firearms before, though those chosen to lead units and companies in particular often had some experience in street fighting and the use of light arms. Little was done to overcome this shortcoming. Training was rudimentary and consisted of little more than drill.[33] Columns were also badly equipped. In theory the POUM militia on the Huesca front had its own artillery, machine gunners, sappers and cavalry, but lack of equipment meant that most of these specialised sections amounted to little.[34] In fact, the severe shortage of arms and ammunition seriously limited most militias' ability to put more men at the front. Militia were initially armed with the same Mauser rifles as the regular army, rudimentary hand bombs and a few dozen machine guns and mortars. As late as February 1937, on the Aragon front the POUM, PSUC[35] and the CNT Acaso Column barely had ten rifles for every 17 fighters and one machine gun per 250. Only the Durruti Column was slightly better armed.[36]

Most columns obtained arms on their own initiative, usually as a result of confiscations from barracks during the first days of the war. Even when the central government or bodies like the Catalan Central Militia Committee channelled the supply of arms and munitions, many columns still tried to obtain arms independently. The Iron Column sent representatives to Belgium and the POUM to Mexico to buy arms, but in both cases they came back empty-handed. Durruti went personally to Madrid to get arms and had an inconclusive interview with Prime Minister Largo Caballero. Coinciding with the anniversary of the Russian revolution, a delegation from the Durruti Column even went to Moscow to try to obtain arms.[37]

Providing general equipment and feeding the volunteers also proved very difficult. Such was the lack of the most basic ordnance that *Nosotros* member Antonio Ortiz was given a *Michelin Guide* to orient him when he left Barcelona at the head of the CNT's Second Column.[38] According to George Orwell, the militia was lacking in more or less every form of basic equipment necessary for a modern army: binoculars, telescopes, periscopes, maps, range-finders, lanterns, electric torches, lights, wire cutters, gun oil or armourer's tools.[39] Columns were given food by the peasants. Where it was not given it was usually paid for if not directly expropriated, as was particularly the case if the local peasantry was seen as conservative or insufficiently anti-fascist.

Discipline had negative connotations for many militiamen, especially in the CNT columns. In an attempt to counter this, Durruti argued discipline was 'no more than respect for one's own and others' responsibility'. He was 'against barrack-style discipline but also against badly understood freedom that cowards tend to turn to in order to duck out [of their responsibilities]'.[40] In general, discipline was maintained through the militia's political commitment rather than blind obedience. Militia officers had to depend on their own force of personality and prestige to be obeyed.[41]

The militias' limitations were most evident when fighting over open terrain. Thus in the south they were, with few exceptions, brutally swept aside as Franco's Army of Africa pushed up the peninsula. The already fragile morale of the militia forces was further undermined by the trail of terror left by Franco's army. Fear of capture and certain death contributed to disorderly and disastrous retreats on occasion. In contrast, untrained workers showed they could fight well defensively, as was the case at Irún in the Basque Country, at the town of Sigüenza to the north of Madrid and at the Rio Tinto mines in Andalusia. In the north, the Basque and Asturian militias initially held up the fascist advance, but were soon overstretched. One of few offensive actions by the militia, the attempt to retake Mallorca and Ibiza, failed without sea or air back-up against stronger Italian forces.

The largest concentration of militia forces was in eastern Aragon where, by October 1936, the front stretched nearly 500 km from Teruel to the Pyrenees. But the initial push of the first weeks soon became bogged down due to lack of suitable arms and coordination and the ineptitude, if not treachery, of professional military advisers. All three provincial capitals, Saragossa, Huesca and Teruel, remained besieged until the fascist offensive of 1938.

More than on any other front, in Aragon the militias saw their role as spreading the social revolution as much as combating fascism. The relative passivity of the front also provided more time for the installation of libertarian communism in the rear. As the militia advanced in the summer of 1936, they set up revolutionary committees, helped collectivise the land and eliminated enemies. One of the first actions of the Durruti Column was to issue a decree abolishing private property. Whether collectivisation was 'imposed' or 'spontaneous' depended on such factors as class structure and types of landownership. Outside pressure to collectivise was greatest near the front or where the CNT had not existed before the war. But above all, the demise of Republican legality in eastern Aragon was more important than the presence of the armed CNT militias.[42]

Militia forces also sought to guarantee the revolution in the rear. The Iron Column sent expeditions back to Valencia to suppress 'fascist' newspapers, destroy the archives of the 'state and capitalist institutions' and demand that the police forces be disbanded and their members sent to the front. Iron Column fighters also released 'social prisoners', much to the alarm of the middle classes and the Popular Front.[43]

THE TOMB OF FASCISM

Where popular mobilisation and the militias were to play a decisive role was Madrid, which by late October 1936 was threatened by the rebel army. An army of 30,000 could not capture a city of one million prepared to defend itself. But this was no ordinary military victory. In contrast to the rest of the war, the defence of Madrid was based on what former communist leader Fernando Claudin termed 'the spirit of proletarian revolution'.[44]

The Republican government's decision to establish the Popular Army (see below) was too recent to make any real impact on the situation. The city's defences were hardly prepared; its troops were disorganised. There was a shortage of rifles and ammunition and no anti-aircraft cover. Military commanders had little or no idea of the scale, disposition or readiness of forces at their disposal. Many political leaders thought Madrid was doomed and on 6 November the government fled to Valencia. A junta made up of party, union and military representatives now took over the defence of the capital. As Pierre Broué points out:

> 'placed at the head of the capital at a time when the government's departure in fact left the initiative to those who wanted to fight, the Junta became, as a result of its language and its methods, a genuinely revolutionary government . . . To defend Madrid, its defenders had to be galvanized into action. The Junta realised this: hence there were no speeches about the legality of the government or respect for law and order and property. It did not hesitate to appeal to the workers of Madrid to glorify the proletarian revolution they were carrying out . . . the Junta employed methods that the . . . CNT and POUM had advocated elsewhere . . . arming the people, omnipotence of the Committees, action by the masses, and summary revolutionary justice.'[45]

Once the decision had been made to defend the city, two options were posed: stopping the enemy outside the city in the Tajo Valley or building defences and avoiding open conflict. The communists, the newly arrived Soviet advisers and the anarcho-syndicalists favoured the second option, which was adopted. The discovery of the fascist battle plan on a dead officer aided the city's defence.

Thousands of citizens were mobilised both as militia and to dig trenches. Recruitment centres were established in the offices of the workers' organisations. Barricades were erected in every street and in every threatened district; they were often built by women and children. District, house and block committees were set up and 'took on the immediate tasks of defence, antiaircraft observation, and surveillance of suspects'.[46] Workers left for the front in the outlying neighbourhoods of Madrid with no arms. Volunteers recovered the weapons of dead and wounded soldiers. CNT leaders, pistols in hands, forced those retreating to return to the frontline. Anarchist and POUM columns also arrived from Catalonia. The Durruti Column would soon play a central role in 'epic fighting' in the University City, where they suffered heavy losses.[47]

Everything was valid in defence of the city: propaganda about Moroccans raping women and children; repeated promises of external aid; or the heroic example of the International Brigades.[48] Improvised theatre companies performed the play *Four Shock Battalions!* in working-class districts. Orders for mobilisation were constantly broadcast over the radio. For the first time in the history of war, a civilian population was subject to systematic bombardments from the air, but this initially caused anger and determination to resist rather than demoralisation.

The battle of Madrid saw the timely arrival of the first significant international aid for the Republic: Soviet arms and aircraft and the first units of the International Brigades. Organised and led by the communists, although relatively few in number the Brigades would play an important role both as shock troops and in raising morale. Soviet propaganda – posters, literature, films – flooded the city.[49] The heroic defence of Petrograd in the Russian civil war was presented as an example to emulate. This use of the Russian revolution to inspire Madrid's defenders contrasted with the professed aim of the Republican government to be defending democracy. As Broué concludes, 'never again, during the whole Spanish Civil War, did the Communists join the fight with such ferocity. Never again did the Russians repeat the efforts they made for Madrid in November 1936 . . .'[50]

On 23 November the fascists halted their attack on the capital, but Republican forces were too depleted to mount a serious counter-offensive. Having failed to take Madrid in a frontal assault, the rebels were forced to change their strategy. The war now became one of attrition, affecting the whole population, in which large-scale manoeuvres and set-piece battles dominated.

THE PEOPLE'S ARMY

In the first weeks of the Spanish revolution many workers' leaders argued that there should be no turning back from the militia system as the basis of a new proletarian army. As a leader of the *Nosotros* group, and future government minister, Juan García Oliver had stated on 10 August 1936: 'The Madrid government believes that an army with a non-revolutionary outlook can be formed to combat fascism. The army must have no other expression than that which emanates from the people's voice and it must be 100 per cent proletarian.'[51] A few days later the left socialist daily *Claridad* declared that 'to think of replacing the militias with another kind of army to control their revolutionary action is to think in a counter-revolutionary way'.[52]

However, the military situation did not favour the militias. Thanks to massive aid provided by their Italian and German backers the balance between the two opposing armies had decisively swung in favour of the fascists. Most anarchist military leaders, after experiencing the slaughter of their troops at the hands of a better trained and equipped enemy, did what they could to make their militia more effective and soon favoured a stricter code of discipline. In September 1936, the CNT called for the creation of a 'war militia' which would include conscription but be under the control of the unions and preserve the election of officers, a single pay scale and the absence of badges of rank. Parallel to this, the anarcho-syndicalists advocated the formation of a defence junta based on the unions and the Republican parties, the latter representing the 'petty bourgeoisie'. As the socialists would not countenance a government that excluded the workers' political parties, the CNT's proposals came to nothing. Instead a new Popular Front government was formed under the left socialist Francisco Largo Caballero. On 30 September it decreed the conversion of the militias into a regular army based on an organisational plan drawn up by Soviet military advisers.[53] The new Popular Army was to be based on traditional forms of military discipline and hierarchy, conscription and have a centralised high command. The Communist Party's militia, the Fifth Regiment, served as a model and its officers were to hold key positions of command in the new army.[54]

Its defence of military orthodoxy and the prestige gained from Soviet aid soon meant that the PCE was the dominant political force in the new army. By March 1937, according to the party's own figures, 131,600 of its 249,140 members were at the front.

Six months later it was reported that 87 of 130 commanders were communists or sympathisers, as were 321 of the 715 commissars named by the Ministry of Defence during 1937.[55]

In some ways the Popular Army did differ from other modern armies. Units often maintained the ideological allegiances of the former militia. Officers from a working-class background, who had previously led the militia, held important posts of command. Often leading through example, they were among the most effective officers in the Popular Army.[56] Further proof that this was no ordinary bourgeois army was the presence of commissars in its ranks, albeit that officially this was presented as inspired by the Napoleonic example rather than the Soviet.[57]

Yet despite such differences from military orthodoxy, the Popular Army represented a break with the revolutionary nature of the militias. As Michael Alpert points out, the new army 'lacked the revolutionary fervour, the sense of common purpose and the ready acceptance of discipline that in real revolutionary armies has made up for the lack of military experience and often material'.[58] Instead, militarisation has to be seen in the context of the rebuilding of the Republican state to the detriment of the social revolution and, consequently, of a war which was decidedly non-revolutionary in its aims and methods.

By November 1936 the CNT leadership clearly favoured militarisation, though it tried to placate opposition by claiming that it would not change the nature of the Confederation's columns as they would keep the same commanders and names. The government stipulated that those columns that did not accept militarisation would receive neither arms nor supplies and militiamen would no longer be paid. Such threats, along with the pressure for anti-fascist unity and the fear of being sent to other units, convinced most anarchist militia to accept their conversion into troops of the new army.

Arguments in favour of militarisation were strengthened by the military situation. So in the south and Extremadura where the advance of the Army of Africa had been virtually unstoppable, there was little opposition in the ranks of anarcho-syndicalist militia. Resistance was centred on the Aragon front where there was 'an explosion of bad feeling' over such aspects as the introduction of epaulettes and saluting and, above all, the fact that militarisation was imposed without consulting the rank and file. In contrast to other CNT leaders, Durruti, despite favouring more efficient military organisation, opposed the Militarisation Decree. His Column's War Committee declared on 20 October that it did not believe militarisation would improve their ability to fight and instead would create 'suspicion, reticence and repulsion' which could lead to a 'true state of disorganisation'. It concluded: 'This Committee, echoing the clamour of protest . . . about the Decree, sees it as necessary not to accept it.' An alternative to the government's new Military Code, proposed by the Column's International Group, which suppressed saluting and defended equal salaries, freedom of discussion and democracy, was adopted unanimously by a meeting of *Centuria* leaders on 22 December.[59]

Although militarisation was gradually imposed, dissent continued. About 1,000 members of the Durruti Column requested to leave the front. In March 1937 several hundred members of the Column in the Gelsa sector abandoned their positions after having reached an agreement with their commanders about their replacement. The Gelsa fighters had been among the first to propose the reorganisation of the militia and the establishment of a collective general staff based on delegates of different columns, but they rejected militarisation. They now returned to the rear, taking their weapons with them, and would form the nucleus of the Amigos de Durruti group which would play a leading role in the fighting in Barcelona two months later.

Opposition to militarisation was particularly strong in the Iron Column. Its delegates were at the forefront of protests at a meeting of CNT columns on 5 February 1937 in Valencia where the anarcho-syndicalist leadership was attacked for being too concerned about the war and not enough about the revolution.[60] Army discipline, according to the Iron Column's newspaper, meant the 'maiming of [the personality] . . . What men need is not discipline but stimulus, an example of bravery, of abnegation, of disinterest, generosity . . .' Instead, militiamen should voluntarily cede to the orders given by those accepted as military technicians due to their knowledge.[61] Nevertheless, further military setbacks and the collapse of opposition in other columns meant that in late March the Iron Column finally accepted militarisation, becoming part of the 41st Division. The last bulwark against militarisation had fallen.[62]

The POUM was also critical of the implications of militarisation under the auspices of the Republican state. In January 1937 the party's military conference rejected the Popular Army as bourgeois. Instead, the POUM called for the formation of a 'regular revolutionary proletarian army' based on the experience of the Russian revolution. This would combine the political and voluntary nature of the militias with a centralised command system, which in turn would be subordinated to a workers' and peasants' government. Officers would have no privileges. Soldiers' committees would exist at all levels and exercise political control over military 'technicians' (professional officers). These committees in turn would, with their worker and peasant counterparts, form the basis of the workers' government.[63] But without the formation of such a revolutionary government in the rear the party had no alternative to accepting militarisation, and its column on the Aragon front was transformed into the 29th Division in April 1937.

The events of May 1937, with street fighting in Barcelona between revolutionaries, many former militiamen and government forces, marked the end of the revolutionary process. Inside the army the revolutionary left had long since lost the initiative. On the Aragon front the news from Barcelona caused disquiet, but discipline held firm. Only a few hundred, mainly CNT fighters, left the front before being turned back at Lerida with guarantees that there would be no reprisals against the workers' organisations.

In the aftermath of the May fighting the main victim was the POUM, which was banned and its leaders imprisoned on 16 June. The day before, troops of the party-led 29th Division had been thrown into action as part of the offensive on Huesca. They fought bravely and sustained heavy losses over the next two days unaware that their party was being repressed as a 'fascist' organisation in the rearguard. Upon returning to the rear, the 29th Division was disbanded and its commanders arrested.

POLITICS AND WAR

The capacity and limitations of the new army would soon mark the character and development of the war. Once organised it was shown to be capable of launching effective and, at times, devastating offensives which repeatedly threw back the fascist forces. However, a pattern was soon established whereby the Popular Army was unable to follow up these attacks due to the lack of reserves and equipment. The overwhelming superiority of the rebel army would then impose itself and the lost ground would be regained, all at a terrible cost for both sides, but with the difference that the Republican army had far greater difficulty in replacing its losses in both men and materiel.

The Republic also faced great logistical and organisational difficulties. Massive and swift transfers of men to threatened parts of the front were exacerbated by the bad state of roads and railways. Brigades, divisions and corps were set up without the benefit of existing administrative organisation or bases. Units might be formed on paper, often without arms or officers to command them. Republican officers often showed little initiative due to both a lack of training and the conservatism of commanders who insisted on keeping a tight control over lower ranks. Worse still, while competent officers were sometimes overlooked because of political bias inside the General Staff, others were given commands beyond their capacity. The rapid creation of training schools only partly helped overcome the low quality of Republican officers. It was not until January 1938 that former militia officers were allowed to advance beyond the rank of major, even though some of them were already commanding divisions and army corps.[64]

For the Popular Front government to maintain middle-class support at home and win over the democracies abroad, its war aims had to be seen to be defending liberal democracy. By extension any remaining influence of the revolutionary left over the army had to be broken. So it was politics not military strategy that determined that arms were not sent to the Aragon front or to Malaga.[65] Similarly, the proposed offensive on Extremadura in the spring of 1937 was rejected by the Soviet advisers as it would have strengthened Largo Caballero's position in a government where the more moderate elements, aligned with the communists, wanted him removed.[66]

A particularly clear example of how the Popular Front subordinated its military strategy to its political aims was the restricted use of the Republican navy to avoid alarming the imperial powers. By transferring ships from the Mediterranean to Cantabria in the first weeks of the war, allowing Italian and German ships to reach Andalusia and North Africa unhindered, the Republican government made what was 'maybe the major [tactical] mistake of the war'. The Madrid government 'did not dare to . . . convert the Straits of Gibraltar into a war zone'. It is also quite feasible that Soviet advisers insisted that the Republican fleet be used only to escort incoming arms shipments rather than attack fascist ships. Likewise it appears that the Republican air force was instructed not to attack German planes or ships during the early weeks of the war so as not to enter into conflict with Hitler's government.[67]

For the Republic to fight a well-equipped regular army such as Franco's, it either had to have at its disposal a similar force or use irregular methods. An alternative strategy, according to the military historian Antony Beevor, would have been to have fought a largely defensive war punctuated by multiple and rapid incursions by both regular troops and guerrilla units into the sparsely defended parts of an extremely long and undermanned front. Such a strategy would have tied down large numbers of fascist forces and avoided the massive destruction of loyalist troops and materiel which eventually undermined the Republic's ability to resist. In particular, guerrilla actions, however limited by repression, could have mobilised political sympathy in the enemy rearguard in support of subversion.[68]

Later in the war the communists promoted the formation of guerrilla units; the NKVD[69] chief in Spain, Alexander Orlov, would claim to have been in charge of such operations. Apparently, Stalin recommended the use of guerrilla warfare, as did the most influential Comintern representative in Spain, Palmiro Togliatti. However, such initiatives were too limited and came too late to make any real impact on the war.[70]

Guerrilla tactics were hardly used, despite suitable terrain, due to the political priorities of a Republican government determined to keep tight control over the army and hence avoid the mass radicalism that had characterised the first months of the war. In particular, 'the essential independence of guerrillas was anathema to both the authoritarian centralists of the government and to the conservative officers who organised the Republican army'.[71] Fear of alarming the democracies was a further factor which determined that such a strategy was not developed, and led even Largo Caballero, despite his leftist rhetoric, to oppose the formation of a guerrilla army.[72] Even most anarchist leaders did not seem to realise that a guerrilla campaign in Aragon would have forced the fascists to concentrate troops there, as well as leading to fewer losses than the type of frontal assaults the militia tended to launch on defended positions.[73]

Thus the transformation of the militias into a regular army has to be seen in the context of the changing political situation in the Republican zone. Having harnessed the initial enthusiasm of the first days of the anti-fascist struggle, the militias, with the necessary leadership and organisation, could have been converted into the army of the revolution. That this did not happen was due to the political orientation of the main workers' organisations. There could be no revolutionary army without revolutionary power, but for the main revolutionary organisation, the CNT, the establishment of such a power meant breaking with their most cherished principles in that the anarchists rejected the existence of all states and, by extension, the 'taking of power'. Instead the Popular Army was built on the backs of the militia. So although it included many of the same military leaders who had risen from the ranks of the workers' movement and was based overwhelmingly on working-class recruits, it was the army of a bourgeois state. An army committed to defend Republican democracy not only from fascism but also, if need be, from the social revolution of 1936.

NOTES

1. In 1898 Spain lost control of Cuba and the Philippines to the United States.
2. There were another 4,838 officers and 50,392, mostly local, troops in Morocco; Stanley Payne, *Los militares y la política en la España contemporánea*, Paris: Ruedo Ibérico, 1968, p. 432.
3. Michael Alpert, *El ejército republicano en la guerra civil*, Madrid: Siglo veintiuno, 1989, pp. 5, 12.
4. Michael Alpert, 'Soldiers, politics and war', in Paul Preston, ed., *Revolution and War in Spain 1931–1939*, London: Taylor & Francis, 1984, p. 203.
5. The Popular Front electoral coalition was organised towards the need of 1935 on the basis of the middle-class (liberal) Republican parties, the socialists and the communists.
6. Paul Preston, *The Spanish Civil War: Reaction, Revolution and Revenge*, London: Harper, 2006, p. 102.
7. Michael Alpert, *El ejército republicano en la guerra civil*, Madrid: Siglo veintiuno, 1989, p. 59; Antony Beevor, *Battle for Spain: The Spanish Civil War 1936–1939*, London: Phoenix, 2006, p. 57; Paul Preston, *Las derechas españolas en el siglo XX: autoritarismo, fascismo y golpismo*, London: Routledge, 1994, pp. 95–6.
8. The Assault Guards were a paramilitary police force organised in 1931 and generally led by officers loyal to the Republic.
9. Confederación Nacional de Trabajo.
10. José Manuel Marquez Rodríguez and Juan José Gallardo Romero, *Ortiz. General sin dios ni amo*, Barcelona: Hacer, 1999, p. 49; Antonio Pedraza Fontecha, 'Anarcosindicalismo y violencia: la gimnasia revolucionaria para el pueblo', *Historia Contemporánea* 11, 1994, pp. 173–4.
11. Federación Anarquista Ibérica: radical anarchist federation.
12. Agustín Guillamón, *Los Comités de Defensa de la CNT en Barcelona (1933–1938)*, Barcelona: Aldarull, 2011, pp. 23–4; Márquez and Gallardo, *Ortiz. General sin dios ni amo*, pp. 82–6.
13. Confederación Española de Derechas Autónomos.
14. José C. Guibaja Velázquez, 'La tradición improvisada: el socialismo y la milicia', *Historia Contemporánea*, 11, 1994, pp. 110–14.
15. Enrique Lister, *Memorias de un luchador. Los primeros combates*, Madrid: G. del Toro, 1977, pp. 59–60; other sources suggest that the party's influence in the ranks before the war was minimal, see Juan Andrés Blanco Rodríguez, *El Quinto Regimiento en la política militar del PCE. en la guerra civil*, Madrid: UNED, 1993, p. 23.
16. Juventud Socialista Unificada (JSU).
17. Dolores Ibárruri et al., eds., *Guerra y Revolución en España 1936–1939*, Volume 1, Moscow: Editorial Progreso, 1966, p. 272.
18. Partido Obrero de Unificación Marxista.
19. Andrew Durgan, *B.O.C. El Bloque Obrero y Campesino 1930–1936*, Barcelona: Laertes, 1996, pp. 478–80.

20. Agustín Guillamón, *Barricadas en Barcelona. La CNT de la victoria de Julio de 1936 a la necesaria derrota de mayo de 1937*, Barcelona: Ediciones Espartaco Internacional, 2007, pp. 36–8.
21. Alpert, *El ejército republicano*, p. 22.
22. Walther L. Bernecker, *Guerra en España 1936–1939*, Madrid: Editorial Sintesis, 1996, p. 39.
23. Alpert, *El ejército republicano*, pp. 320–2.
24. *Comité Central de Milicies Antifeixistes*; on the CCMA, see Guillamón, *Barricadas en Barcelona*, pp. 70–126; Andrew Durgan, 'Workers' democracy in the Spanish revolution, 1936–1937', in Immanuel Ness and Dario Azzellini, *Ours to Master and to Own. Workers' Control from the Commune to the Present*, Chicago: Haymarket Books, 2011, pp. 154–5; on the militias in Aragon, see Judit Camps and Emili Olcina, *Les milicies catalanes al front d'Aragó*, Barcelona, Laertes, 2006.
25. Eladi Mainar, *De milicians a soldats. Les columnes valencianes en la guerra civil española (1936–1937)*, Valencia: Universitat de Valencia, 1998, p. 54.
26. Márquez and Gallardo, *Ortiz. General sin dios ni amo*, p. 6.
27. Mary Nash, *Rojas. Las mujeres republicanas en la guerra civil*, Madrid: Taurus, 1999, pp. 93–8.
28. Gema Iglesias Rodríguez, 'Derechos y deberes de las mujeres durante la guerra civil española: "los hombres al frente, las mujeres en la retaguardia"', *Las mujeres y la Guerra Civil Española. III Jornadas de estudios monográficos. Salamanca, octubre 1989*, Madrid: Ministerio de Cultura, 1991, p. 111; Julián Casanova, *De la calle al frente. El anarcosindicalismo en España (1931–1939)*, Barcelona: Crítica, 1997, p. 168; Mainar, *De milicians a soldats*, p. 6; Nash, *Rojas*, pp. 93, 97.
29. Andrew Durgan, *The Spanish Civil War*, Basingstoke: Palgrave Macmillan, 2007, pp. 85–6, 106, 120–1.
30. Mainar, *De milicians a soldats*, pp. 149–51.
31. José Peirats, *The CNT in the Spanish Revolution*, Volume 1, Hastings: Meltzer Press, 2001, p. 204; Beevor, *Battle for Spain*, pp. 140, 195.
32. Mainar, *De milicians a soldats*, pp. 35, 59–60.
33. Alpert, *El ejército republicano*, p. 35; Ramon Brusco *Les milicies antifeixistes i l'exèrcit popular a Catalunya*, Lleida: Edicions El Jonc, 2003, p. 69; George Orwell, *Orwell in Spain*, London: Penguin, 2001, p. 36.
34. Andrew Durgan, 'Les volontaires internationaux des milices du POUM', in Stéfanie Preszioso et al., eds., *Tant pis si la lutte est cruelle. Volontaires Internationaux contre Franco*, Paris: Éditions Sylleps, 2008, pp. 185–6.
35. Partit Socialista Unificat de Catalunya: Catalan Communist Party.
36. José Maria Maldonado, *El frente de Aragón. La guerra civil en Aragón (1936–1938)*, Zaragoza: Mira Editores, 2007, p. 140.
37. Miquel Amorós, *La revolución traicionada. La verdadera historia de Balius y Los Amigos de Durruti*, Barcelona: Virus, 2003, p. 148.
38. Márquez and Gallardo, *Ortiz. General sin dios ni amo*, p. 110.
39. Orwell, *Orwell in Spain*, p. 56.
40. Amorós, *La revolución traicionada*, p. 146.
41. Orwell, *Orwell in Spain*, p. 279; Peirats, *The CNT in the Spanish Revolution*, p. 170; Brusco, *Les milicies antifeixistes*, p. 61.
42. Walther L. Bernecker, 'La revolución social', in Stanley Payne and Javier Tusell, eds., *La guerra civil. Una nueva visión del conflicto que dividió España*,

Madrid: Temas de hoy, 1996, p. 521; Julián Casanova, *Anarquismo y revolución en la sociedad rural aragonesa 1936–1938*, Madrid: Siglo ventiuno, 1985, pp. 119–29.

43. Mainar, *De milicians a soldats*, pp. 71–2, 74; Amorós, Miquel, 2009, *José Pellicer. El anarquista íntegro. Vida y obra del fundador del la heroica Columna de Hierro* (Virus), pp. 141–70.
44. Fernando Claudin, *The Communist Movement. from Comintern to Cominform*, London: Penguin, 1975, p. 238.
45. Pierre Broué and Emile Témime, *The Revolution and Civil War in Spain*, London: Faber, 1972, pp. 244–5, 247.
46. Ibid., p. 247.
47. The death of Durruti on 20 November, in confused circumstances, demoralised many anarchist volunteers, many of whom demanded to return to Aragon as they did not feel safe in the capital, or even abandoned the column altogether.
48. Andrew Durgan, 'Las Brigadas Internacionales', in Antonio Liz et al., eds., *Barbarie fascista y revolución social*, Huesca: Sariñena Editorial, pp. 188–9.
49. Daniel Kowalsky, *La Unión Soviética y la Guerra Civil Española*, Barcelona: Crítica, 2004, pp. 153–62; Robert G. Colodny, *El asedio de Madrid* (1970), Ruedo Ibérico/Transaction, 2009, p. 46.
50. Broué and Témime, *The Revolution and Civil War in Spain*, p. 245.
51. Peirats, *The CNT in the Spanish Revolution* , pp. 154–5.
52. Alpert, *El ejército republicano*, p. 37.
53. Kowalsky, *La Unión Soviética*, pp. 262–4.
54. Blanco, *El Quinto Regimiento*, p. 376.
55. Angel Viñas, *El escudo de la República. El oro de España, la apuesta soviética y los hechos de mayo de 1937*, Barcelona: Crítica, 2007, p. 445; Ferrando Hernández Sánchez, *Guerra o revolución. El Partido Comunista de España en la guerra civil*, Barcelona: Crítica, 2010, pp. 353–4.
56. Michael Alpert, 'Soldiers, politics and war', in Paul Preston, ed., *Revolution and War in Spain 1931–1939*, London: Taylor & Francis, 1984, p. 213.
57. Helen Graham, *The Spanish Republic at War 1936–1939*, Cambridge: Cambridge University Press, 2002, pp. 146–7.
58. Alpert, 'Soldiers, politics and war', p. 220.
59. Amorós, *La revolución traicionada*, pp. 147, 151, 154.
60. Julián Casanova, *De la calle al frente. El anarcosindicalismo en España (1931–1939)*, Barcelona: Crítica, 1997, p. 189.
61. Mainar, *De milicians a soldats*, p. 130.
62. In August 1937, after having failed to carry out its part in an attack on the main road to Zaragoza and taking heavy casualties, the former Iron Column, now the 83rd Brigade, was dissolved. A report by the Brigade stated that their 'humanitarian principles' had led them to have a naïve view of war and 'the majority of our brigade had not been at the level of circumstances . . . war has shown us the need for iron discipline', Mainar, *De milicians a soldats*, pp. 138–9.
63. Víctor Alba, ed., *La revolución española en la práctica. Documentos del POUM*, Madrid: Júcar, 1977, pp. 182–90; Reiner Tosstorff, *El POUM en la revolució espanyola*, Barcelona, Editorial Base, 2009, pp. 155–70.
64. Michael Alpert, 'The clash of Spanish armies: contrasting ways of war in Spain 1936–1939', *War in History*, 6(3), 1999, pp. 337, 345.

65. Even sources hostile to the revolution recognise that the Aragon front was starved of arms, for example Antonio Elorza and Marta Bizcarrondo, *Queridos camaradas. La Internacional Comunista y España 1919–1939*, Barcelona: Planeta, 1999, p. 314.
66. Beevor, *Battle for Spain*, pp. 307–8.
67. Alpert, 'The clash of Spanish armies', pp. 334-6, 346.
68. Beevor, *Battle for Spain*, pp. 349–50; Abraham Guillen, *El error militar de las 'izquierdas'*, Barcelona: Hacer, 1980, pp. 22–3.
69. Soviet secret police.
70. John Costello and Oleg Tsarev, *Deadly Illusions*, London: Century, 1993, pp. 269–72; George Esenwein and Adrian Shubert, *Spain at War: The Spanish Civil War in Context 1931–1936*, London: Longman, 1995, p. 153.
71. Michael Alpert, 'Soldiers, politics and war', p. 221.
72. Guillen, *El error militar*, p. 27.
73. Amorós, *La revolución traicionada*, p. 150; Beevor, *Battle for Spain*, pp. 229–30.

BIBLIOGRAPHY/FURTHER READING

Víctor Alba, ed.., *La revolución española en la práctica. Documentos del POUM*, Madrid: Júcar, 1977.

Michael Alpert, 'Soldiers, politics and war', in Paul Preston, ed., *Revolution and War in Spain 1931–1939*, London: Taylor & Francis, 1984.

Michael Alpert, 'The Spanish army and the Popular Front', in Martin Alexander and Helen Graham, eds., *The French and Spanish Popular Fronts. Comparative Perspectives*, Cambridge: Cambridge University Press, 1989.

Michael Alpert, *El ejército republicano en la guerra civil*, Madrid: Siglo veintiuno, 1989.

Michael Alpert, 'La historia military', in Stanley Payne and Javier Tusell, eds., *La guerra civil. Una nueva visión del conflicto que dividió España*, Madrid: Temas de hoy, 1996.

Michael Alpert, 'The clash of Spanish armies: contrasting ways of war in Spain 1936–1939', *War in History*, 6(3), 1999.

Miquel Amorós, *La revolución traicionada. La verdadera historia de Balius y Los Amigos de Durruti*, Barcelona: Virus, 2003.

Miquel Amorós, *José Pellicer. El anarquista íntegro. Vida y obra del fundador del la heroica Columna de Hierro*, Barcelona: Virus, 2009.

Antony Beevor, *Battle for Spain: The Spanish Civil War 1936–1939*, London: Phoenix, 2006.

Walther L. Bernecker, *Guerra en España 1936–1939*, Madrid: Editorial Sintesis, 1996.

Walther L. Bernecker, 'La revolución social', in Stanley Payne and Javier Tusell, eds., *La guerra civil. Una nueva visión del conflicto que dividió España*, Madrid: Temas de hoy, 1996.

Juan Andrés Blanco Rodríguez, *El Quinto Regimiento en la política militar del PCE. en la guerra civil*, Madrid: UNED, 1993.

Pierre Broué and Emile Témime, *The Revolution and Civil War in Spain*, London: Faber, 1972.

Ramon Brusco, *Les milicies antifeixistes i l'exèrcit popular a Catalunya*, Lleida: Edicions El Jonc, 2003.

Judit Camps and Emili Olcina, *Les milicies catalanes al front d'Aragó*, Barcelona, Laertes, 2006.

Julián Casanova, *Anarquismo y revolución en la sociedad rural aragonesa 1936–1938*, Madrid: Siglo ventiuno, 1985.

Julián Casanova, *De la calle al frente. El anarcosindicalismo en España (1931–1939)*, Barcelona: Crítica, 1997.

Fernando Claudin, *The Communist Movement. From Comintern to Cominform*, London: Penguin, 1975.

Robert G. Colodny, *El asedio de Madrid* (1970), Ruedo Ibérico: Transaction, 2009.

John Costello and Oleg Tsarev, *Deadly Illusions*, London: Century, 1993.

Andrew Durgan, *B.O.C. El Bloque Obrero y Campesino 1930–1936*, Barcelona: Laertes, 1996.

Andrew Durgan, *The Spanish Civil War*, Basingstoke: Palgrave Macmillan, 2007.

Andrew Durgan, 'Les volontaires internationaux des milices du POUM', in Stéfanie Preszioso et al., eds., *Tant pis si la lutte est cruelle. Volontaires Internationaux contre Franco*, Paris: Éditions Sylleps, 2008.

Andrew Durgan, 'Workers' democracy in the Spanish revolution, 1936–1937', in Immanuel Ness and Dario Azzellini, *Ours to Master and to Own. Workers' Control from the Commune to the Present*, Chicago: Haymarket Books, 2011.

Andrew Durgan, 'Las Brigadas Internacionales', in Antonio Liz et al., eds., *Barbarie fascista y revolución social*, Huesca: Sariñena Editorial.

Antonio Elorza and Marta Bizcarrondo, *Queridos camaradas. La Internacional Comunista y España 1919–1939*, Barcelona: Planeta, 1999.

George Esenwein and Adrian Shubert, *Spain at War: The Spanish Civil War in Context 1931–1936*, London: Longman, 1995.

Antonio Pedraza Fontecha, 'Anarcosindicalismo y violencia: la gimnasia revolucionaria para el pueblo', *Historia Contemporánea*, 11, 1994.

Helen Graham, *The Spanish Republic at War 1936–1939*, Cambridge: Cambridge University Press, 2002.

José C. Guibaja Velázquez, 'La tradición improvisada: el socialismo y la milicia' *Historia Contemporánea*, 11, 1994.

Agustín Guillamón, *Barricadas en Barcelona. La CNT de la victoria de Julio de 1936 a la necesaria derrota de mayo de 1937*, Barcelona: Ediciones Espartaco Internacional, 2007.

Agustín Guillamón, *Los Comités de Defensa de la CNT en Barcelona (1933–1938)*, Barcelona: Aldarull, 2011.

Abraham Guillen, *El error militar de las 'izquierdas'*, Barcelona: Hacer, 1980.

Ferrando Hernández Sánchez, *Guerra o revolución. El Partido Comunista de España en la guerra civil*, Barcelona: Crítica, 2010.

Dolores Ibárruri et al., eds., *Guerra y Revolución en España 1936–1939*, 3 volumes, Moscow: Editorial Progreso, 1966.

Gema Iglesias Rodríguez, 'Derechos y deberes de las mujeres durante la Guerra Civil española: "los hombres al frente, las mujeres en la ret Guardia"', *Las mujeres y la Guerra Civil Española. III Jornadas de estudios monográficos. Salamanca, octubre 1989*, Madrid: Ministerio de Cultura, 1991.

Daniel Kowalsky, *La Unión Soviética y la Guerra Civil Española*, Barcelona: Crítica, 2004.

Enrique Lister, *Memorias de un luchador. Los primeros combates*, Madrid: G. del Toro, 1977.

Eladi Mainar, *De milicians a soldats. Les columnes valencianes en la Guerra Civil española (1936–1937)*, Valencia: Universitat de Valencia, 1998.

José Maria Maldonado, *El frente de Aragón. La guerra civil en Aragón (1936–1938)*, Zaragoza: Mira Editores, 2007.

José Manuel Marquez Rodríguez and Juan José Gallardo Romero, *Ortiz. General sin dios ni amo*, Barcelona: Hacer, 1999.

Mary Nash, *Rojas. Las mujeres republicanas en la guerra civil*, Madrid: Taurus, 1999.

George Orwell, *Orwell in Spain*, London: Penguin, 2001.

Stanley Payne, *Los militares y la política en la España contemporánea*, Paris: Ruedo Ibérico, 1968.

José Peirats, *The CNT in the Spanish Revolution*, Volume 1, Hastings: Meltzer Press, 2001.

Paul Preston, *Las derechas españolas en el siglo XX: autoritarismo, fascismo y golpismo*, London: Routledge, 1994.

Paul Preston, *The Spanish Civil War: Reaction, Revolution and Revenge*, London: Harper, 2006.

Reiner Tosstorff, *El POUM en la revolució espanyola*, Barcelona, Editorial Base, 2009.

Angel Viñas, *El escudo de la República. El oro de España, la apuesta soviética y los hechos de mayo de 1937*, Barcelona: Crítica, 2007.

7
Never 'One Hand': Egypt 2011

Philip Marfleet

For Egypt's military elite the revolution which began in January 2011 was an earthquake. It removed the head of the armed forces, President (and Air Chief Marshal) Husni Mubarak, and soon threatened the foundations of the accustomed order – a regime in which the army had played a leading role for almost 60 years. For senior officers everything was at stake: their authority, their privileges, their security and the state itself. During the first 18 months of the revolution they survived, protecting the core of the old order and their place within it. They were shaken and uncertain, however, pursuing a series of changing strategies against the movement from below. This chapter examines the armed forces as an institution, the nature of military authority and the people's challenge to military rule.

The revolution had begun with demands to remove a dictator; within months there were insistent calls to remove the dictatorship in the form of the ruling military elite. The speed of change was remarkable. In January 2011 millions joined the activists of Tahrir Square in asserting solidarity between the military and the movement of the streets in the face of attacks by riot police and thugs, affirming: 'The army and the people are one hand'. Within nine months demonstrations had a different tone: following sustained attacks on protestors by military police under the command of the Supreme Council of the Armed Forces (SCAF), activists insisted: 'The police and the army are one filthy hand.' On the anniversary of the revolution huge crowds in city centres across the country demanded an end to military rule: *yasqut, yasqut hukm il-askar* ('Down, down with military rule'). The officers remained in power, urgently seeking accommodation with a newly elected Islamist government but still confronted by a mass movement of increasing radicalism which challenged political principles embedded in the Egyptian state.

For SCAF leader Field Marshal Mohamed Hussain Tantawi the army expressed the interests of the nation. Those challenging his troops were 'subversive elements' whose activities would not be tolerated: he pledged to confront anyone who sought 'to drive a wedge between people and the armed forces'.[1] Amnesty International recorded scores of cases in which troops attacked demonstrations and seized people from the streets and from their homes. Thousands were sentenced by military courts operating in secret. 'Plus ça change,' said Amnesty: 'The euphoria of the uprising has been replaced by fears that one repressive rule has simply been replaced with another.'[2] But Tantawi did not attempt a frontal assault on the mass movement or prevent elections, which in November and December 2011 produced Egypt's first relatively free national polls. Hoping to come to terms with the Islamists, he shaped the electoral process to favour their parties and candidates. Under this new arrangement Egypt's military men intended that a controlled 'opening' and tame parliament would leave the old system – and their own privileges – largely untouched. For some of those analysing the strategies of SCAF this was consistent with the idea of a 'deep state' – the existence of an inner group of top officers and security chiefs who had been the real power behind Mubarak and now made carefully calculated decisions about how to ensure continued control.[3] It was much more likely, however, that Tantawi and his colleagues had undertaken a huge gamble. The civilian arm of the old regime, the National Democratic Party (NDP), had been dismantled, its offices destroyed and its senior officials sent for trial. In efforts to contain a highly mobilised population, SCAF now sought new allies which could mobilise their own constituencies in the mass movement – most importantly the Islamists, Mubarak's historic foes. Could the Muslim Brotherhood assist in halting the revolution, above all in restraining an increasingly confident working class?

ARMY AND PEOPLE

As the revolution unfolded, Egyptian politics polarised around the issue of military rule. How had senior officers gained such power and privilege? From where did they derive their authority? Both the military elite and the mass movement made claims about such authority: for Tantawi, the armed forces represented the nation and had authority to act on its behalf; for the activists of Tahrir, the army had responsibilities to the people and must identify with their movement for change. What historical developments lay behind such claims?

Tantawi and his associates in SCAF were initially a shadowy group. For weeks after the overthrow of Mubarak individual identities were unknown: eventually it became clear that among the Council were heads of the army, navy and air force, and a clutch of major generals responsible for security in each region of Egypt. On 10 February 2011 they issued a first public statement:

'Based on the responsibility of the Armed Forces, and its commitment to protect the people, and to oversee their interests and security, and with a view to the safety of the nation and the citizenry, and of the achievements and properties of the great people of Egypt, and in affirmation and support for the legitimate demands of the people, the Supreme Council of the Armed Forces convened today, 10 February 2011, to consider developments to date, and decided to remain in continuous session to consider what procedures and measures that may be taken to protect the nation, and the achievements and aspirations of the great people of Egypt.'[4]

The 'continuous session' meant that, in effect, SCAF had declared ownership of the Egyptian state and of the country's politics. On 11 February it facilitated the removal of Mubarak; within a week it had suspended the constitution and was attempting to halt public protests and strikes. 'Normality has been restored,' said SCAF, 'all groups and sectors of society [sh]ould work together to support this positive progress and the efforts of the Supreme Council of the Armed Forces to realized [sic] the ambitions and aspirations of the people.' The generals also threatened to intervene against 'irresponsible persons [who] commit illegitimate acts'.[5]

Here there was an echo of another key episode in modern Egyptian history, when the army had seized power 60 years earlier. Members of the Free Officers movement who launched a successful coup on 23 July 1952 were unknown to all but a handful of their colleagues. They too issued proclamations about political change, asserting an identity of interest between the army and the people; they also suppressed popular mobilisations, assaulting strikers and peasant activists. Their coup followed years of planning by a small group of middle-ranking officers pledged to secrecy and committed to exclude all others from their project. The historian Raymond Baker suggests they were 'elitist military conspirators' determined to restrict involvement of the mass of people in national politics.[6] Here similarities with events in 2011 come to an end, however. The Free Officers were beneficiaries of years of struggle by the mass of Egyptians against colonial rule and a corrupt and enfeebled monarchy. In the absence of effective organisation within the nationalist movement itself, from either the left (the communist movement) or the right (the Muslim Brotherhood), the Free Officers had eventually seized their moment. The coup was greeted with popular enthusiasm: one of the main problems identified by its leader and later Egypt's president, Gamal Abdel-Nasser, was keeping supporters among the general public off the streets. Here he could rely on both the communists and the Muslim Brotherhood – each had sympathisers among the Free Officers and believed the coup would serve its own interests.[7]

The Free Officers removed King Faruq and declared a republic. Over the next few years they brought to an end seven decades of British military occupation, first obtaining withdrawal of British troops from all areas of the country except the Suez Canal Zone and, following the Suez War of 1956, securing the exit of British, French and Israeli forces. The military command, and Nasser in particular, accumulated enormous prestige. Seen as leaders of an authentically independent state and of an emerging pan-Arabism, they were projected onto the world stage as key figures within the movement for a 'third' way, independent of East and West. The Cold War was at its height, and the 1956 victory was also hailed as a triumph for progressive forces against European states and their US allies. In 1955 a conference of non-aligned leaders met in Bandung, Indonesia, giving Nasser a huge audience and placing Egypt at the forefront of states which had bettered their colonial rulers. When the Non-Aligned Movement was formed in 1961, Nasser was its pre-eminent figure.

'SOCIALISM' AND NATIONAL UNITY

Tantawi's SCAF of 2011 was a junta seeking to save the military elite and its allies from a powerful insurrectionary movement. Nasser's Free Officers constituted a more complex and contradictory body, one with strong anti-imperialist credentials but which progressively alienated more and more Egyptians as it pursued a particular vision of national development. Throughout the 1950s and 1960s the Free Officers followed the principles which had guided their conspiracy, developing a highly elitist project in which senior officers and a new cadre of bureaucrats directed the economy and the political system. According to Nasser, the 'revolution' of 1952 had been enacted 'in a democratic spirit' and had received 'genuine popular backing'.[8] He denied that it was non-participatory and insisted that the whole process of national development was conducted by and through the people:

> 'A revolution is not the work of one individual, nor of one group. The validity of a revolution lies in its degree of popularity. Also in the extent to which it is an expression of the will of the masses, and in the extent to which it mobilises them to rebuild the future.'[9]

While the Free Officers suppressed workers' and peasants' own initiatives, which they feared might derail their 'revolution', they were also under intense pressure to deliver economic and social reform. Within weeks of taking power they announced a land reform: the first meaningful distribution of land in Egypt and an act of immense significance in the countryside. This restricted the scale of landholdings, directly challenging traditional landowners and foreign investors in the cotton plantations of the Nile delta. Millions of hectares came under state control and were redistributed among the *fellaheen*, the cultivators, giving the regime an instant base in rural communities. The Reform was limited and carefully controlled, however. Only about 15 per cent of cultivable land was taken from large landowners and distributed to smallholders, and the principle of private ownership was retained.[10] Peasants were organised into local cooperatives; membership was compulsory for all those gaining lands released by the reform and the co-ops were run by appointed supervisors responsible to the Ministry of Agrarian Reform. The Free Officers ensured that land remained private property regulated nationally by a system of 'strong government tutelage'.[11]

The Free Officers were sympathetic to private capital and, during their early period in power, did much to accommodate both local and foreign business. In 1953 they introduced Law 430, giving new companies a tax holiday on all profits for seven years. Despite later nationalisations of foreign holdings and of some significant areas of local capital they attempted to cohabit with Egyptian landowners, merchants and industrialists.[12] On this issue Nasser was clear: writing in 1962, at the height of his nationalisation programme, he maintained: 'The private sector has its effective role in the development plan and must be protected to fulfil that part.'[13] His issue with Egypt's businessmen was less a matter of ownership than of their effectiveness in the national project: in advancing development he wanted them to show some independence of foreign capital. Private enterprise, he said, had been incapable of shouldering the needs of the nation and the role of the state was to accelerate development, bringing together elements of Egyptian society in a common project of 'national class unity'.[14] The key aim was 'democratic interaction between the various component elements of the nation, namely the farmers, workers, soldiers, intellectuals and capital'.[15] By such means Egypt would progress towards 'socialism' – a system defined primarily by improvements in material life, including better education, housing and healthcare.[16]

National unity was to be guaranteed by the army which, said Nasser, was 'the tool of the popular will'.[17] Initially, the Free Officers ruled by asserting their authority within the military. On taking power in 1952 they established an Executive Committee, known after January 1953 as the Revolutionary Command Council – a model for the SCAF of 2011. In 1956 Nasser and other senior officers resigned their military commissions, arguing that they should take up civilian roles in national politics. But this was a notional shift: the army remained in control of key institutions and more than a decade after the 1952 coup almost half of all ministerial positions and almost all provincial governorships were held by serving or former officers.[18] Military men meanwhile colonised the political arena. They suppressed the activities of Egypt's main political currents, the Islamists and the communists, becoming more and more intolerant of independent organisation and of criticism of any kind. Hundreds of communists were imprisoned in remote locations such as Kharga in the Western Desert: these were in effect concentration camps in which student activists, worker militants, writers and academics were incarcerated for years, sometimes alongside Islamists whom they had earlier viewed as their enemies. There were so many activists of left and right in prison that they constituted 'a virtual counter-society'.[19] Some key figures were executed, notably the leading Islamist ideologue Sayyid Qutb, whose prison writings were to have a huge impact in Egypt and abroad.[20] Many members of the Brotherhood fled Egypt, most to Saudi Arabia, as the Islamists were reduced to a shadow of the movement that had dominated anti-colonial struggles in the 1930s and 1940s.

In 1953 the Free Officers established the Liberation Rally, intended to draw the people behind the new military leadership. Nasser observed: 'The Liberation Rally is not a political party. Its creation was prompted by the desire to establish a body that would organise the people's forces and overhaul the social set-up.'[21] Three years later the regime founded the National Union through which Egyptians were to combine in support of the army during the Suez conflict. In 1962 Nasser initiated the Arab Socialist Union (ASU), a body which more closely resembled a conventional political party but which had no active membership. In 1965 Nasser admitted, 'The fact is we have no internal organization, except on the books.'[22] All these bodies were shell organisations: they had formal structures but were closed to most Egyptians. The purpose was to inhibit independent political activity, part of an approach often described as corporatism, in which the state establishes structures which privilege certain political currents (or at least their leaders) with the aim of achieving control over the latters' own constituencies. The most striking success for the Egyptian regime saw the Egyptian Communist Party (ECP) dissolve itself on the basis that Nasser's regime represented progressive forces in power (notwithstanding that many ECP activists were still in the army's prisons). In 1964 leading members of the ECP leadership joined the ASU, where they were given token positions from which they conducted ideological work on behalf of the regime. It was one of the lowest points in the history of communism in the Middle East but appeared to confirm the effectiveness of Nasser's strategy of incorporation. By similar means the regime absorbed figures in the workers' movement: in exchange for job security, inflated salaries and other privileges they operated the Egyptian Trade Union Federation (ETUF) as an arm of the state.

'MILITARY SOCIETY'

During the 1940s Egyptian politics had been open, vigorous and increasingly radical. The historian Robert Stephens describes the closing years of the decade as a period of 'revolutionary ferment'.[23] Millions of people participated in demonstrations, rallies and marches against the British occupation, while industrial struggles intensified to the extent that key centres of strike action became ungovernable.[24] A key aim of the Free Officers was to bring stability and order. They intervened not only against British colonialism but also to invigorate Egyptian capitalism, which they intended to assist by disciplining the population and mobilising its resources for the project of development. The masses soon became an instrument for consolidation of a state capitalism in which power and privilege lay with a new military-bureaucratic class.

In the drama of independent national development the masses were allocated non-speaking parts. They were summoned to tasks determined by those in authority, so that the energies of the movement which had presented the Free Officers with their chance to seize power were soon exhausted. Writing in 1968, the former communist Anouar Abdel-Malek argued that in the course of just 15 years Egypt became a 'military society' in which 'the main forces of the national movement, employed one after another as need dictated, [were] eventually eliminated or smashed'. Egypt, he said, had fallen into the hands of 'a devouring bureaucracy . . . let loose with the immunity of autocracy'; the people had been subordinated to the interests of a military-bureaucratic elite which 'determined the objectives and modes of national action': they were present merely 'to supply the manpower'.[25]

Independence under military rule, he argued, had produced a contradictory situation. On the one hand, there had been clear progress in some areas of economic development and in welfare, education and public health. On the other hand, those in power had seized a disproportionate share of national resources which they mobilised for purposes alien to the interests of the majority:

'the share of the state apparatus – not only the army but also the various security and police forces and the mushrooming economic bureaucracy – is truly gigantic and a number of the old rich are still where they were , even if under another name . . .

'. . . the group in power has no socialist roots in its thinking, it resorts to quasi-socialist schemes and formulas in order to attract the masses, which are deeply angered by the dictatorship, and it uses them to cloak what is in reality planning and statism [so] establishing this enormous bureaucratic and security apparatus with all its privileges.'[26]

POPULISM AND WAR

The American academic Raymond Hinnebusch describes the Nasser regime as a definitive case of 'authoritarian populism'.[27] Operating on the basis that reform and development require strong leadership, he suggests, such regimes concentrate power in the hands of politicians or military officers of middle- or lower-middle-class background, often headed by a charismatic leader.[28]

They rule through the army and the bureaucracy by means of a single party and corporatist political structure. This sociological characterisation, avoiding pressing questions about the class nature of such regimes, nonetheless captures key features of many states which emerged in Africa, Asia and the Middle East in the post-colonial era. In the case of Egypt the regime was elitist and increasingly authoritarian, justifying concentration of power in the military apparatus through a specific form of populism – that which presented society as engaged in continuous conflict with the imperialist powers and with its neighbour Israel.

The importance of the Palestine issue in Egyptian politics cannot be overstated. The young men who established the original Free Officers group had been strongly influenced by the efforts of Palestinian nationalists to oppose British colonialism and Zionist settlement. During the 1930s and 1940s the Palestinians had been backed in Egypt by the Muslim Brotherhood, with which a number of the officers, including Nasser, were associated. They were appalled by the conduct of Arab governments during the conflict of 1948 from which Israel emerged as an independent state. Stephens comments sympathetically on Nasser's assessment of the 1948 events as the outcome of an imperialist initiative in which the Western powers – chiefly Britain – combined with 'self-seeking or complaisant Arab governments' and the Zionist movement.[29] Like millions of Egyptians, the Free Officers believed that enfeebled Arab armies, ill-directed and compromised by their political leaders, had surrendered Palestine and that the only way to redeem the land and restore the self-respect of the Arab world was by replacing local regimes and mobilising against the Israeli state.

Once in power, however, the Free Officers took a much more conservative approach. Strong on pro-Palestinian rhetoric, Nasser followed a cautious, calculated policy towards Israel. This infuriated large numbers of Egyptians: when in 1954 key figures of the new regime, including Nasser, visited Cairo University they were jeered and told: 'Give us arms for the [Suez] Canal and for Palestine.'[30] Nasser made extravagant promises on Palestine while keeping a low profile militarily and even maintaining links with the Israeli government through diplomatic contacts in Europe. The Suez victory of 1956 eased pressure on the regime; at the same time it raised expectations of what might be achieved. Nasser channelled these sentiments towards support of the army as guardian of the nation's honour and dignity, and a focal point around which other Arab states should mobilise to defend Palestine. In 1958 Egypt unified with Syria to form the United Arab Republic (UAR) – a project accomplished by integrating two armies under Egyptian control. By 1961 the UAR had collapsed but Nasser was more and more committed to using the armed forces as a key instrument of politics at home and abroad; in 1962 he sent troops into Yemen to support the republican cause, eventually committing some 40,000 men.[31] Egypt was now on a permanent war footing, the regime insisting that the fate of the people was inextricably linked to that of the army.

Huge sums were channelled into military spending: over 15 years from 1952 this increased by some 300 per cent.[32] The military budget funded not only arms and equipment but also a new officer elite. The Free Officers had occupied middle ranks of an army subservient to the colonial power, organising their coup in part to reform the military apparatus. Motivated primarily by nationalist sentiment, they purged the army command and set out to construct armed forces fit to lead independent development. A decade later those promoted to the senior ranks were being inducted into new networks of privilege. They received special bonuses and had access to exclusive social clubs, shops and holiday villages; on retirement, many senior officers moved into key positions in the state bureaucracy, creating relationships across the military and civilian sectors which provided opportunities for lucrative commercial activity. Baker quotes a contemporary observation by Soviet analysts (the Soviet Union then being the key supplier of arms and training for the Egyptian forces): 'They [Egyptian officers] use their privileges for the improvement of their own well-being . . . officer businessmen [are] more interested in business than in the military preparation of soldiers and sergeants.'[33]

These developments took place as nationalisations of foreign capital were enriching the most innovative members of the Egyptian bourgeoisie. The exit of Egypt's European communities provided opportunities to enter key areas of commerce and industry; at the same time, the state apparatus expanded rapidly, offering private capital new means of 'integrating and surviving' within and alongside the new structures of the state.[34] Growth of the armed services was accompanied by massive profiteering in construction and provision of services, facilitated by links between private business and members of what Malak Zaalouk calls the new 'state bourgeoisie':

There were significant overlaps and alliances between both: i.e. some members of the state bourgeoisie were engaged in

private enterprise, while alliances, interlinkages and interde-
pendencies existed between the two groups – some by virtue of
mutual business interests, others by virtue of kinship, or the social
background of the top managerial elite . . .'[35]

Contrary to most external assessments of Nasserism, which
saw private capital obliterated by zealous radicals, the state sector
encouraged diverse forms of profit-seeking. The military elite was
part of this process: while it called on the population to rally behind
a project of national redemption led by the armed forces, senior
military men became part of a ruling class which cohabited with
private business and enjoyed more and more privilege vis-à-vis the
mass of the people.

The military elite faced growing dangers, however. After a decade
of frustration and broken promises about confronting Israel,
Palestinian activists had taken the initiative. In 1964 they began
guerrilla attacks on Israel, starting a process of radicalisation in
Palestinian refugee camps which brought thousands of young people
into the ranks of the *fedayeen* – the fighters, or redeemers/sacrificers.
In response Nasser created the Palestine Liberation Organisation
(PLO) under the conservative Palestinian politician Ahmed Shuqairi,
who aimed to assist the Egyptian regime in containing the new
movement. Such was the impact of the guerrillas, however, that the
PLO was soon under independent Palestinian control, the armed
struggle against Israel providing a sharp contrast to the inaction of
the Arab states and a focus for renewed radicalism. Israeli forces
attacked Palestinian villages in the West Bank, then in Jordan,
prompting the Jordanian monarch, King Hussein, to criticise
Nasser for inaction – in effect, the Arab rulers were displacing
onto one another responsibility for their own ineffectiveness on
the Palestine issue. Nasser intensified his rhetoric vis-à-vis Israel,
which responded with its own threats. In 1967 the Israelis launched
a massive pre-emptive strike on Egyptian airfields and by land into
Egypt, Jordan and Syria: within days they had won a crushing
victory. At a stroke Israel increased by more than three times the
territory under its control.

In the case of Egypt, Israel seized all of Gaza and Sinai. It was
a disaster for an Egyptian regime which had identified the armed
forces with independence, national integrity and the entire agenda
for development. Friday, 9 June 1967, when Nasser accepted
defeat, was 'Black Friday', said Abdel-Malek: 'The military power
elite had lost, at one stroke, all pretension of being recognised

as a possible political leadership for Egypt [and] inflated hopes and real achievements were seriously called in[to] question.'[36] Nasser survived as President, his reputation as leader of the first post-colonial government enough to save his personal reputation, but the strategy to which he was committed had been damaged beyond repair.

INFITAH

In February 2011 the generals announced that they were formally taking control of Egypt in order to fulfil historic commitments, including 'the responsibility of the Armed Forces . . . to protect the people'.[37] Here they invoked memories of the Nasser era, of confrontations with colonial powers and with the idea of military leadership as the embodiment of the people and its interests. The mass movement promptly challenged the army on just these terms. As tanks entered Tahrir Square, activists demanded that troops must choose between Mubarak, the riot police and the *baltigayya* (thugs) on the one hand, and the protestors on the other. The slogan which rose from the streets went to the heart of problems which had beset Egyptians for 60 years: 'The army and the people are one' proposed that the armed forces should support the uprising; it also raised in an acute form the whole question of military rule. Consistent with a long tradition of political wit and popular sloganeering, it used allusion to contest the role and status of the military. Were the army and the people really 'one'? If not, to whom would the generals give their allegiance? Who had legitimacy now – the officers or the people?

In 1967 defeat by Israel had exposed senior officers as beneficiaries of military-bureaucratic rule who enjoyed new privileges without delivering on promises of national security, Arab unity and solidarity with Palestine. This was soon reflected in a nationwide movement of student protest. One participant recalls that it was 'a summing up of the outrage that spread all over the country after the 1967 defeat . . . an expression of discontent with a whole style of rule of which the military defeat was but one feature'.[38] Protests spread to major workplaces: for the first time in 15 years there were significant strikes, posing a threat so serious that key figures of the regime, including Nasser, visited the industrial centre of Helwan to intervene directly with worker activists.[39] These events were harbingers of much wider and more intensive struggles throughout the 1970s.

Nasser died in 1970, succeeded as President by Anwar Sadat, one of the original Free Officers. He had long embraced a more conservative agenda, maintaining links with influential members of the old bourgeoisie and with senior technocrats at the interface of the state and private capital. In a declaration of intent, one of his first acts as President was to return property seized from wealthy families under the partial nationalisations of the early 1960s. Sadat soon moved against 'radicals' associated with Nasser's economic policies and with his orientation towards the Eastern Bloc. Their places were taken by the new President's allies and clients, so that the Free Officers 'were destroyed as a cohesive political force dominating the apex of power'.[40] Sadat moved quickly to formalise networks of patronage within and outside the bureaucracy, facilitating links between senior military men, the old landowning aristocracy, entrepreneurs who had survived the Nasser era and merchants, traders and commercial intermediaries. At the same time, he assaulted the left, arresting student activists, radical academics and journalists. In 1973 he closed campuses and purged the ASU of dissident members. But Egyptian society was in a febrile state: despite repression, student and worker activism continued and Sadat was faced with multiple challenges to his legitimacy as Nasser's successor. His solution was a dual strategy: mobilise national sentiment once more by means of war and reshape economic and foreign policy with a sharp turn away from the state-centred model of development towards the market. In 1973 Egyptian forces crossed the Suez Canal to strike at the Israeli army in Sinai. The conflict almost ended disastrously for Sadat, but Egyptian troops remained in Sinai and an oil boycott organised by the Gulf States gave him some leverage over the United States and hence Israel. Sadat dubbed himself 'Hero of the Crossing' and set out to exploit his advantages. In 1974 he declared an *infitah* ('opening' or 'open door') through which, he said, Egypt would now welcome foreign imports and investment, reversing 20 years of statist policies and embracing the market locally and internationally.

Sadat was a pioneer of what would shortly be termed neo-liberalism – his *intifah* was an early version of Thatcherism in Britain and Reaganomics in the United States. The impact was profound: the old bourgeoisie was back on centre stage, together with a new generation of aggressive import–export merchants, commission agents and speculators, soon dubbed the 'fat cats' or the 'Sadat class'. The military elite was part of this process: its members had influence or even control over state budgets, which they now used freely to obtain commission from contractors and suppliers. Sadat legitimised and encouraged public–private enterprise: building on networks established during the Nasser era, senior ranks of the armed forces were key players in the rush to profit. When workers' protests continued and in 1977 erupted into a mass movement of opposition to IMF-inspired cuts to food subsidies, Sadat and the generals sent tanks and troops onto the streets. Hundreds died during the '*intifada* of bread', as the army backed the President, his allies in a reconfigured ruling class and the IMF.

MUBARAK AND THE 'CRONIES'

Sadat did not break from Nasser's economic policies: rather, he accelerated trends already present, changing the balance between the state and private capital. In the case of Egypt's foreign policy, however, he abandoned most of Nasser's agenda: most importantly, in 1977 he visited Jerusalem to strike a deal with the Israeli government. At a stroke he removed Egypt and its armed forces from the conflict over Palestine. This mocked the Free Officers' commitment to solidarity with the Palestinians. If Nasser had ruled by means of 'authoritarian populism', Sadat was content with mere authoritarianism, abandoning the notion that the people and the army shared an interest in confronting both colonial and Zionist enemies. For Nasser, the assertion of *karama* (dignity) had been a key component of the nationalist agenda; for Sadat, the rule of the army and its allies was enough. Accommodation with Israel also achieved reorientation from East to West: Sadat had expelled Nasser's Soviet military advisers in 1972; now he moved into formal alliance with the United States, promptly receiving military aid, which brought vast quantities of weaponry. Over the next 30 years Egypt was to receive some $62 billion in economic aid and military assistance from Washington.[41]

Among Sadat's ploys against student and worker activism was rehabilitation of the Islamist movement. He welcomed back exiled members of the Muslim Brotherhood and encouraged them, together with radicals of the *jihadi* tendency, to organise as a counterbalance to communists and Nasserists whom he blamed for dissidence in general and the 1977 uprising in particular.[42] In 1981, as Sadat took the salute at an extravagant military parade in Cairo, he was killed by a team of Islamist soldiers under the command of a junior officer, Khalid Islambouli.

Sadat's replacement, Husni Mubarak, was a career officer who had risen to senior status in the late 1960s – exactly the period when the crisis of Nasserism was most acute and when the armed forces were forging new relations of privilege with Egypt's traditional bourgeoisie. He inherited Sadat's economic agenda and his vision of foreign policy: Egypt was to be a friend of the West and a good neighbour to Israel. The priorities were stability, growth and control over an angry and restless population. Mubarak immediately launched a nationwide campaign of repression: all manner of people, real and imagined opponents of the regime, were seized and imprisoned. In 1984 he ordered troops into the Delta city of Kafr al-Dawwar where workers led protests against government plans to cut healthcare and pensions. The events were testimony to immense pressures among workers, peasants and the poor: Joel Beinin describes 'a three-day urban insurrection, during which workers and urban crowds cut telephone lines, started fires, blocked transportation and destroyed train carriages before a massive crackdown by security forces restored order'.[43] Two years later the regime faced an even more alarming protest in the form of a nationwide revolt by its own foot-soldiers – the riot police of Amn al-Markazi (Central Security). Tanks and artillery were brought in as the army crushed the protests using extreme violence. The episode held important lessons: often viewed as a single coherent institution, the forces of the state had fractured at the base. Police conscripts, little different from those compelled to join the armed forces, had mutinied en masse, their officers helpless to contain the protests and requiring intervention by the army proper.

Control of the barracks, streets and workplaces was particularly important to a regime that Mubarak now steered unwaveringly towards private capital and the world market. He negotiated a series of loans with the IMF, of which the most important, the Economic Reform and Structural Adjustment Programme (ERSAP) of 1991, bound the regime to accelerate neo-liberal policies. The regime threw its energies into a hectic programme of deregulation and privatisation, preparing to dismantle a host of state-owned companies, including most public utilities. Momani comments on its presentations to the IMF of a 'bold and aggressive privatisation plan' and offers to sell 'one [public] company per week'.[44] At this point, with George Bush Senior bragging of a New World Order under Washington's leadership, Mubarak was emerging as a key figure in US plans at a global level. He combined a zealous commitment to the free market with an ultra-authoritarian political regime bound to the United States by military and intelligence ties. A contemporary analysis by US army intelligence lauded Egypt's forces as the core component of a stable political system, 'an entity that is supportive of national goals, responsible to civilian control and without overt interest in political dominance'.[45] The armed forces were, in fact, not only at the heart of the apparatus of repression but also key players shaping economic policy. Their role was obscured by secrecy surrounding the state in general and the military establishment in particular: the army's economic activities were classified as state secrets and investigation could lead to imprisonment and worse. Robert Springborg was among the first to identify its role in privatisation, describing a 'horizontal expansion' of the armed forces into key areas of the economy during the 1990s.[46] Later assessments confirm the consolidation of this 'officer economy', a process in which 'The army's tentacles . . . grasped large shares of the civilian public sector as part of the 'privatisation' process of the 1990s'.[47]

Over the past 20 years the armed forces have entered every area of economic activity, becoming what Springborg calls Egypt's 'Military Incorporated'.[48] Marshall and Stacher identify involvement in arms production, construction, shipbuilding, oil and gas, railway engineering, IT, docks and container services, finance and real estate. The generals have also entered a host of joint ventures with private capital, including investors from the Gulf States such as the Kharafi group of Kuwait, a leading player in the oil engineering business whose links to the military were described by a former minister as a 'model of cooperation' between the state and the private sector.[49]

By the mid-1990s, suggest Henry and Springborg, Egypt was in the grip of 'a nexus of cronies, officers, bureaucrats and public sector managers'.[50] The term 'crony' was to recur repeatedly as a means of characterising businessmen associated with the President and his inner group of allies, especially the Mubarak family. Entrepreneurs such as the iron and steel tycoon Ahmed Ezz were given leading positions in the ruling NDP, sitting within a network of privilege and power which included senior officers and civilian officials. When Mubarak fell in 2011 media worldwide took up the theme: Ezz and others were 'crony capitalists' who had exploited their political influence to damage the wider society. The *New York Times*, for example, located them at 'the intersection of money, politics and power' and 'self-dealing, crony capitalism and corruption'.[51] If they were 'cronies', however, the entire Egyptian ruling class was implicated: for decades the army elite had used its position to forge close relations with the private sector, producing a hybrid capitalism in which those who controlled the state facilitated and benefited from ever-expanding business activity which was integrated more and more fully with the international system.

REVOLUTION

The army and the people have never been 'one hand'. Many Egyptians retain memories of an era in which the country's military rulers asserted commitments to independence and Arab unity, and in which reform brought change in the countryside and new systems of education and healthcare. In the 1950s Nasser captured popular aspirations for change, exploiting his opportunity to place the armed forces in command of a centralised and increasingly authoritarian regime. The distance between the people and their military rulers widened quickly and within a generation Nasser's legitimacy had diminished; for activists in the universities and industrial workplaces, it was exhausted. Sadat never enjoyed his predecessor's popularity: there was a mood of grim satisfaction when he was assassinated in 1981. Mubarak appeared as a faceless officer-technocrat who inherited power without authority: he was of a new generation shaped within the military elite, pursuing government as if by right. Each of the Presidents of the post-independence era used the army systematically against the people, sometimes on a massive scale and with lethal force. Nasser initiated the era of independence by ordering the execution of strike leaders at the Kafr al-Dawwar textile mill: Mustafa Khamis and Muhammed al-Baqari were hanged six weeks after the 'revolution' of July 1952. In 1977 Sadat assaulted the *intifada* of bread; throughout his presidency Mubarak used the army to contain struggles from below, including those originating within the apparatus of state.

In 2011, however, the army did not at first intervene against the demonstrators of Tahrir. Some accounts of the events see Egypt's generals as content with an opportunity to remove Mubarak, his family and the 'cronies' of the NDP. Marshall and Stacher comment that 'SCAF was no disinterested arbiter of the political transition. The furore over the obscene wealth of Mubarak's private-sector cronies presented the military with a golden opportunity to eliminate rivals.'[52] On this view, key figures of the military had grown anxious about the activities of Mubarak's inner circle, which was seizing opportunities formerly distributed more evenly among the country's rulers. They therefore arranged for Mubarak to be removed and his sons and associates arrested and put on trial, providing a public spectacle they hoped would deflect public interest away from the military leadership. The military placed itself 'above' events in the streets, adopting a posture of concerned attention but refraining from intervention.

This view, like that of the 'deep state', attributes too much to the generals. More plausible is the suggestion that, shaken by the fall of Ben Ali in Tunisia and by the scale of protest in Egypt, they hesitated to risk a conscript army in the streets. Informed perhaps by the Auxiliary Forces Mutiny of 1986, when a key component of the security services disintegrated, they decided to sacrifice Mubarak in the interests of maintaining their own authority. As the revolution unfolded they faced a series of crises: assaults by the people on the NDP and Central Security; campaigns against corrupt officials, managers and police officers; strikes across industry; repeated mass demonstrations at parliament, ministries and security centres. Their responses were haphazard and uncertain: increasingly they intervened directly, sending military police to assault activists and killing hundreds of demonstrators. Thousands were arrested and sent for trial in military courts, prompting the assessment of Amnesty International that 'one repressive rule has simply been replaced with another'.[53] At the time of writing, the army has not succeeded in containing the revolutionary movement or asserting its own legitimacy as a national leadership: on the contrary, more Egyptians have taken up demands that the rule of the army must come to an end.

More carefully calculated is the generals' electoral strategy: an agreement with the Muslim Brotherhood to ease the latter's access to parliament by means of a favourable electoral process. In January 2012, the Brotherhood entered the Majlis al-Shaab (Lower House) with a comfortable majority, committed to a business-friendly economic policy and an agreement to deal respectfully with the armed forces. After decades of mutual hostility the Brothers and the army seemed set for cohabitation in government. With the revolutionary process continuing, however, this alliance was also under immense pressure from below. Committed to the same neo-liberal policies which had brought millions onto the streets, and to further measures of austerity, it faced the prospect of renewed mass opposition. Would the generals of SCAF continue to refrain from a full assault on the movement from below, or would their historic commitment to order, control and self-enrichment dictate a different agenda?

The officers hesitated. As presidential elections approached they mocked the idea of full civilian government, insisting that military men would retain key powers, including control of military budgets and foreign policy. In June 2012 they launched a 'soft coup', dismissing parliament and issuing a constitutional decree restricting the authority of the President. For many Egyptians, including supporters of the Muslim Brotherhood, this was the prelude to a full military offensive. Rallying behind the Muslim Brotherhood candidate for president, Mohamed Mursi, huge demonstrations assembled in Tahrir Square, their main slogan asserting unity against SCAF: 'Liberal, secular, Islamist, revolutionary – all one hand against military rule.' Army commanders were again confronted by the challenge of the streets, declining to risk a conscript army against popular mobilisations which at any time might stimulate mass strikes and a further threat to their own interests.

At the time of writing [July 2012] the generals have retreated from their immediate threat to the revolutionary movement. They have reluctantly conceded the presidency to Mursi and appear to be preparing for a long battle with the Muslim Brotherhood over presidential powers and further parliamentary elections. Above all, SCAF is determined to protect its economic interests. The military's investments, they say, will be secured at all costs: according to a leading figure in the army command, General Mahmoud Nasr, 'this money is not the state's . . . but the result of our sweat from 30 years of labour.'[54] Nasr insists that the armed forces will fight, 'in order not to allow any party whatever it might be to come near our projects'.[55] It is only a matter of time before the revolutionary movement confronts a military command at the heart of the dictatorship and of the structures of economic privilege.

NOTES

1. Egypt Independent, 'Tantawi: We will confront attempts to divide people and army', *Egypt Independent/Al Masry al Youm*, 19 October 2011.
2. Amnesty International, *Broken Promises: Egypt's Military Rulers Erode Human Rights*, London: Amnesty International, 2011, pp. 5, 24.
3. Issandr El Amrani, 'Sightings of the Egyptian deep state', *Merip*, 261, Winter 2011.
4. SCAF Statement of 10 February 2011, *New York Times*, 2011.
5. SCAF Statement of 14 February 2011, *New York Times*, 2011.
6. Raymond William Baker, *Egypt's Uncertain Revolution Under Nasser and Sadat*, Cambridge, MA: Harvard University Press, 1978, p. 26.
7. For a fuller account of the Free Officers Movement, see this volume chapter 12.
8. Gamal Abdel-Nasser, 'The National Charter', in A. M. Said, *Arab Socialism*, London: Blandford Press, 1972, p. 105.
9. Ibid.

10. Those with five *feddan*s or less made some gains. In 1952 they had represented 94 per cent of owners, controlling 35 per cent of the cultivated area. After the first reforms they owned 52 per cent of cultivated land. Middle peasants, those with 11–50 *feddan*s, gained the most: after the reforms they accounted for 3 per cent of all landowners, owning 24 per cent of the cultivated area. See Ray Bush, 'The land and the people', in Rabab El-Mahdi and Philip Marfleet, eds., *Egypt: The Moment of Change*, London: Zed Books, 2009, p. 53.
11. Baker, *Egypt's Uncertain Revolution*, p. 202.
12. For a detailed account of Nasser's economic policies, see Malak Zaalouk, *Power, Class and Foreign Capital in Egypt: The Rise of the New Bourgeoisie*, London: Zed Books, 1989.
13. Nasser, 'The National Charter', p. 115.
14. Ibid., p. 110.
15. Ibid.
16. Ibid., p. 120.
17. Ibid, p. 103.
18. Between 1962 and 1967, 27 of 65 men holding ministerial positions were former officers; 22 of 26 governors were active or retired military men. Baker, *Egypt's Uncertain Revolution*, pp. 48–9, 55.
19. Ibid., p. 299.
20. Qutb is usually viewed as the originator of ideas about *jihad* as a confrontation between committed Muslim activists and impious Muslims in authority in the modern state. His book *Signposts on the Road*, written in prison, was a foundational text for Islamists who formed activist cells in Egypt during the 1970s. Khalid Islambouli of the Jihad group assassinated President Anwar Sadat in 1981. See Gilles Keppel, *Muslim Extremism in Egypt: The Prophet and Pharaoh*, Berkeley, CA: University of California Press, 1985.
21. Quoted in Derek Hopwood, *Egypt, Politics and Society 1945–1990*, London: Routledge, 1993, p. 87.
22. Quoted in Baker, *Egypt's Uncertain Revolution*, p. 96.
23. Robert Stephens, *Nasser*, Harmondsworth: Penguin, 1971, p. 63.
24. For more on this, see Joel Beinin and Zachary Lockman, *Workers on the Nile*, Princeton, NJ: Princeton University Press, 1987.
25. Anouar Abdel-Malek, *Egypt, Military, Society: The Army Regime, the Left, and Social Change under Nasser*, New York: Vintage Books, 1968, p. 367.
26. Ibid., pp. 368–9.
27. Raymond Hinnebusch, *Egyptian Politics under Sadat*, Cambridge: Cambridge University Press, 1985, p. 2.
28. Ibid.
29. Stephens, *Nasser*, p. 86.
30. Baker, *Egypt's Uncertain Revolution*, p. 37.
31. Stephens, *Nasser*, p. 427.
32. Spending increased from an estimated 3.9 per cent of GNP to 12.3 per cent of GNP. See Baker, *Egypt's Uncertain Revolution*, p. 56.
33. Ibid., pp. 59–60.
34. Zaalouk, *Power, Class and Foreign Capital in Egypt*, p. 35. Many Europeans had settled in Egypt in the mid-nineteenth century, largely in response to opportunities provided by the cotton boom and opening of the Suez Canal. Most left in the 1950s and 1960s, as the Nasser regime nationalised their businesses. Egypt's Jewish communities, including those with an historical presence in the country

over millennia, also left. See Joel Beinin, *The Dispersion of Egyptian Jewry: Culture, Politics, and the Formation of a Modern Diaspora*, Berkeley, CA: University of California Press, 1998; Timothy Mitchell, *Rule of Experts: Egypt, Techno-Politics, Modernity*, Berkeley, CA: University of California Press, 2002.

35. Zaalouk, *Power, Class and Foreign Capital in Egypt*, pp. 35–6.

36. Abdel-Malek, *Egypt, Military, Society*, p. xiii.

37. SCAF Statement of 14 February 2011, *New York Times*.

38. Fouad Zakariya, quoted in Ahmed Abdalla, *The Student Movement and National Politics in Egypt*, London: Al Saqi, 1985, p. 152.

39. Ibid., p. 156.

40. Hinnebusch, *Egyptian Politics under Sadat*, p. 44.

41. Jeremy Sharp, *Egypt–US Relations*, Brief for Congress, Washington, DC: Congressional Research Service, 2004, pp. 27–9.

42. While clamping down on all forms of public protest and arresting all manner of suspected oppositionists, he argued that 'Those calling themselves Nasirists' were attempting 'to bring back detention camps and a socialism of poverty for everyone'. Quoted in Hinnebusch, *Egyptian Politics under Sadat*, p. 72.

43. Joel Beinin, 'Workers' struggles under "socialism" and neoliberalism', in Rabab El-Madi and Philip Marfleet, eds., *Egypt: The Moment of Change*, London: Zed Books, 2009, p. 72.

44. Bessma Momani, *IMF–Egyptian Debt Negotiations*, Cairo Papers in Social Science, 26(3), Cairo: The American University in Cairo Press, 2005, p. 66.

45. Stephen Gotowicki, *The Role of the Egyptian Military in Domestic Society*, Washington, DC: Institute of National Strategic Studies, National Defense University, 1994.

46. Robert Springborg, *Mubarak's Egypt: Fragmentation of the Political Order*, Boulder, CO: Westview Press, 1988, p. 107.

47. Shana Marshall and Joshua Stacher, 'Egypt's generals and transnational capital', Middle East Research and Information Project, MERIP 262, 2012.

48. Nadine Marroushi, 'US expert: leadership of "Military Inc." is running Egypt', *Egypt Independent*, 26 October 2011.

49. Marshall and Stacher, 'Egypt's generals and transnational capital'.

50. Clement Henry and Robert Springborg, *Globalization and the Politics of Development in the Middle East*, Cambridge: Cambridge University Press, 2001), p. 155.

51. Kareem Fahim, Michael Slackman and David Rohde, 'Egypt's ire turns to confidant of Mubarak's son', *New York Times*, 6 February 2011.

52. Marshall and Stacher, 'Egypt's generals and transnational capital'.

53. Amnesty International, *Broken Promises*, pp. 5, 24.

54. General Mahmoud Nasr, quoted in International Crisis Group, *Lost in Transition: The World According to Egypt's SCAF*, Brussels: International Crisis Group, 2011, p. 23.

55. Ibid.

BIBLIOGRAPHY/FURTHER READING

Ahmed Abdalla, *The Student Movement and National Politics in Egypt*, London: Al Saqi, 1985.

Amnesty International, *Broken Promises: Egypt's Military Rulers Erode Human Rights*, London: Amnesty International, 2011.

Anouar Abdel-Malek, *Egypt, Military, Society: The Army Regime, the Left, and Social Change under Nasser*, New York: Vintage Books, 1968.

Gamal Abdel-Nasser, 'The National Charter', in A. M. Said, *Arab Socialism*, London: Blandford Press, 1972.

Raymond William Baker, *Egypt's Uncertain Revolution under Nasser and Sadat*, Cambridge, MA: Harvard University Press, 1978.

Joel Beinin, *The Dispersion of Egyptian Jewry: Culture, Politics, and the Formation of a Modern Diaspora*, Berkeley, CA: University of California Press, 1998.

Joel Beinin, 'Workers' struggles under "socialism" and neoliberalism', in Rabab El-Mahdi and Philip Marfleet, eds., *Egypt: The Moment of Change*, London: Zed Books, 2009.

Joel Beinin and Zachary Lockman, *Workers on the Nile*, Princeton, NJ: Princeton University Press, 1987.

Ray Bush, 'The Land and the People', in Rabab El-Mahdi and Philip Marfleet, eds., *Egypt: The Moment of Change*, London: Zed Books, 2009.

Issandr El Amrani, 'Sightings of the Egyptian deep state', *Merip*, 261, Winter 2011.

Egypt Independent, 'Tantawi: We will confront attempts to divide people and army', *Egypt Independent/Al Masry al Youm*, 19 October 2011.

Kareem Fahim, Michael Slackman and David Rohde, 'Egypt's ire turns to confidant of Mubarak's son', *New York Times*, 6 February 2011.

Stephen Gotowicki, *The Role of the Egyptian Military in Domestic Society*, Washington, DC: Institute of National Strategic Studies, National Defense University, 1994, fmso.leavenworth.army.mil/documents/egypt/egypt.htm.

Clement Henry and Robert Springborg, *Globalization and the Politics of Development in the Middle East*, Cambridge: Cambridge University Press, 2001.

Raymond Hinnebusch, *Egyptian Politics under Sadat*, Cambridge: Cambridge University Press, 1985.

Derek Hopwood, *Egypt, Politics and Society 1945–1990*, London: Routledge, 1993.

International Crisis Group, *Lost in Transition: The World According to Egypt's SCAF*, Brussels: International Crisis Group, 2011.

Gilles Keppel, *Muslim Extremism in Egypt: The Prophet and Pharaoh*, Berkeley, CA: University of California Press, 1985.

Nadine Marroushi, 'US expert: leadership of "Military Inc." is running Egypt', *Egypt Independent*, 26 October 2011.

Shana Marshall and Joshua Stacher, 'Egypt's generals and transnational capital', Middle East Research and Information Project, MERIP 262, 2012.

Timothy Mitchell, *Rule of Experts: Egypt, Techno-Politics, Modernity*, Berkeley, CA: University of California Press, 2002.

Bessma Momani, *IMF–Egyptian Debt Negotiations*, Cairo Papers in Social Science, 26(3), Cairo: The American University in Cairo Press, 2005.

Jeremy Sharp, *Egypt–US Relations*, Brief for Congress, Washington, DC: Congressional Research Service, 2004.

Robert Springborg, *Mubarak's Egypt: Fragmentation of the Political Order*, Boulder, CO: Westview Press, 1988.

Robert Stephens, *Nasser*, Harmondsworth: Penguin, 1971.

Malak Zaalouk, *Power, Class and Foreign Capital in Egypt: The Rise of the New Bourgeoisie*, London: Zed Books, 1989.

Guerrilla Wars and the
Limits of Imperial Power

8
People Change: American Soldiers and Marines in Vietnam 1965–73

Jonathan Neale

The American troops flew into Vietnam in chartered aircraft with civilian pilots and crew. Helen Tennant Hegelheimer worked on these flights for two years:

> 'When I was a young gal I watched The Mickey Mouse Club and they did a program on what it was like to be a stewardess. I was absolutely glued to the TV set. After that, I cannot remember a time I did not want to be a stewardess.
>
> 'On the California to Japan leg of the flight, the troops did a lot of letter writing. Guys would ask me, "Is this a good letter? If you received this, would you wait for me?" At first I read the letters, but they really pulled at your heart, so after a while I would just pretend to read them and say they were perfect.
>
> 'It was the senior stew[ardess]'s position to be on the top of the ramp when the men got off in Vietnam. But when we were about two hours out she would usually ask for a volunteer to take the forward door. All you had to do is stand at the door and say good-bye, but nobody wanted that job. It's nothing disparaging to the other gals, but many just couldn't do it. I'd always take the forward door and I was good at it.
>
> 'I never said "good-bye" or "good luck." I would shake their hand, look them in the eye, and say, "See you later." They really wanted somebody to look at them.
>
> 'I saw eyes full of fear, some with real terror. And maybe this sounds crazy, but I saw death in some of those eyes. In that moment, at the top of the ramp, I was their wife, their sister, their girlfriend, and for those troops who had no one else – and there were many – I was their mother. That was the most important thing I've ever done. I can't imagine anything more important than to nudge a troop into war. If he wasn't okay I was nudging

173

him to his death. I don't think there was one of us didn't want
to keep them on the plane. That's why some of the girls were in
the back in the bathrooms crying.

'The first thing we'd ask when we arrived in Vietnam is, "Are
we taking troops out?' If you took a hundred and sixty-five men
in and a hundred and sixty-five out, you could really fool yourself
into believing they were all coming home.

'You did not want to be on that airplane if we flew back empty.
There were five stewardesses and we didn't even sit with each
other. And when we got back to Japan we drank even heavier.'[1]

THE VIET CONG

People change. This chapter is about how the American soldiers
and marines changed in Vietnam. First I explain how and why they
were forced to fight a particularly cruel war. Then I tell the story of
how they eventually rebelled and ended that war.[2]

To understand both the cruelty and the rebellion, we have to
start with the nature of the Vietnamese resistance. Resistance began
in 1945 as a communist-led uprising against French colonialism.
After eight years of war the Vietnamese had won. But international
negotiations between the United States, France, the Soviet Union
and China ended with a compromise. Vietnam was divided: North
Vietnam would be communist; South Vietnam would be a military
dictatorship allied with the United States.

Most communists went north, but some stayed in the south. The
new Southern government arrested about 90 per cent of them, many
of whom were killed in prison. The reason was land. During the
war against the French, the communists had controlled many of
the southern villages. Where they had control, they drove out the
landlords. Tenants had previously paid about two-thirds of the crop
in rent. Now, with the landlords gone, tenant farmers tripled their
income. For people on the edge of hunger this was an enormous life
change. The new Southern government was based on the support
of the old landlords and restored them to power in the villages. To
do that, they had to break the communists.

The communist cadres were under orders from the new party
government in the North not to resist, but they fought anyway. A
peasant revolt, led by local communists, began to spread across
the South. The party in the North changed course and backed it.

The peasants started driving out the landlords and sharing the
land again in the late 1950s. By 1964 the communist-led 'Viet Cong'

guerrillas controlled much of the countryside. It was clear that the Southern government would fall soon.

From 1960 on, the United States had had small forces in South Vietnam. Then, in 1965, Washington sent 500,000 troops to prevent the fall of the Southern government.

The nature of the Vietnamese resistance, however, set strong limits on US strategy. This was a land war, not simply a war of national resistance. By 1965 the Viet Cong had the support of a large majority of villagers. Because of the land, many of these villagers were prepared to fight for many years, very bravely.

Some of the resistance were regular army troops from North Vietnam, but the majority of the fighters were Southern peasant guerrillas in the Viet Cong. Altogether, they had about 250,000 full-time fighters. Only about a sixth of the 500,000 Americans were combat troops. The general expectation in counter-insurgency is that the occupier must heavily outnumber the guerrillas to win. In this case, the North Vietnamese soldiers and Viet Cong outnumbered US combat soldiers by about three to one. They controlled most of the villages and enjoyed strong popular support. Crucially, women, the elderly and children were prepared to stay in the villages and died in large numbers.

Support was not entirely one-sided. The Southern government had a real base among the landlords and business people. Nor did the Viet Cong control the cities, and only once tried to fight there. The Southern government was able to conscript soldiers; 250,000 died in the South Vietnamese army, four times as many as the Americans fighting alongside them. Even late in the war, American soldiers could walk the streets of Saigon city unarmed.

But the Southern government and their US allies did not control the villages. The Pentagon strategy followed from this. If they could not win over the peasants, they would have to terrify and break them. And as they could not win fighting man to man, they would use their two great advantages – fire power and air power.

Washington's strategy was to kill very large numbers of Vietnamese in order to break their will to fight. The primary weapon was bombing from the air and the main target was rural North Vietnam.[3] American pilots were reluctant to bomb small peasant houses, so they went for the larger targets. In the countryside, these were mainly government offices, schools, temples and hospitals. There was also heavy bombing of Viet Cong-controlled areas in the South, designated 'free fire zones'. In all, American bombers killed about two million people over ten years.

THE GROUND WAR

The ground war killed fewer, but was crucial to the experience of the US troops, because that is where they were. The strategy was the same as the air war – to use overwhelming fire and air power to kill large numbers. This made the ground war very cruel. That cruelty, however, did not come from the personalities of the troops. It came from the top. In the opinion of the generals and politicians in charge, it was the only way they could win the war.

It was a bureaucratic army. The crucial paperwork was called the 'body count'. The officer in each unit had to submit a report every evening recording how many his men had killed. These reports then went up to battalion level, were phoned through to the embassy in Saigon and added up there. The total body count was on the desk of the Secretary of Defense in Washington the next morning.

Philip Caputo was a marine lieutenant. He arrived in Vietnam in 1965:

'General Westmoreland's strategy of attrition also had an effect on our behaviour. Our mission was not to win terrain or seize positions, but simply to kill: to kill Communists and to kill as many of them as possible. Stack 'em like cordwood. Victory was a high body-count, defeat a low kill-ration, war a matter of arithmetic. The pressure on unit commanders to produce enemy corpses was intense, and they in turn communicated it to their troops.'[4]

Enlisted men served twelve-month tours of duty in Vietnam. Officers served six months, so they could all get a crack at war experience for their careers – 'get their tickets punched'. They knew an officer's career would go nowhere without a good body count.

The pressure downwards was relentless. Many soldiers and officers faked their numbers, counting every dead civilian as a Viet Cong guerrilla, counting dead buffaloes, dead dogs, body parts, drops of blood, or simply made up the numbers.

Conscientious officers tried to keep accurate records and insisted on proof. This explains the stories told by soldiers who served in different parts of Vietnam of an officer at the end of the day sitting behind a table counting a pile of ears. It wasn't sadism or souvenirs. Just paperwork.

The body count also pushed officers to tolerate cruelty and random killing. Every unit, like every workplace anywhere, had someone capable of evil if they were allowed. And in Vietnam US soldiers were not punished. This made most other soldiers nervous. Michael Clodfelter, an infantryman in the 101st Airborne, arrived in 1965

> 'expecting to encounter uniformed communist hordes, but found this strange small people wearing peasant garb and those inscrutable smiles. [We] found it hard to believe that these weak, undernourished-looking peasants could really present a threat and a danger to all of our battalions of big, husky, heavily armed GIs. It seemed a laughable country and a laughable war . . . until we started running into explosive evidence of the enemy's existence, until we started becoming a part of the red results of their cunning and courage. And then, slowly . . . our vision blurred, clouded over, and re-focussed. Where before we had found it difficult to see the enemy anywhere, now we saw him everywhere. It was simple now: the Vietnamese were the Viet Cong, the Viet Cong were the Vietnamese. The killing became so much easier now.'

Atticus Tate, one of the men in Clodfelter's platoon,

> 'wasn't like the rest of us, we said, not even like those of us who, under the burdens and blows we had to take, sometimes gave in to the temptation to cruelty. He enjoyed the killing. We hated him because what he had done we could do. Maybe one more month in Nam, one more buddy blown apart by a booby trap, maybe the Tate would come out in all of us.'[5]

Tate began bringing in the scalps of the Vietnamese he killed to confirm the body count to the officers. Many of Clodfelter's fellow soldiers were reluctant to do this, but his unit had a low body count and their officers were pressing them to kill more. When an elderly villager failed to warn them of the presence of two Viet Cong ahead, the Americans went back and killed him. Someone then pointed out they needed proof for the officers. They didn't scalp him, but they did cut off his ears and took them back to the officers.

However, shooting people was not the main source of the body count. The main strategy, pushed from the top, was for soldiers and marines to go out on patrol. The guerrillas would then attack them and the Americans would call in air support or artillery. In effect, the soldiers and marines were bait.

Michael Call of the 25th Infantry Division remembered the constant fear of land mines:

'We begin to walk with our eyes fixed on the ground, looking for some tell-tale sign we should avoid. I ask myself: "Is that little thing ahead the three prongs of a Bouncing Betty [mine] or just three blades of grass?" As my right foot moves in front of my left foot, I carry on a debate in my mind on whether I should place it down on that rock just ahead of behind it. Or in front of it. Or on that side of it. But now I face another dilemma. If I choose to step to the side of the rock, which side do I choose. These gooks are very clever. They must figure out I still want to place my foot on hard ground. So, maybe they put the mine under a rock. Maybe I should move over to the left a little or to the right. Then again, why not place my foot in the step of the guy ahead of me. But he is already too far ahead. And if you walk too close to him, he will get pissed off because if I trip a mine he'll get blown away too. What do I do with my right foot? I say, "I can't stand on my left foot forever." I finally put my right foot down and nothing happens. My next decision is what to do with my left foot, which, in the act of walking, comes up when the right foot goes down.'[6]

About a quarter of American combat deaths came from stepping on mines. But several things made mines loom larger in the imagination than that. Constant fear accompanied every step. Disabling, but not fatal, wounds from mines were more common and often resulted in amputations or paralysis. Moreover, whenever an American stepped on a mine, his fellow soldiers knew that every Vietnamese they had passed on patrol knew where the mine was. Every person in the village knew, because the Viet Cong told them or left markers – otherwise they would have stepped on the mines too. In the instant after the explosion, the soldiers felt rage towards the villagers. Sometimes they reacted immediately by beating or killing someone. More often, they suppressed the rage and carried it with them. But they had learned – every child and every grandmother is an enemy.

Nearly a fifth of American deaths were from 'friendly fire' – the air support and artillery they called in. But the experience of being bait was not just frightening – it was not what being a soldier was supposed to be about, and it made the troops enraged with the generals. What made it worse was that the GIs knew they were on the wrong side. The way they usually put it when they came home was that the enemy were the only people in the country who knew what they were fighting for. Thomas Giltner was a platoon leader. He remembered:

'We faced mostly local VC, peasants armed with World War II rifles and no heavy weapons. They were taking on the best army in the world. They received their training from the local cadres. We respected them from day one. They did an awful lot with awful little.

'They were tremendously inventive. We used to capture home-made rifles created out of metal pipes and bits of fence post. We never put out antipersonnel mines: we knew they would be dug up and used against us. Claymores were strictly accounted for, but they were still stolen. The Vietnamese were just so ingenious. We all knew they are poor, not stupid.'[7]

Jeri Luici was an infantryman:

'We humped in just before dawn, and fighting was still going on. There were over a hundred bodies. Later that day we found more surface graves.

'To give you an idea of how steadfast the people we were fighting were, I found a dead VC medic who had tied himself to a bamboo clump, with a morphine syringe stuck in his arm, as he was bleeding to death. He had an RPG at the ready with the safety off. Another guy was clutching one of our claymores: he was going to try to detonate himself on our perimeter. Amazing.'[8]

The soldiers and marines could also see the poverty of the people they were fighting. A reporter tells the story of one American soldier. When he came home his family met him at the airport:

'They drove home in silence and sat together in the kitchen, and his mother, in passing, apologized for there being "nothing in the house to eat." That did it; he broke. Raging, he went from cupboard to cupboard, shelf to shelf, flinging doors open, pulling down cans and boxes and bags, piling them ever higher and higher on the table until they spilled over onto the floor and everything edible in the house was spread out in front of them.'

'I couldn't believe it,' the soldier told the reporter.

'I'd been over there . . . killing those poor bastards who lived in their tunnels like rats and had nothing to eat but mud a few goddam mouldy grains of rice, and who watched their kids starve to death or go up in smoke, and she said nothing to eat, and I ended up in the kitchen shouting: Nothing to eat, nothing to eat.'[9]

Imagine what his mother felt.

Many of the soldiers were also upset because the poverty of the Vietnamese reminded them of their own childhoods. The GIs and marines in combat were working-class – 80 per cent of them had fathers who were manual workers; 20 per cent had white-collar fathers, usually doing low-level, routine jobs. Half of Americans in their generation had started college, but only a fifth of soldiers in Vietnam. Seven per cent of them had graduated and almost all of those were officers.

The GIs were very aware that the American class system had put them in Vietnam. Here is a fire-fighter talking to a psychologist in 1970. His son 'Ralph' had died in Vietnam:

'I'm bitter. You bet your goddamn dollar I'm bitter. It's people like me who gave up their sons for the country. The business people, they run the country and they make money from it. The college types, the professors, they go to Washington and tell the government what to do.

'But their sons, they don't end up in the swamps over there, in Vietnam. No sir. They're deferred, because they're in school [college]. Or they get sent to safe places. Or they get out with those letters they get from their doctors. Ralph told me. He told me what went on at his physical. He said most of the kids were from average homes, and the few rich kids there were, they all had big-deal letters, they weren't "eligible" for the army for health reasons. They looked eligible to Ralph. Let's face it: if you have a lot of money, or if you have the right connections, you don't end up on the firing line in the jungle over there, not unless you want to. Ralph had no choice. He didn't want to die. He wanted to live. They just took him. It's the Ralphs of America who pay every time.'[10]

In Vietnam the Ralphs were frightened, in danger and pushed into cruelty. Being sent there was part of their punishment for being working-class. And they knew it. Many of them had grown up the hard way. They could see themselves in the poverty of the Vietnamese children.

The troops had expected to be greeted by children and to give them candy. Their fathers and uncles told them about the kids in Europe in the Second World War. But these children were resentful beggars. And the troops learned that the children knew where the mines were, and waited for the soldiers to die.

Seeing themselves in those children is the only way to explain a 'game' reported from many parts of Vietnam. An army combat engineer testified in 1972:

'We threw full C-ration cans at the kids on the side of the road. They'd be yelling out, "Chop, chop; chop, chop," and they wanted food. Well, just for a joke these guys would take a full can . . . and throw it as hard as they could at a kid's head. I saw several kids, heads split wide open, knocked off the road, knocked into the tires of the vehicle behind.'

A marine:

'When they originally get in the country [Americans] feel very friendly toward the Vietnamese and they like to toss candy at the kids. But as they become hardened to it and kind of embittered against the war, as you drive through the village you take the cans of C-rats and the cases and you peg 'em at the kids; you try to belt them over the head. And one of the fun games that always went was you dropped the C-rats cans or the candy off the back of your truck so that the kid will have time to dash out, grab the candy and get run over by the next truck.'[11]

In 1975 a peasant woman in central Vietnam told an American researcher:

'I was walking along the road with my son, who was wearing a hat. There was a string to hold the hat to his chin. One of the American soldiers grabbed the hat, and pulled my son up and under the wheels of the truck. The truck stopped, but it was too late.'[12]

But the same experience that was driving working-class Americans to play these 'games' were also turning the troops against the war. The two American witnesses, the army combat engineer and the marine, were both testifying before a war crimes investigation in 1971 set up and run by the Vietnam Veterans Against the War.

It is not that there were cruel and brutal American 'redneck' soldiers and good anti-war soldiers who rebelled against the war. The same people did both. And they were cruel for the same reason they rebelled – that was the nature of the war they were forced into.

Ron Kovic, for instance, was the son of a supermarket worker. He joined the marines out of high school, was promoted to sergeant and did two tours of duty in Vietnam, where he was paralysed from the waist down. Kovic went to a facility in Mexico that helped disabled American veterans have a holiday where they could drink and have sex with mostly kindly prostitutes. He went drinking with another veteran, 'Charlie'. In the last brothel they went to,

> 'Charlie got in a wild fight with one of the whores. He punched her in the face because she laughed at him when he pulled down his pants and told her he couldn't feel his penis anymore. He was crazy drunk and kept yelling and screaming, swinging his arms and his fists at the crowd.
>
> [Charlie screamed] "That goddamn fucking slut! I'm going to kill that whore for ever laughing at me. That bitch thinks it's funny I can't move my dick. Fuck you. Fuck all of you goddamn motherfuckers! They made me kill babies! They made me kill babies."'[13]

Kovic, watching, could not move. Charlie was saying what he had been thinking for a while. Soon after, Kovic joined the Vietnam Veterans Against the War.

THE ANTI-WAR MOVEMENT

It is hard for soldiers in any war to refuse to fight, even if they think a war is wrong. They face being thought cowards if they refuse individually. If they refuse together, they face long incarceration in brutal military prisons. And they face being shot by officers on the field of battle. Refusal to join the army, or desertion, is one thing. Refusal of battle is another – particularly if an enemy is firing on you and your closest friends, the people you rely on to save your life.

This is part of the reason refusal of battle is unusual. But there is another reason. A soldier refusing to fight has to be willing to kill the officer or sergeant issuing the order, and to do so immediately before he is killed himself. This is a very difficult thing to do. Loyalty to the unit and to everyone in it is a central moral value for soldiers and essential to survival. Moreover, the soldier has to know that his fellow soldiers will back him, that they will not turn him in, and that if comes to a fight, they will shoot alongside him. This means that soldiers feel their way towards revolt. They need a deep moral knowledge that this war is wrong. And they need to know the people around them feel the same.

For all these reasons, revolt on the battlefield is rare. But the US soldiers and marines did it on a large scale. One reason was the courage and endurance of the Vietnamese peasants. Without that, the body count would have won the war.

The second reason was the anti-war movement in the United States. That movement, however, had a complex relationship with the troops. On the one hand, the movement was enormous and lasted for years. There were teach-ins at hundreds of universities and colleges, some of them attracting thousands of students. There were thousands of demonstrations over seven years. One of them, in Washington late in 1969, was the largest protest ever in the United States up to that time, three or four times the size of Martin Luther King's March on Washington. In the spring of 1970 more than four million college students went on strike against an invasion of Cambodia that would extend the theatre of war.

Nowadays that movement is often portrayed as the work of students worried they would be drafted and die. But a decade before a similar numbers of Americans had died in the Korean War. That was similar to Vietnam in other ways too – the enemy were communists, the United States had the draft, American bombers killed about two million people and the majority of the dead were civilians. Moreover, within three years most Americans thought the troops should be brought home, Dwight Eisenhower was elected President on a promise to do just that and he then ended the war in a negotiated 'tie'.

But there were no protests, no open opposition to the Korean war. Yet this was at the height of the Cold War. Some people were patriotic and some were scared. The difference with Vietnam was that the Civil Rights movement had broken anti-communism. And the people who opposed the war vociferously did so because they thought it was wrong.

The anti-war movement was magnificent in many ways, but there was an enormous weakness – class. We heard earlier from a fire-fighter whose son was killed in Vietnam. Here is his wife talking in 1970 about the anti-war protest movement: 'I think my husband and I can't help but thinking that our son gave his life for nothing, nothing at all.' She told her husband that she thought the protesters wanted

> 'the war to end, so no more Ralphs will die, but he says no, they never stop and think about Ralph and his kind of people, and I'm inclined to agree. They say they do, but I listen to them, I watch them; since Ralph died I listen and watch as carefully as I can. Their hearts are with other people, not their own American people, the ordinary kind of person in this country. I know when someone is worrying about me and my children, and when he says he is, but he's really elsewhere with his sympathy. Those people, a lot of them are rich women from the suburbs, the rich suburbs. Those kids, they are in college.
>
> 'They don't come out here and try to talk to us. I'm against this war too – the way a mother is, whose sons are in the army, who has lost a son fighting in it. The world hears those demonstrators making a noise. The world doesn't hear me, and it doesn't hear a single person I know.'[14]

She was broadly right. Not everyone, but a majority of the protestors believed they were better than 'rednecks'. They also believed that educated people were more likely to be against the war and that the peace movement was in a minority. In fact, by 1967 most Americans wanted an end to the war. That was two years after 500,000 troops had been sent. And less educated people were more likely to be against the war. This was because the uneducated knew more than the educated. They understood more about power in the United States – it is easier to understand these things from the bottom looking up. But the less educated were also talking directly to large numbers of people who had been in Vietnam. Those people were telling their friends and families it didn't feel like a good war.

THE SOLDIERS' REVOLT

So there was a deep fissure between the peace movement and the troops. This was not because of a lack of class politics but because of the class politics of the educated. Even so, the soldiers' revolt would not have happened if the peace movement had not organised for so long, so deeply and so publicly. Everyone knew the arguments against the war and were aware that many people believed them.

The ideas of the anti-war movement also penetrated the armed forces in two main ways. First there were the African-American troops. By and large, they understood it was a racist war and had serious issues already with American patriotism. As teenagers many of them had been in the northern urban ghetto riots, which were a central part of the African-American revolt of the 1960s. And Martin Luther King, their most respected leader, had come out against the war publicly in 1967.

Until King's first anti-war speech black soldiers and marines had been in combat in much larger proportions than in the general American population. King pointed this out in his speech and the Pentagon moved immediately to hold down the proportion of black troops in the frontline. Nevertheless, in many different accounts of the revolt in the ranks, groups of African-American soldiers are central. They are always groups. Sometimes, on bases in Germany in particular, black soldiers or marines would fight in bars against white non-commissioned officers over the music on the jukebox, but never in Vietnam. And again and again, the black soldiers were bringing white soldiers with them against the war.

The other bridge from the peace movement to the armed forces was the coffee houses just outside the bases. The coffee houses were often founded by socialists or anarchists with class politics or by pacifists with commitments to all humanity. They provided a quiet place for soldiers to talk to each other and to peace activists. The coffee house people were a minority in the larger movement, but they were key.

Then there were the 'underground' newspapers produced by rank-and-file soldiers, sailors, marines and airmen themselves. These newspapers were illegal, they usually only came out for a few issues and the editors were often heavily punished. Frank Cortright helped produce one and later wrote about them. He counted 245 different ones. Some of the names give a flavour of the movement:

Fatigue Press, Fort Hood, Texas.
FTA (Fuck the Army), Fort Knox, Kentucky
Napalm, Fort Campbell, Tennessee
The Man Can't Win if You Grin, in Okinawa, Japan
Kill for Peace, by marines at Camp Drake, Japan
Duck Power, by sailors in San Diego
All Hands Abandon Ship, by sailors in Newport, Rhode Island
Fat Albert's Death Ship, by sailors in Charleston, Massachusetts
Blows Against the Empire, Kirtland Air Force Base, New Mexico
FTA with Pride, by soldiers in Heidelberg, Germany
Stuffed Puffin, Keflavik Air Force Base, Iceland.[15]

PINKVILLE

The persistent courage of the peasants, the long anti-war movement, the African-American soldiers and the underground newspapers – all these led to revolt on the battlefield. But it was what the US troops finally did in Vietnam that made the most difference.

I will start with a unit serving near the village of My Lai in central Vietnam in 1969. The year before My Lai had been caught up in a series of coordinated massacres. In January 1968, the Viet Cong had mounted an armed insurrection in the main cities of South Vietnam during the New Year 'Tet' celebrations. After days, or in one case weeks, of fighting, the US troops had defeated those uprisings. This was a major defeat for the Viet Cong and the North Vietnamese army. They never recovered their position in many parts of the countryside, but they still had the support of the majority of the villagers. The Americans had 'won'. But if they ever left, the communists would 'win'.

In two provinces in central Vietnam, authority was restored in the three months after Tet by mass killings. We know of 43 villages in the region where 20 or more people were killed at once and 14 villages where more than 100 were killed. These particular killings were coordinated by the South Korean military – South Korean troops were helping their US allies.[16] These were not random cruelties; they were ordered by senior officers and directed at villages where many or most of the younger men were with the guerrillas. The people killed were the elderly, women and children who remained. The intention was not revenge, but terror. And it partly worked. Many guerrillas left the area or stopped fighting.

One of these villages, My Lai, had been under the control of Korean troops, but had been passed on to US troops the month before the massacre there. Most of the 143 dead in My Lai were killed in three large groups, by a small number of soldiers commanded by one officer. All the troops had been summoned to a council of war by their officers the night before and told to go in killing. The unit's colonel was flying over the village in a helicopter throughout the slaughter and refused to intervene when a helicopter crew begged him to.

This massacre, and only this one, was exposed the next year in the American press. One soldier, the most junior lieutenant, was convicted of misdeeds. The Vietnam Veterans Against the War picketed his trial, arguing that he was being made a scapegoat for the senior officers. The following year Tim O'Brien was a solider on patrol near My Lai, which he called 'Pinkville'. At first O'Brien and his unit behaved in the established manner:

'Along the way, we encountered the citizens of Pinkville, the non-participants in the war. Children under ten years, women, old folks who planted their eyes in the dirt and were silent. "Where are the VCP?" Captain Johansen would ask, nicely enough. 'Where are all the men? Where is Poppa-San?" No answers.

'Not until we ducked poppa's bullet or stepped on his land mine. In the next days it took little provocation for us to flick the flint of our Zippo lighters. Thatched roofs took the flame quickly, and on bad days the hamlets of Pinkville burned, taking our revenge in fire. It was good to walk from Pinkville and to see fire behind Alpha Company. It was good, just as pure hate is good.

'We walked to the other villages, and the phantom Forty-Eighth Viet Cong Battalion walked with us. When a booby-trapped artillery round blew two popular soldiers into a hedgerow, men put their fists into the faces of the nearest Vietnamese, two frightened women living in the guilty hamlet, and when the troops were through with them, they hacked off chunks of their thick black hair. The men were crying, doing this. An officer used his pistol, hammering it against a prisoner's skull.'[17]

This fits the pattern of helplessness and cruelty we have been describing. But something quite different was starting to happen in O'Brien's unit at the same time. The first week O'Brien was with his unit they came under mortar fire. O'Brien scrambled out of his barracks with his rifle, his helmet and his boots. But 'no one else came out of the barracks. I waited, and finally one man came out, holding a beer. Then another man, holding a beer.'

'They sat on the sandbags in their underwear, drinking beer and laughing, pointing out at the paddies and watching our mortar rounds land. Later two or three more men straggled out. No helmets, no weapons. They laughed and joked and drank. The first sergeant started shouting.'

He was ordering them to fight. 'But the men just giggled and sat on the sandbags in their underwear. A lieutenant came by. He told the men to get their gear together, but no one moved, and he walked away.' Then, 'the lieutenant hurried back. He argued with a platoon sergeant, but this time the lieutenant was firm. He ordered us to double-time out to the perimeter. Muttering about the company needed a rest and this had turned into one hell of a rest and they'd rather be in the boonies [Vietnamese countryside], the men put on their helmets and took up their rifles and followed the lieutenant. Three of the men refused and went into the barracks and went to sleep.'[18]

Those three men were not disciplined. For discipline was beginning to run the other way. The first sergeant in O'Brien's company was white. He had the power to approve transfers to the rear, which got men out of combat, and he would only transfer white men. One day he was killed on patrol. That night the company dug foxholes, and then O'Brien stayed up talking with a black friend.

'He told me that one of the black guys had taken care of the first sergeant. It was an M-79 round, off a grenade launcher. Although the shot was only meant to scare the top sergeant, the blacks weren't crying, he said. He put his arm around me and said that's how to treat whitey when it comes down to it. In two weeks, a black first sergeant came to Alpha [Company]'.[19]

Fragging had begun. Fragging was a new word for killing officers or sergeants – usually for ordering men out on patrol. Killing someone in your unit was not something soldiers did lightly. Where they could, they usually warned people. In 1969 and 1970 Lamont Steptoe was an officer in the 25th Infantry. He remembered that

'generally there was a pattern. If you were fucking with the men, they would generally warn you. When you came back to our bunk there would be a tear gas canister.
'The next time there would be a booby trap, which when you tripped it would let you know it could have been real. The third time would be the real thing. It's not like you weren't warned.'[20]

Mark Jury was a photographer in the army in Vietnam in 1969 and 1970, taking pictures around the country:

'Fragging is an institution in Vietnam. If the lifers [career non-commissioned officers] make life unbearable, the kids will warn him with a CS [tear gas] grenade. If he persists, they'll frag him with a real grenade. In the field there's no problems. If and when a lifer is assigned to a combat company, he's put in shape quickly; the kids have the option to simply kill him during a fire fight.'[21]

John Lindquist was a marine in 1969: 'One time they tried to frag the lifer's hooch, it didn't work because the grenade didn't go off. The lifers sat up all night with a rifle waiting for somebody to try it again so they could blow them away.' Also, 'they tried to get this guy' from the Criminal Investigation Division. But the grenade exploded on a gunnery sergeant 'who had nothing to do with it and he lost a leg. That rubbed me the wrong way.' And, 'when I was down in Quang Tri they had three fraggings of first sergeants in 3rd Division.'

The battalions were separated by concertina wire so they would night fight each other. Once Lindquist and his friends were 'listening to Deep Purple and through the top of our hootch comes about five rounds of M16. They could have been lower.' 'Somebody could be dead or wounded because somebody's fighting next door with other marines. The ground was no longer really working.'[22] Another marine recalled:

'We started having war calls, which is like at midnight everybody in the outfit starts screaming, "Gooks in the wire" . . . and then you try to kill all the lifers you don't like. So we tried to get the CO a couple of times with a machine gun. One time his rack took nine holes. His cot, nine bullet holes.

'So one night this guy named H booby-trapped his tent. And in the morning when we woke up it wasn't his CO that got it. It was the executive officer Captain J. Captain K was the one we wanted to get. But J, it was good to get J 'cause he sucked too. They threatened to press charges against the whole outfit for mutiny. They were trying to figure out a way they could keep it hush-hush. Nobody wants to know the Marine Corps mutinied.'[23]

In 1969 *Playboy* interviewed Lieutenant Colonel Herbert. He said that in his battalion of the 173rd Airborne

'there had been two attempts on the previous commander's life. There had been quite a few fraggings in that battalion, of both officers and senior enlisted men. One man had both his legs blown off by a grenade, and a Claymore mine had been thrown right at the tactical operations center – a mine to kill the staff, for Christ's sake.'[24]

And in O'Brien's unit, patrolling My Lai, there was something that sounds a great deal like a fragging. Colonel Daud liked combat assaults from helicopters:

> 'More Combat Assaults came in the next few days. We learned to hate Colonel Daud and his force of helicopters. When he was killed by sappers in a midnight raid, the news came over the radio. A lieutenant led us in a song, a catchy, happy celebrating song: Ding-dong, the wicked witch is dead. We sang in good harmony. It sounded like a choir.'[25]

A midnight raid by sappers, indeed. It is not possible to find exact numbers for fraggings, but the numbers we do have are very large. One estimate is that there were between 800 and 1,000 attempted fraggings. The army reported 563 fraggings for 1969 and 1970 combined, and 363 courts martial for fraggings between 1970 and 1972. Most fraggings we have accounts of, however, did not result in courts martial. And as the army photographer Mark Jury said, it was easier to kill someone on patrol. Miguel Lemus, for example, was in the 25th Infantry. His unit came back from a hard patrol and 90 of them sat down to smoke cannabis together:

> 'This officer tried to be a hero – bust ninety guys. We were along the trenches and they shot him. They threw him over a trench and shot him with a machine gun. No one said anything. Someone called on the radio and told them the captain had been shot by gooks.'[26]

We can expect that at least half, perhaps more, of the killings happened in this way. So perhaps several thousand attempted fraggings or warnings, and perhaps 1,000 killed over four years. That is not an exact number. But remember that these killings were confined to officers and sergeants, very much a minority, and that there were never more than 80,000 combat troops at any one time. It was enough to discipline the other officers and sergeants. The US armed forces stopped fighting. In some units they refused outright, but more often they left base, found a place to sit down and called in false reports.

By June 1971 Marine Colonel Robert Heinl was writing in the *Armed Forces Journal* that 'by every conceivable indicator, our Army that now remains in Vietnam is in a state approaching collapse, with individual units avoiding or having refused combat, murdering their officers and non-commissioned officer, drug-ridden and dispirited where not near mutinous.'[27] This was an official journal of the armed forces. The army had stopped fighting, and mutiny was spreading. The marines, always tougher when they set out to do something, were withdrawn that year, the soldiers the next year. Between them, the Vietnamese peasants, the American protestors and the American marines and soldiers ended the war.

NOTES

1. Christian G. Appy, *Patriots: The Vietnam War Remembered from All Sides*, New York: Penguin, 2003, pp. 106–9.
2. For a more detailed account, see Jonathan Neale, *The American War: Vietnam 1960–1975*, London: Bookmarks, 2001; or the second edition, *A People's History of the Vietnam War*, New York: The New Press, 2003.
3. The Chinese government had stationed tens of thousands of soldiers in the Northern cities, and if the American bombers killed them this would mean a war with China that the United States was unlikely to win. This was not widely publicised at the time, but the US government knew it. This was why bombing focused on the countryside and Haiphong harbour.
4. Philip Caputo. *A Rumor of War*, New York: Holt, 1997, pp. xvi–xviii.
5. Michael Clodfelter, in John Pratt, *Vietnam Voices: Perspectives on the War Years 1941–1982* , New York: Penguin, 1984, pp. 601–6. For more detail, see the excellent memoir by Michael Clodfelter, *Mad Minutes and Vietnam Months*, Jefferson, NC: McFarland, 1988.
6. Eric Bergerud, *Red Thunder, Tropic Lightning: The World of a Combat Division in Vietnam*, Boulder, CO: Westview Press, 1993, p. 133.
7. Ibid., pp. 200–1.
8. Ibid., p. 229.
9. Peter Marin, 'Coming to terms with Vietnam', *Harpers*, 1980, quoted in Appy, *Patriots*, p. 296.
10. Robert Coles, *The Middle Americans: Proud and Uncertain*, Boston, MA: Little, Brown, 1971, p. 131.
11. Both testimonies from Vietnam Veterans Against the War, *The Winter Soldier Investigation*, Boston, MA, 1972, quoted in Christian G. Appy, *Working Class War: American Combat Soldiers and Vietnam*, Chapel Hill, NC: North Carolina University Press, 1993, pp. 294–5.
12. James Trulllinger, *Village at War: An Account of Revolution in Vietnam*, New York: Barnes & Noble, 1980, p. 117.
13. Ron Kovic, *Born on the Fourth of July*, New York: Pocket Books,1976, p. 111.
14. Coles, *The Middle Americans*, pp. 133–4.
15. David Cortright, *Soldiers in Revolt: the American Military Today*, Garden City, NY: Doubleday, 1975.

16. For details, see Heonik Kwon, *After the Massacre: Commemoration and Consolation in Ha My and My Lai*, Berkeley, CA: University of California Press, 2006; Michael Bilton and Kevin Sim, *Four Hours in My Lai*, New York: Viking, 1992; and Larry Colburn, 'They were butchering people' and Michael Bernhardt, 'The portable free-fire zone', both in Appy, *Patriots*, pp. 346–53.

17. Tim O'Brien, *If I Die in a Combat Zone, Box Me Up and Take Me Home*, New York: Delacorte Press, 1973, pp. 120–2.

18. Ibid., pp. 79–80.

19. Ibid., p. 173.

20. Richard Moser, *The New Winter Soldiers: GI and Veteran Dissent during the Vietnam War*, New Brunswick, NJ, Rutgers University Press, 1996, p. 49.

21. Mark Jury, *The Vietnam Photo Book* (1971), New York: Vintage, 1986, p. 40.

22. Moser, *The New Winter Soldiers*, pp. 50–51.

23. Ibid., p. 50.

24. Quoted in Cortright, *Soldiers in Revolt*, p. 45.

25. O'Brien, *If I Die in a Combat Zone*, pp. 113–14.

26. Charley Trujillo, *Soldados: Chicanos in Vietnam* , San Jose, CA: Chusma House, 1990, p. 35.

27. Robert Heinl, quoted in Joel Geier, 'Vietnam: the soldiers' rebellion', *International Socialist Review*, 9, 1999, p. 38.

9
Crazy Little Armies: Guerrilla Strategy in Latin America 1958–90

Mike Gonzalez

In one sense, guerrilla warfare has been a feature of Latin American history from the moment of the Spanish Conquest. It took 40 years for Spain to overwhelm the Mayas of southern Mexico, and the Tarascans of the north were never conquered fully by them. In Chile, the Araucanians under Caupolican learned to ride the Spanish horses the better to resist the invaders. Communities of escaped slaves (*palenques*) waged war on their ex-masters across the continent. In the eighteenth century the great indigenous rebellions led by Tupac Amaru and Tupac Katari held the colonists at bay for many years. And the wars of independence were rarely fought in set-piece battles; rather, they were conducted by mobile forces using their speed and knowledge of the territory to outwit a colonial army – the horsemen that rode with Artigas in Uruguay or Bolivar and Paez in Venezuela, for example. Perhaps by then they had assimilated the experiences of the guerrillas of the Spanish peninsula fighting the invading forces of the French, their experience commemorated in Goya's 'Disasters of War' series.

The list can continue and repeat itself across the ages. During the Mexican revolution (1910–17) the army of the south under Emiliano Zapata waged guerrilla war from a base in Morelos, Mexico for much of its brief history, while Pancho Villa's exploits in the north seem to belong to a history of guerrilla warfare despite the extravagant uniforms his men wore and the military rituals he so enjoyed. In times of war and occupation, the tactics of guerrilla war have re-emerged, from France to the Philippines, where the experience of guerrilla war found expression in William Pomeroy's *Guerrilla Warfare*.[1] But it is perhaps Mao Zedong's writings of the mid-1930s on guerrilla warfare in China that were more widely disseminated and thus more influential, summed up in his famous adage: 'The enemy advances, we retreat; the enemy camps, we harass; the enemy tires, we attack; the enemy retreats, we pursue.'[2]

FROM COLOMBIA TO CUBA

For most external observers, guerrilla warfare in Latin America follows the Cuban experience and is a phenomenon primarily of the 1960s. In this framework, the definitive text is Che Guevara's *Guerrilla Warfare*, a manual to be read alongside his memoir, *Reminiscences of the Cuban Revolutionary War*. There is no doubt that Guevara's writings had an enormous influence on a generation of young revolutionaries and served to define and shape one kind of modern guerrilla warfare. While their experiences left stories of courage and self-sacrifice which have influenced Latin America's subsequent political history, the strategy produced few successes. It is not only the revolutionaries who pore over these writings, but also the enemies of change, the military strategists of the School of the Americas and their Latin American allies. The counter-guerrilla strategies of the 1960s could rely on the resources of the state and of its military advisers to the north, while the guerrillas could depend only on what they could acquire by stealth or confrontation and what supplies the local population could or would offer them. This was the first lesson of guerrilla warfare, which Mao had underlined – that the guerrilla fighter in the population must be like a fish in the sea. The Vietnam war, and particularly the actions of the Vietcong in the South, gave meaning to the Chinese leader's advice and showed that the world's most powerful army could be maddened and traumatised by its inability to distinguish the fighters from the people, as they all wore black pyjamas.

It is a matter of argument when and where modern guerrilla warfare began in Latin America. With the irregular forces in the Mexican revolution perhaps, or with Augusto Cesar Sandino, whose 'crazy little army'[3] fought a small-scale guerrilla campaign against the US occupying forces in Nicaragua in the early 1930s. The Cuban revolution inspired the creation of guerrilla organisations in most countries of Latin America through the 1960s. But these groups, based for the most part on the ideas of Che Guevara and his concept of the guerrilla *foco*, were not the first to organise a military response against their governments. The Fuerzas Armadas de la Revolucion Colombiana (FARC), for example, were formed under that name in 1966, but they had existed in a different form since the mid-1940s.

The reasons for their emergence – as Peasant Self-Defence Leagues under the leadership of the Communist Party – are specific to Colombia. And an examination of their history emphasises what any history of the Latin American guerrillas must acknowledge – the particularity of each organisation, even though they may share certain external features and common tactics. Though the issue will be addressed more carefully below, the fundamental problem with the emergence of a common practice based on Cuba in my view is to be found in the failure to acknowledge specificities.

Colombia's is a history of violence almost without parallel in Latin America – and remains so. It is a violence of landowners against peasants and agricultural workers in the battle to control the production of coffee and bananas, which later is transformed into an equally brutal struggle for control of the burgeoning market for marijuana and cocaine. In the 1920s and 1930s, and in response to the dramatic modernisation of the national economy, social conflict intensified. The indigenous rebellion of Quintin Lame set a precedent, but from 1919 onwards the key labour struggles and conflicts took place in the coffee and banana enclaves, culminating in the famous 1928 strike of banana workers at the United Fruit Company's Ciénaga plantation. Having promised negotiation, the government sent heavily armed troops to mow down the workers and their families who had gathered in the town square.

The 1930s can be seen as a progressive interlude under the Liberal presidency of López Pumarejo. But the early 1940s saw a violent counter-revolutionary movement in which the landowners, the conservative forces and the Church mobilised to claw back what they felt they had lost. The high levels of mobilisations of peasants and workers had faded in the previous period; faced with new attacks, however, they reorganised and fought back. Their struggles found a figurehead in the radical Liberal lawyer Jorge Eliecer Gaitán. Gaitán was that rare thing in Colombia – an honest politician who had come to identify with the majority population, not as a revolutionary but as a Liberal committed to a democratic vision. (He refused to leave the Liberal Party despite its violent and corrupt history.) Gaitán himself had talked about the double reality of his country – the political reality of party politics and battles for power and a real Colombia of extreme poverty and social conflict. He identified himself with that 'real' Colombia and gathered its support for his presidential bid in the elections of 1948. He did not win but enjoyed the overwhelming support of organised workers and the rural and urban poor. His popularity was unprecedented, and when he was assassinated in October 1948, the effect was to launch Colombia into renewed and relentless violence. For three days crowds of enraged Gaitán supporters roamed the streets of the capital, looting and burning in protest. The *Bogotazo*, as it came to be called, ushered in a period called in Colombia *La Violencia* (The Violence), a generic name for a period of bitter confrontations, revenge killings and land grabs. What was unleashed was a process of staggering violence and sadistic cruelty – not just killing, but torture and persecution. Local scores were settled, landlords terrorised populations to claw back land, while the politicians whose machinations had set all this in motion disclaimed any responsibility. Tens of thousands fled from their homes as the armed gangs financed by the landowners wreaked havoc on their behalf.

In this situation, communities of peasants organised in their own defence and took refuge in areas of the country which later came to be called 'independent peasant republics'.[4] The most famous of these was Marquetalia, a community of some 40 or so peasants working the land who came to symbolise the republics and the vicious assault on them when, in 1964, they were surrounded by troops and bombed by the Colombian air force. Those who fled later formed part of a broad front of peasant organisations called the Bloque Sur, which two years later became the FARC.

The legendary leader of the FARC, Manuel Marulanda, or 'Tirofijo' ('Sureshot'), was himself a peasant and a leader of the self-defence forces. He was to become a member of the Communist Party in the early 1950s, perhaps as a result of the successful organisation of the defence of the community of El Davis under communist leadership. Thus, although the FARC occupy a prominent role in the roster of guerrilla organisations of the 1960s, their origins lie in the mobilisations of the peasantry against the violence of the powerful. Jenny Pearce adds that the Communist Party in the late 1950s was committed to a return to electoral politics as soon as the Conservative and Liberal Parties reached an agreement (in 1956) to alternate power and set aside party political rivalries. The Violence, however, continued unabated – and it was the violence of the state at Marquetalia and elsewhere that drove the FARC and the Communist Party back to the armed rural enclaves. The ELN (National Liberation Army) was formed in the mid-1960s under Fabio Vasquez, a peasant leader, but under the influence of Cuba and with quite a different social composition. There were also Maoist guerrillas, the EPL (Popular Army of Liberation) in a rural enclave around Córdoba.

The FARC's overwhelmingly peasant membership, its origins in rural struggles and conflicts, and the nature of its leadership, make it an exception in the history of Latin America. It is, to all intents and purposes, an armed mass movement under communist leadership. The conditions which gave birth to the guerrillas, the breakdown of central authority in Colombia and the extreme violence of its social conflicts remain the case today. In the 1980s and 1990s the expanding drugs trade created its own powerful paramilitary forces, independent of and in collusion with the state. Like the landowners of a previous age, they too employ terror to control the land where the marijuana and coca are grown. The FARC's rural base has enabled it to control significant territories, the heirs to the 'independent peasant republics'.

Whatever its contradictions, the support the FARC still enjoys suggests that it continues to represent an important chapter in the history of communal self-defence, which remains necessary against the background of continuing violence.

The Venezuelan guerrillas, led by Douglas Bravo and (until his murder in 1966) Fabricio Ojeda also emerge in the specific context of Venezuelan history, albeit more directly influenced by the Cuban experience. That history is told in detail elsewhere in this volume,[5] but it is important to underscore the fact that its roots are the peasant community, and its struggles allowed the Venezuelan guerrillas to survive a period of intense persecution and the severe weakening of its urban base. Furthermore, its composition – which included peasants, military officers and soldiers, urban workers, students and intellectuals at different times – distinguish the Venezuelan guerrillas in other ways. Yet for clear historical reasons, the Venezuelan guerrillas were able to attract significant support within the military in a way that does not seem to have been possible in Colombia.

THE INFLUENCE OF CHE GUEVARA

On 1 January 1950 Cuba's dictatorial ruler Fulgencio Batista fled Cuba for the safe haven of the Dominican Republic, ruled by the sadistic Rafael Trujillo. The young bearded revolutionaries who entered Havana that day in triumphant procession proclaimed the beginning of a new era in Latin America. Their youth and militancy struck chords across the continent with the young people who had demonstrated against US vice-president Richard Nixon the previous year. And their revolution caused considerable apprehension in Washington: Cuba[6] after all had been an economic colony of the United States since the war for independence from Spain had ended by driving Cuba into the sinister embrace of the United States in 1899. Cuba was just 112 km from the Florida coast, which gave it some strategic significance, and its sugar supplied the sweet tooth of North America. After the social upheavals of the mid-1930s, in which he first figured as a radical, Batista's corrupt and repressive regime had served the purposes of the colossus of the north very well – he was, as Franklin Roosevelt once said of another military dictator, 'a son of a bitch but *our* son of a bitch'.

A week after Batista's departure, Fidel Castro, the head of Cuba's Rebel Armed Forces and of the 26 July Movement (M-26 J), entered Havana to assume his role as the leader of the Cuban revolution. Just over two years earlier, in December 1956, 82 armed men had disembarked in a swamp from the motor vessel *Granma* to establish a first guerrilla encampment in Cuba's Sierra Maestra range. They were met by Batista's forces and 18 survived, among them Fidel, his brother Raúl and the Argentinian Ernesto 'Che' Guevara. The M-26 J had support among a small group within the armed forces, but more significantly an urban movement whose acknowledged leader was the young teacher and union activist Frank País. This was not the only armed opposition the Batista regime faced. The Directorio Revolucionario attempted to assassinate the dictator in March 1957 in a daring assault on the presidential palace. The attempt failed and the leader of the group, José Antonio Echeverria, was killed. The group nevertheless went on to establish its own guerrilla cell in the province of Escambray. The general strike called by the M-26 J in April 1958 was a failure, and as a result the tension between urban and rural wings of the resistance over where its leadership should be located was resolved in favour of the mountains and a guerrilla strategy. In the mid-1950s the widespread dissatisfaction of the Cuban population with Batista found several other expressions, in student protest and the largely middle-class Civic Resistance Movement. But in reality the movement was fragmented, with no strong political organisations at its heart. Although Cuba had a strong trade union tradition, the Communist Party which provided many of its leaders was no longer a radical force by this time. On the contrary it had reached an accommodation with Batista in the previous decade, and had become corrupt and bureaucratic as a result. The nationalist parties, particularly the Ortodoxos to which Fidel belonged, had disintegrated by the early 1950s, when Batista's 1952 coup pre-empted the elections of that year.

Castro was to have been a candidate in those elections. Instead he organised an assault on the Moncada barracks to capture arms. The attack on 26 July 1953 was a failure and a number of the attackers were killed. Castro himself was arrested and put on trial, delivering from the dock his speech 'History will absolve me', which set out the basic principles of his movement: hostility to the United States, a commitment to the nationalisation of Cuban assets and an end to the corrupt Batista regime. Amnestied two years later, Castro went to Mexico where he began to gather the men and resources for the *Granma* expedition. He secured material and political support from several wings of the anti-Batista opposition, including political opponents based in Miami, such as former President Prío Socarrás.

Established in the Sierra Maestra, the guerrillas began to attack army outposts in search of weapons and to seek the support of the local peasantry in this, the poorest part of the island. While some recruits were of peasant origins, the small fighting force consisted largely of students, intellectuals, and so on from the city. But the guerrillas faced not only the Batista military but also the hostility of Cuba's Communist Party, who rejected M-26 J as another group of 'petty bourgeois adventurists'. They would later send one of their leading members, Carlos Rafael Rodríguez, to accompany Fidel, as well Raúl Castro, who in 1958 established a second guerrilla column. Raúl was the only member of the guerrilla leadership who maintained close contact with the Communist Party. At the same time, Che and Camilo Cienfuegos, a Cuban revolutionary who had joined Castro in Mexico, were sent to build guerrilla cells (*focos*) in Escambray and to try to unite with the other guerrilla groups there. The fall of Batista came extremely rapidly. The military operation to root out the guerrillas in April 1958 was a failure and it became clear that his armed forces were falling apart, a process hastened by the realisation in the United States that the corruption and ineffectiveness of the regime were now so public that Batista had become an undesirable ally. Arms sales ceased and support quietly withdrawn.[7]

The victory of the guerrillas was the result of a number of factors: the collapse of the Batista regime; the disintegration of its armed forces; the lack of any social support from the middle classes or Cuban capital, especially after the withdrawal of US support; and the last-minute conversion of the Communist Party all contributed to the victory. And through the first year of the new regime, Castro devoted himself to building a machinery of power which would enable him to take full control. He declared en route to Havana that January that he had no interest in power; 52 years later that seems disingenuous at best. Castro and Guevara went to New York to speak at the United Nations and created a great stir in Harlem, where they moved having rejected the US government's preferred option, the Waldorf Astoria, as too expensive and almost certainly bugged. More importantly, the news of the Cuban revolution spread at speed through a younger Latin American generation whose attitudes to US imperialism in the region had been expressed in demonstrations and protests wherever a representative of Washington appeared.

It would be hard to overestimate the impact of the Cuban revolution or the level of support the overthrow of Batista enjoyed in those first months. It was unclear, however, what political direction Castro was likely to follow, beyond a general determination to reform agriculture and introduce measures of social justice. The new President, Manuel Urrutia, was a respectable figure and a judge, but his role was essentially ceremonial. The Agrarian Reform of May 1959 was directed at the large sugar plantations, the bulk of them foreign-owned. The new state, for its part, purged of the pro-Batista elements in the security apparatus and the government, was to replicate the command structure of the rebel army. This reflected the battle within the guerrilla forces before Batista's fall between the urban movement (based on working-class activity) and the rural guerrillas (based on the actions of the guerrillas themselves with peasant support).

Through 1959–60, Castro was building a new power structure as all those that had previously existed were systematically dismantled and replaced with organs linked directly to Castro and the new state. There was still no dominant political organisation, but Castro was keeping his distance from the communists at this stage. By the second half of 1959, however, it was clear that Washington's response would be extremely hostile and directed at bringing down the new regime as quickly as possible. It would employ economic instruments (freezing the sugar quota and severing economic relations with Cuba from January 1960), diplomatic weapons (using the Organization of American States to isolate Cuba in Latin America), military pressure (developing counter-guerrilla forces across the continent and linking further military aid to breaking contacts with Cuba) and political manipulation (through US President Kennedy's Alliance for Progress which offered an alternative programme for gradual social change sustained by US aid and administered by friendly governments). Half a million Cubans – the middle class, Cuban capitalists, many professionals and those who in one way or another, through business connections or the Mafia, had served US interests on the island – left the island in that first year.

In February 1960 the visit of a high-level Soviet delegation offered Cuba an alternative means of economic survival – though it came with hidden costs. By now, revolutionaries from Latin America were flocking to Cuba in search of a strategy that would allow them to repeat the Cuban experience. Their principal mentor was Che Guevara. His *Guerrilla Warfare*[8] was not simply an account of the Cuban experience, it was an instruction manual – or at least that is how it was read.

Guevara's vision was of 'a method for achieving political power' in which 'The guerrillas are the fighting vanguard of the people . . . armed and ready to carry out a series of warlike actions with the sole possible strategic goal of taking power. They are supported by the worker and peasant masses of the region'.[9] He goes on:

> 'The Cuban revolution has made three fundamental contributions to the technique of revolutionary movements in Latin America. First, the popular movements can win a war against the army; second, one does not always have to wait for all the conditions for the revolution to be in place – the insurrectionary *foco* will create them; and third, the field of armed struggle must fundamentally be the countryside.'

The key ideas here are that the *foco* can create the conditions for revolution and that the vanguard acts with the *support* of the masses. The active protagonist of the revolutionary process, therefore, is the group of revolutionaries themselves – the role of the mass movement is an ancillary one of support and supply. Guevara, unlike Castro, described himself as Marxist, a communist. Yet his interpretation of Marxism removed from it its central tenet, that 'the emancipation of the working class must be the act of the working class itself'. The theory, or technique, offered by Guevara derives its authority, of course, from his role in the Cuban revolution.

Nothing accords authority like a successful revolution. But the victory of the Cuban revolution cannot be attributed to the guerrilla strategy alone. In fact, the strategy would normally involve a long period of accumulation of forces, of achieving roots among the (in this case rural) population and a long-term attrition of the armed forces of the state. That the Cuban revolution succeeded so quickly

202 ARMS AND THE PEOPLE

is due to other factors: the extreme weakness of the Cuban state; the reality of an army led by paid mercenaries whose rank and file were certainly not held together by a strong sense of national pride; and the changing attitude of the United States towards Cuba. In other words, in the Cuban case, as in that of Nicaragua which we discuss below, it was the weakness of the enemy that ensured victory. It is possible that over time the rebel army would have grown in number and that its assaults on the armed forces would have worn them down. But there is a serious gap in the argument; where is the political work within the mass movement that can prepare it to take advantage of that weakness or make it an active protagonist in the demise of the state? The *foco* theory assumes that the active component of the guerrilla strategy is the guerrillas themselves; in other words, it is a military rather than a political strategy. And it did succeed in Cuba. It could not be exported and applied in the same way to the rest of Latin America, yet it was. However, the guerrilla movements that emerged in the 1960s seeking to reproduce the Cuban experience were not like the Colombian organisations or even the Venezuelan, with their roots in popular resistance. Instead, interpreting the idea that the 'objective conditions need not exist' as a kind of shortcut which obviated the need for long, patient work at the grass roots, a generation of courageous and committed young people took to the mountains.

This was consistent with a central feature of Guevara's vision – internationalism. From the outset he argued that an isolated Cuban revolution would fail. The training of Latin American guerrillas in Cuba was entirely in step with that view and Guevara's own life is evidence of his deep commitment to the principle.[10] Yet the historical evidence tells a different story, in part at least because the enemy, the states and armed forces of Latin America also learned their lessons well. The role of Regis Debray, a postgraduate student from Paris who caught Castro's attention and produced two key documents, 'The Long March in Latin America' (the title a deliberate echo of the Maoist experience) and his short but influential book *Revolution in the Revolution*, is important. For in many ways it was Debray, building on the views of Guevara, who argued that Cuba could provide a *model* for other Latin American revolutions. Debray's is the voice of a Third Worldism whose starting point was certainly hostility to Stalinism and the gradualism and opportunism of the European communist parties. The word 'voluntarism' is often used in relation to this moment in Latin America – and indeed more generally. And insofar as it points to the notion that the will and sacrifice of individual revolutionaries could accelerate processes of change irrespective of the real condition of the mass movements and working-class organisations, it seems to be accurate.

In fact, while the new revolutionaries were impatient to reproduce the Cuban experience in their own countries, the new Cuban government gave quite qualified support to their efforts.[11] Nonetheless, the use of Guatemalan territory to launch attacks on Cuba inspired the creation of Guatemala's first guerrilla organisations, led by two dissident army officers, Marco Antonio Yon Sosa and Luis Augusto Turcios Lima, both of whom had participated in a failed coup against the Ydígoras military regime. Their early actions in 1962 were no more successful, and both leaders withdrew to reconsider their strategies. Yon Sosa emerged with a new programme, openly socialist and clearly influenced by Trotskyism. Turcios Lima, for his part, remained closer to the Guatemalan Communist Party (the PGT).

The events of October 1962 changed Cuban attitudes to the guerrilla struggle. From early in 1960 Cuba was developing an increasingly close relationship with the Soviets, reflected in their internal influence, particularly in relation to economic policy. With characteristic pragmatism, and given the hostility of radical nationalists like himself to the Cuban communists, he maintained some degree of distance from the communists. But he could not escape the increasing dependence on Soviet support and their increasingly central role in internal decision-making. The missile crisis, however, culminated in an agreement between Washington and Moscow to remove the missiles on the island, which was reached over the heads of the Cuban leadership. In August 1961, Castro had declared the revolution 'Marxist-Leninist'; in the wake of the missile crisis, and what he saw as the cynical attitude of the Soviets, he turned towards Latin America in search of the expanding revolution.

Cuban influence in the rest of the continent derived, of course, from the revolution of 1959 and the representation of its methods in the writings of Guevara and Debray. Debray was insistent on the autonomy of the guerrilla *foco* as a tactical question. Yet it also had serious political implications. The argument was put forward, in fact, in the context of deepening tensions with the communist parties of the continent, none of which ever gave priority to the armed struggle or saw it as the key strategy.[12] While formally they gave political support, the period after 1962 marked a withdrawal of support from the armed struggle. Douglas Bravo is adamant that this was the direct result of the negotiations between Kennedy and

Khrushchev during the missile crisis, since the Soviets agreed to withdraw support for the guerrillas in exchange for an agreement not to invade Cuba and to withdraw US bases from Turkey.

The reality is that the subsequent guerrilla operations were quickly isolated and abandoned by their putative political allies. Across most of the continent the guerrillas came from dissident groups within the mass populist parties like Apra in Peru or Acción Democrática in Venezuela. And as in Cuba the social composition of the guerrilla groups was overwhelmingly urban and middle- or lower-middle-class.[13] This was true of Guevara too, whose contact with the organisations of the working class had been severely limited.

Although they were deeply critical of what were seen as reformist methods and Stalinist gradualism, the guerrillas remained dependent on networks of political support linked to the populist or communist parties. Yet the experience of Guevara in Bolivia demonstrated how fragile that support really was and how distant the guerrillas were from the working class and socialist movements to which they paid homage. The tragic fate of these guerrilla *focos*, poignantly exemplified in the fate of Guevara himself, is the most telling argument against the concept of the *foco* itself. A rural guerrilla can only be based within the peasant movement; it can only exist in that environment and with that degree of support and protection. In this Mao was clearly right. But the possibility of survival over time, in isolation and abandoned by the major political forces, is minimal.

Two cases might seem to contradict this interpretation. In Nicaragua, the FLN (National Liberation Front) became the Sandinista National Liberation Front in 1967. By then, however, the discovery of the Sandinista nucleus at Zacapa by the ruthless Somoza National Guard virtually eliminated the movement. Its founder, Carlos Fonseca, was killed in the encounter and its remaining leaders jailed and horribly tortured or exiled. Yet in 1979 the Sandinistas led the successful overthrow of the hated Somoza dictatorship. It cannot be claimed, however, that this was the result of a guerrilla strategy. In fact, the FSLN leadership split into three factions and rarely met until a popular rising in the town of Masaya in 1978 forced a reunification.

One faction, under the charismatic Tomas Borge, had argued for a prolonged people's war against the dictatorship. A second, the Proletarian Tendency led by Jaime Wheelock, advocated a longer-term socialist political strategy. The Third Tendency, as it was called, promoted a dual strategy of acts of armed propaganda[14] along with the active mobilisation of sympathetic opinion outside the country behind a project of democratic reform. If the revolution succeeded, however, it was because a series of factors combined to make it possible: the internal erosion and corruption of the Somoza regime; the growing opposition of the Nicaraguan bourgeoisie, exemplified by the conservative newspaper editor Pedro Joaquín Chamorro, whose murder in January 1978 sparked the Masaya rising and who had consistently attacked Somoza; and the spontaneous reaction against the worsening living conditions suffered by the majority of the population, exacerbated by the effects of the 1972 earthquake and the open theft of foreign aid to its victims by Somoza and his people.

The second example of a highly successful guerrilla organisation was the Tupamaros of Uruguay, an urban guerrilla group with huge popular support. It originated among the agricultural workers of the north of the country but quickly moved its base of operations to Montevideo, the national capital. It recruited widely among the same intellectual and student circles as other movements, but they remained in the city conducting their normal activities. The response of the Uruguayan state made a mockery of its persistent claims to be the Switzerland of Latin America. José María Bordaberry was elected President in 1971; two years later he took dictatorial powers and initiated a reign of terror designed to root out and destroy the Tupamaros. The silence he imposed on the media in Uruguay was exemplified in the large blank sections that appeared regularly in newspapers forbidden to publish certain items. The military regime lasted until 1990 and was particularly brutal, but perhaps overshadowed and hidden by its larger counterparts in Argentina and Uruguay. It is ironic, of course, that in the Uruguay of 2012, many ex-Tupamaros are in positions of political power.

THE SECOND WAVE

In 1967 Che Guevara was killed in Bolivia; his attempt to build a guerrilla base there had been a disaster. In the following year, Fidel Castro's speech supporting the Russian invasion of Prague was in some ways a declaration of failure – the failure of the strategy of exporting revolution which had briefly driven the Cuban government in the aftermath of the missile crisis. Cuba's return to the Soviet fold was a political as well as an economic decision, an acknowledgement that Cuba's survival depended on the support of the USSR. The further implication was that its foreign policy would now be shaped by Soviet ambitions. If Cuba had symbolically, and to some extent materially, sustained the guerrilla groups, it was now withdrawing from that involvement.

Weakened by the assaults of increasingly sophisticated counter-guerrilla operations and by their own isolation, the guerrillas of the 1960s were largely immobilised by the end of the decade. Yet the struggle in Central America in the 1980s would reveal that in Guatemala and El Salvador resistance had continued in circumstances in which democratic political activity was virtually impossible. Military regimes protecting the interests of the wealthy and the powerful, and often holding profoundly racist attitudes, had no compunction in assaulting indigenous communities and terrorising organised workers. In these circumstances, guerrilla struggles re-emerged, particularly in those two countries. But their underlying strategies were different from those of the 1960s. The guerrillas of El Salvador were not small, mobile groups but mass armed movements, defending significant territories under their control.[15] In post-Vietnam America the trauma of defeat obsessed the political leadership, and the presidential campaign of Ronald Reagan in 1980 promised to restore the United States' prestige in the world. The defeat of the burgeoning social movements of Central America seemed a relatively easy way to demonstrate in 'its own backyard' the United States' continuing global vocation. It financed and supplied the Nicaraguan counter-revolutionaries and the repressive military dictatorships of Guatemala and El Salvador throughout the 1980s. The response in the latter two was closer to Vietnam than to Cuba in that it was a civil war conducted largely in rural areas rather than the construction of guerrilla *focos*.

In Guatemala, the mass base of the armed resistance was largely the oppressed indigenous communities. In Peru, the Shining Path organisation (Sendero Luminoso) began its slow, patient organising work in the 1970s before emerging as an insurrectionary army in 1983. Sendero was a unique organisation, though it arose from the same wellspring as the Maoist guerrillas that had emerged earlier in Colombia and Peru. Its doctrinaire Maoism and intransigence towards any other organisation on the left have produced widely varying analyses of its origins and direction. For the ten years or so of its existence before the arrest and detention of its leader, Abimael Guzman ('President Gonzalo'), it mounted increasing numbers of well-oiled urban operations, but its base was in Peru's poorest and most oppressed region, Ayacucho. Its members came largely from a group of younger educated people from indigenous communities who had responded to the promise of education and professional employment that came from the Velasco government of 1968, a progressive military regime. By the mid-1970s, the promise of integration that this implied had been definitively broken. Velasco's successors were military men of the right. For that generation there was little to hope for and nothing to lose. The curious utopia that Sendero offered, puritanical and rigid, opened another horizon it seemed. As an organisation they were also autonomous and independent, self-sustaining both economically and ideologically – the collapse of Maoism had little or no effect on them. The assumption internationally was that it was a messianic cult following Guzman, and the appalling violence of government repression against them stirred very few in the human rights field. Yet if Sendero was violent and oppressive in its relations with the peasant communities, the response of successive governments, particularly that of Alberto Fujimori, in repressing them was state terror on a grand scale. Sendero has become less active, but it remains in existence.

Across the region, the political panorama has changed dramatically in the first decade or so of the twenty-first century. Mass movements have arisen across the continent, combining demands for social justice, communal rights, cultural recognition and national control of natural resources. They have carried to power new representatives able to speak with their voice and have fought to retain the capacity to act independently when they ceased to do so. As ever their erstwhile oppressors have not simply been content to pass on the baton; they have used their economic and ideological power and mobilised their weapons of every kind. The state has once again turned its guns against them. But the most important weapon these movements have discovered is their own power to mobilise tens of thousands and affect directly, through their actions, the political process.

It is likely that, sooner or later, they will be obliged to become a people under arms. Their success will not depend on their will or their self-sacrifice alone but on their ability to transform their conditions of life and the values and interests that shape their world. And they themselves will be the protagonists of that history.

NOTES

1. Pomeroy was an American communist who fought with the Huk guerrillas in the Philippines.
2. Mao Tse-tung, 'A single spark can start a prairie fire', *Selected Works*, Volume I, Peking: Foreign Languages Press, 1965, p. 124.
3. The term is Gregorio Selser's.

4. See Jenny Pearce, *Colombia: Inside the Labyrinth*, London: Latin America Bureau, 1990, particularly pp. 38–41, 49–66. See also Forrest Hilton, *Evil Hour in Colombia*, London: Verso, 2006, pp. 39–50.

5. See 'An interview with Douglas Bravo by Mike Gonzalez', this volume, chapter 13.

6. On Cuba generally, see Richard Gott, *Cuba a New History*, New Haven, CT: Yale University Press, 2004 and Samuel Farber, *Cuba since the Revolution of 1959*, Chicago: Haymarket Books, 2011.

7. In the *The Fourth Floor* former ambassador Earl T. Smith complains that communist sympathisers had infiltrated the State Department and were undermining Batista – an unlikely scenario. He may have had in mind Herbert Matthews' very sympathetic reporting from the Sierra Maestra, which he published in *Life* magazine in 1958.

8. Che Guevara, *Guerrilla Warfare*, New York: Monthly Review Press, 1961.

9. These and the following quotes are from *Guerrilla Warfare*.

10. There is an enormous literature on Guevara, too copious to cover here. Among them John Lee Anderson's *Che Guevara* is outstanding and, from a very different political standpoint, Jorge Castañeda's *Compañero* is worth reading. See too Mike Gonzalez, *Che Guevara and the Cuban Revolution*, London: Bookmarks, 2003.

11. See Richard Gott's seminal *Guerrillas in Latin America*, Harmondsworth: Penguin, 1970, pp. 37–8.

12. The exception, briefly, was Venezuela; see this volume, chapter 13.

13. Tim Wickham-Crowley, *Guerrillas and Revolution in Latin America*, Princeton, NJ: Princeton University Press, 1992, provides detailed data on the social background of the guerrilla leaders.

14. The most spectacular being the kidnapping of the whole National Assembly and the kidnapping of the guests at a Somocista Christmas party.

15. On the struggles in Central America, see Jenny Pearce, *Under the Eagle: US Intervention in Central America and the Caribbean*, London: Latin America Bureau, 1981; James Dunkerley, *Power in the Isthmus: A Political History of Modern Central America*, London: Verso, 1988; Grace Livingstone, *America's Backyard*, London: Zed Books, 2009.

BIBLIOGRAPHY/FURTHER READING

James Dunkerley, *Power in the Isthmus: A Political History of Modern Central America*, London: Verso, 1988.

Samuel Farber, *Cuba since the Revolution of 1959: A Critical Assessment*, Chicago: Haymarket Books, 2011.

Richard Gott, *Guerrillas in Latin America*, Harmondsworth: Penguin, 1970.

Richard Gott, *Cuba a New History*, New Haven, CT: Yale University Press, 2004.

Che Guevara, *Guerrilla Warfare*, New York: Monthly Review Press, 1961.

Forrest Hilton, *Evil Hour in Colombia*, London: Verso, 2006.

Grace Livingstone, *America's Backyard*, London: Zed Books, 2009.

Mao Tse-tung, *Selected Works*, Peking: Foreign Languages Press, 1965.

Jenny Pearce, *Under the Eagle: US Intervention in Central America and the Caribbean*, London: Latin America Bureau, 1981.

Jenny Pearce, *Colombia: Inside the Labyrinth*, London: Latin America Bureau, 1990.

Tim Wickham-Crowley, *Guerrillas and Revolution in Latin America*, Princeton, NJ: Princeton University Press, 1992.

Counter-Revolution and the Military

10
The Iron Fist: Chile 1973

Mike Gonzalez

Robert Moss, speech writer to Margaret Thatcher, once offered as an example of the headline that would least interest the reading public, 'A small earthquake in Chile'. But the Chilean military coup of 11 September 1973 resonated across the world and provoked intense and often bitter debate throughout the left. In November 1973, Enrico Berlinguer, General Secretary of the Italian Communist Party, used a speech on the Chilean events to launch the concept of the 'historic compromise', based on a coalition of interests between the communists and the Christian Democrats. Chile, he argued, demonstrated that the communists would only ever reach government in coalition with the Christian Democrats. He argued that in a bourgeois democracy a social transformation was impossible without an electoral majority and that its limits would be conditioned by the alliance. In short, some power was better than none. Thus Chile became a byword for the abandonment of the revolutionary project.

In the months and years that followed, Chile was used time and again to demonstrate that reforms might be possible but that any thoroughgoing programme of social change could not carry a majority with it. The argument that then derived from the Chilean experience was that the limits of reform were established by the 'middle sectors' and what they would be prepared to accept.

THE CHILEAN ROAD

The 'Chilean road to socialism' was inaugurated in November 1970, when the socialist Salvador Allende won the presidency of his country with a simple majority. Allende had been a candidate several times in previous years on behalf of various coalitions. This time he was elected as the leader of Popular Unity, a coalition of six parties whose leading members were the Communist Party and the Socialist Party of Chile. His victory occurred in a period of intensifying radicalism and social conflict, following the failure of the previous government under the Christian Democrat Eduardo Frei to carry through its programme of moderate reforms.

In fact, Allende won 36 per cent of the popular vote, which gave him the presidency but left him with a hostile parliament in which his political enemies retained control of the Congress and the Senate. They would systematically use their majority to block the legislative programme Allende had promised to carry through in government. The Christian Democrat presidential candidate, Radomiro Tomic, represented a left current that was sympathetic to some of Allende's aims, but the right-wing National Party's leader, Jorge Alessandri remained irredeemably hostile to Allende's democratic socialist project. And the right wing of the Christian Democrats would reassert its control of the party.

Despite the parliamentary impasse, some early measures were carried through, often by using laws passed during a 13-day socialist republic established in 1932 under Marmaduke Grove. Thus Chile's principal export, copper, was nationalised by unanimous vote in parliament in June 1971. A number of industrial firms were nationalised. A general wage increase was decreed to reactivate Chile's productive sector, and price controls were announced in an attempt to avoid shortages and the consequent inflation. On the land, redistribution measures were set in motion that envisaged the break-up of the big estates within two years and the redistribution of the land in various forms among the rural population.[1]

These measures were certainly intended to limit the power of the wealthiest classes in Chilean society and to increase the role of the state in economic management. But it was very far from a revolutionary programme. In fact, its reforms were aimed at winning over all but the most recalcitrant sections of Chilean capital and reactivating the economy to stimulate production and reduce unemployment. Although Allende was menacingly described by the right-wing press and their foreign sympathisers as 'a Marxist', his interpretation, as he explained in his first message to Congress, was that Marx had offered two roads to revolution, 'the revolutionary way and the pluralist way . . . and Chile is the first nation to conform to the second [pluralist] model of transition to a socialist society'. How profoundly Allende was committed to that pluralist road became very clear when it later emerged that, even before taking office, he had signed a Statute of Guarantees with the opposition, which agreed to respect the independence of the legal system, the armed forces, the press, media, trade unions and 'the existing political system'.

The theory underpinning the agreement stemmed from the proposition, argued by the Communist Party in particular, that power could be won in stages, piece by piece, over the long term. But the bourgeois state and its institutions are a whole, an integrated structure of power, and it was highly unlikely that having lost control of one area the bourgeoisie would not mobilise its other instruments of power to combat any fundamental erosion of the state. And so it was to prove.

These agreements were not widely known among those sectors of the population who had not only campaigned and voted for Allende in 1970, but whose hopes were placed in his government. The Frei administration (1964–70) enjoyed significant support from the US government; it was a central pillar of a strategy of gradual reform conceived as an alternative to the much more radical, anti-imperialist strategies that were gaining support throughout Latin America in the wake of the Cuban revolution of 1959.[2]

The Frei government's programme did obliquely address the frustrations of Chile's majority population. The control of Chile's copper mines – the source of 90 per cent of the country's export earnings – by two US-based multinational companies, Anaconda and Kennecott, was the central issue for any government representing itself as nationalist. Frei's policy of 'Chileanisation', however, never promised nationalisation or state control of the industry, but rather its transfer into the hands of Chilean private capitalists. And the world market for copper remained under the control of the very multinationals that had been excluded from Chile. The second most important issue was land. The patterns of Chilean landownership remained semi-feudal; the majority of Chile's land was held in large estates, with a population of landless labourers or small peasants.[3]

The promise of agrarian reform was central to Frei's programme and was seen as both a modernising and a redistributive measure. It was bitterly opposed by the right, whose support came from the wealthy landed classes, but the legislation was passed through parliament in 1967. Its implementation, however, was systematically blocked by the landowners, aided and abetted by the judiciary, who largely came from the same social class. The reform, therefore, was effectively paralysed. This led to deep rifts within the Christian Democratic Party, which had recruited a number of radical advocates of land reform. They would subsequently leave the Christian Democrats and set up separate organisations – the United

People's Action Movement (MAPU) and the Christian Left (IC), led by Frei's former Minister of Agriculture, Jacques Chonchol – which later joined the Popular Unity coalition. The inaction of government on reform led to a growing number of land occupations and to the radicalisation of peasant farmer and rural organisations under the leadership of dissident Christian Democrats or other left groups.

The promise of economic growth offered by Frei, through a reinvigorated industrial sector, attracted significant numbers of rural migrants who moved to the cities – Santiago and Concepción in particular – in search of work. They settled in the shanty towns (*poblaciones*) in the city's outskirts, taking over vacant urban sites (as urban settlers throughout Latin America were doing at the time), which often brought them into direct confrontation with the military, the police or both in defence of their occupations. The infamous case of the killings at Puerto Montt in 1969 was only one example.

There was a dramatic increase too in trade union activity in the last two years of the Frei regime; the unfulfilled promises of its early years provoked an increasingly militant response. The Chilean Trade Union Federation (CUT), led by the Communist Party, called a general strike in 1968 in response to rising unemployment and dramatic increases in the cost of living. They too were met with repression. The name of Augusto Pinochet, the leader of the 1973 military coup, would first come to public notice in repressing a miners' strike in 1968 at the cost of eight lives. In 1969 and 1970 the number of strikes increased from 1,939 involving 230,725 workers in 1969 to 5,295 mobilising over 316,000 workers in the following year.[4]

The failure to carry through the promised education reform in a country where higher education was largely available only to the middle classes in turn produced a massive response. The agitation for university reform radicalised the student movement, which in 1969 organised a massive march the length of the country culminating in the capital. This restless and militant movement of the young was fertile ground for the growth of the revolutionary left, in particular the Revolutionary Movement of the Left (MIR), which upheld the banner and the example of the Cuban revolution and had some impact among students and the shanty town populations, who were largely outside the influence of Chile's powerful traditional working-class parties, the communists and socialists. The MIR was never a member of Popular Unity.

It was these powerful social forces that carried Allende to the presidency in 1970. His campaign song, performed by the group Inti-Illimani, proclaimed, 'This time it's not just a matter of changing a President / We're going to build a very different Chile.' The cultural life of Chile was a vision of that different future, especially in the music that the movement had brought to the presidential campaign. Quiliapayun, linked to the Communist Party, celebrated working-class history and Inti-Illimani, close to the socialists, set Allende's political programme to music in the 'Canto al programa'. And Victor Jara, the young singer-songwriter who grew up in the slums of Santiago, became an icon for the youth movement.

Allende's promise of a 'Chilean road to socialism' excited enthusiasm and vast expectations. And after two years of mass mobilisations, it was unlikely that the movement would simply retreat, even though the Popular Unity Committees established during the election campaign were disbanded by Allende as soon as the campaign was over. This was particularly true on the land, where a restless peasant movement continued to occupy land without waiting for the relevant legislation to be enacted, especially in areas like Cautín, where the indigenous Mapuche population, for so long marginalised and ignored, moved to reoccupy ancestral territories.

It was only a matter of time before the tensions between the 'parliamentary road' and the expectations and demands of the grassroots would explode. In any event, the Chilean right had no intention of ceding power a little at a time. It began to develop its strategies to bring down the new government even before Popular Unity formally assumed power.

THE CONSTITUTIONAL MYTH

There was a repeated myth about Chilean social history and the role of the state which underpinned Allende's vision of gradual, legal reform and which perhaps explained his readiness to sign the Statute of Guarantees. External commentators regularly cited Chile's democratic credentials – the six-yearly presidential elections, for example. And the second component of the myth, which would have catastrophic consequences, concerned the 'constitutionalism' of Chile's armed forces. It was always argued that Chile's armed forces stood aside from politics, playing no role in the country's political life – and this in a region where the military had repeatedly intervened directly in politics. Bolivia's record of military coups was second to none, for example, and Chile's neighbour, Argentina, had witnessed the direct involvement of the military throughout its history.

Chile, it was argued, was different in this respect – a wilful distortion of the realities of even the most recent past. In 1924, for example, a reluctant Chilean parliament was persuaded to pass a package of social legislation by the menacing presence of military officers occupying the Chamber. One of those involved, Carlos Ibáñez, became President twice. In 1932, Naval Commodore Marmaduke Grove established his 13-day socialist republic; in 1938 a fascist military coup was crushed by then President Aguirre Cerda. In 1946, President Gonzalez Videla called in the army to arrest and detain the leaders of the Communist Party, which had been his ally only weeks before. Time and again, the army had intervened to enforce the power of the state, to repress popular protest and break strikes.[5] But it was true that the Chilean army acted as the guardian of the bourgeois state as a whole rather than defending the interests of any particular fraction of the ruling class, as was the case in Argentina and Colombia.

In the aftermath of the Cuban revolution, the armies of Latin America were assigned a dual role under the provisions of the Interamerican Defence (or Rio) Treaty. They were trained in counter-guerrilla warfare, but they also participated in some of the reform programmes advocated by Kennedy's Alliance for Progress. American academics edited collections of essays on the social role of the military as managers of the new programmes of guided reforms advocated by the Alliance for Progress, but it was clear that the priority was to stem the tide of revolution by means at once military and ideological.

The murder of General René Schneider by a fascist gang in October 1970, before Allende's inauguration, was almost certainly intended to provoke a reaction from the armed forces that would prevent Allende from assuming the presidency. They may have had in mind the triggers that launched the Spanish Civil War.[6] But it was clear that it was a premature action as far as the military command was concerned. After all, Allende himself was a committed parliamentarian who was adamant that all change must come through legal process, and we now know he had acknowledged this in the Statute. Schneider himself was the head of the military academy and, like most of Chile's officer class, had been trained in the United States in counter-guerrilla warfare.

The murder of Schneider was the work of a small group, almost certainly members of the neo-fascist Patria y Libertad (Fatherland

and Freedom) group linked to General Roberto Viaux. It is likely that it was a kidnapping that went wrong when Schneider resisted. It was a reflection, however, of a number of plots and conspiracies intended to prevent Allende from becoming President. The unintended result of the assassination, however, was to legitimise Allende by representing Schneider as the embodiment of the constitutional guarantees that Allende was defending. Despite their Marxist credentials, Allende and his colleagues seemed to be oblivious to the long debate among Marxists regarding the role of the military in defending the bourgeois state, resting as it always does 'in the last instance' on the use of force.

Schneider's death did not deter the organised opposition, however, which continued to plan a systematic campaign of subversion after Allende's accession. In parliament, the right-wing majority maintained an obdurate hostility to almost every presidential initiative, particularly in the economy. Plans to nationalise industry and the banks met with howls of disapproval and allegations of creeping communism. In reality, the decision was made at an early stage to limit nationalisations to 150 key firms.[7] The promised redistribution of land and the creation of state farms on uncultivated land were presented as assaults on the sacred principle of private property, frightening the small farmers who were certainly not likely to be the victims of an agrarian policy directed above all against the big landowners. The powerful Edwards media group, publishers of *El Mercurio*, relentlessly retailed these allegations, and the private television channels faithfully repeated them.

By June 1971, the leadership of the Christian Democratic Party had passed back to Frei, who immediately forged an alliance with the right-wing National Party of Alessandri. Its methods at this stage were political and economic through its control of the state's political and judicial institutions, and its economic power, which remained largely intact. Chile in 1970 laboured under a $2,300 million foreign debt, the result of loans and the high cost of importing technology and know-how. When Allende came to power, less than 3 per cent of industrial enterprises employed almost 50 per cent of the workforce. The same pattern of extreme concentration characterised other areas of the economy. In distribution twelve monopoly firms controlled 43 per cent of all sales, while 67 per cent accounted for less than 5 per cent of total trade. In the finance sector, five banks held the overwhelming majority of deposits. And on the land, where 22 per cent of the workforce were employed, less than 1 per cent of the population owned estates of 200 acres or more and only 4 per cent had holdings of between 50 and 200 acres.[8]

For these powerful sectors, the Popular Unity programme, limited though it was, represented a real threat. Their sabotage began even before Allende's accession, with capital flight, disinvestment, both foreign and domestic, and dramatic reductions in production. It was a sign of things to come. There was a six-month period of grace as the right reorganised its forces, during which the Congress passed a decree nationalising the five mixed enterprises which ran the Chuquicamata copper mines. The National Comptroller (Contralor) set the value of the mines against the excess profits gained over the years by the foreign companies who ran them, and refused compensation of any kind. The copper giants then embarked on a long international legal suit against Chile, combined with a campaign to boycott Chile's production. At the same time their control over the world market brought prices down dramatically, undermining Allende's key strategy to increase copper production and with it augment foreign earnings.

In its first year, the government nationalised around 140 enterprises, in many cases using legislation still on the statute books from the period of Marmaduke Grove which allowed the government to intervene where there was confrontation between workers and management. The general increase in wages, however, stimulated production in an industrial sector with significant unused capacity. New expressions of popular control were also emerging elsewhere. The JAPs (*Juntas de Abastecimiento Popular* – People's Supply Committees) were a government initiative setting up committees in the poorer areas and shanty towns to distribute goods according to need.

The honeymoon period proved short-lived, and the tensions and contradictions within the process quickly surfaced, both between government and opposition and between Popular Unity and its supporters. While Popular Unity insisted that land reform must be conducted within the framework of the law, for example, the landless peasants' organisations were unwilling to wait and continued and intensified their land occupations. In May Allende publicly called on them to stop and wait on the workings of the law. Yet they had voted for Popular Unity precisely because they saw it as a guarantee that, unlike the previous government, Allende would carry through the land reform.

The working class was enjoying the benefits of improved wages, and unemployment fell as the spare capacity in the economy was mobilised to respond to the increased purchasing power of the population. But there were political strains in the situation from the outset. Allende's response to the land occupations and to increasing radicalism in the shanty towns was to call for restraint; all actions should be within the framework of legality which he had guaranteed to the opposition prior to his election. It was true that he had used the term *poder popular* ('people's power') in his earliest speeches. But this was a discourse of government rather than any notion of independent working-class organisation. For many grassroots activists, however, the idea of *poder popular* signified much more than the actions of a sympathetic government. The programme, after all, had promised 'a very different Chile' in which the majority could take collective control of society and economy. The dismantling of the Popular Unity committees, which could so easily have become the embryo of a different social order, caused confusion and perplexity among Allende's supporters. The contradictions made themselves felt immediately, notably on the land. In the working-class movement, however, the official trade union congress (CUT) still maintained firm control, but there was already heated debate as to what 'workers' control' really meant. For the moment, however, full employment plus the firm control of the trade unions under communist and socialist leadership remained a sufficient guarantee of their discipline.

The right, now unified in the pact between the Christian Democrats and the National Party, used the latter part of the year to gather and mobilise its forces. Private investment had all but ground to a halt and was substituted by public funds. The shortages of goods in the face of much higher levels of demand created uncertainties which the opposition skilfully exploited. Fidel Castro's visit in November 1971 to congratulate Allende on his electoral victory provided an opportunity. The well-publicised 'March of the Empty Pots'[9] brought the bourgeoisie onto the streets holding empty pans which they banged with wooden spoons (though many of the bourgeois ladies brought their cooks along too). They were protesting at shortages which we now know were artificially created, as goods were hoarded in warehouses by the large distributors. The protests were then taken up in the parliament, where irate deputies denounced the land occupations and burgeoning strikes. By December the number of strikes reached 1,758 and there had been 1,258 land occupations.[10] The honeymoon, it seemed, was over.

Allende found himself at the first of several critical junctures. The movement that had brought him to power was chafing at the bit, ready to act in anticipation of changes rather than wait for the government to act. And it was anxious to respond to a rising tide of right-wing attacks and mobilisations which intensified in January 1972, beginning with the call for the impeachment of Interior Minister Jose Toha, seen as a radical, for 'insulting the armed forces'. Allende conceded to his dismissal in February, just as the parties of Popular Unity were meeting at El Arrayan to consider how to take the process forward. Should it be 'consolidate to advance' or 'advance to consolidate'? These were the central questions in a debate that began at El Arrayan and continued in June at Lo Curro.

The far left MIR, the Movement of the Revolutionary Left, had been roundly condemned by Allende and his ministers for their activities in the shanty towns and in some of the illegal strikes that had taken place through 1971. In fact, while the MIR was active and supported the militancy of workers and peasants, its political role was far less significant than Allende and the Communist Party claimed. The radicalisation was the result of an independent impulse that derived from the experience of the late 1960s and from the confidence that Allende's election gave to the social movements. The response to the provocations of the right-wing opposition was often spontaneous, given the lack of leadership or direction from the traditional organisations of the left. After all, it was the Communist Party which most vigorously advocated consensual arrangements with the Christian Democrats and counselled against alienating the middle classes by driving the political process too far.

What was becoming clear was that the different political currents within Popular Unity, which had held together during its first year in office, were beginning to diverge as the movements on the ground were becoming radicalised, not only in defence of their specific interests, but also in the battle against the right. The attacks on the MIR served as a veiled criticism of all those groups of Popular Unity supporters who were now escaping its control as they defended and attempted to drive forward the process of political change. There was a noticeable reticence on the part of the Popular Unity leadership, however, to identify the right as those who were subverting the social order – presumably in a bid to maintain the political consensus. The result, of course, was that the right gained in confidence and aggressiveness.

In this atmosphere of increasingly autonomous working-class activity, a parliamentary by-election and elections to the CUT executive in July increased the level of support for Popular Unity. But the paradox is only apparent. Popular Unity remained the only electoral option for the working class who were nevertheless developing other strategies in their increasingly frequent day-to-day struggles. In the mining areas, wildcat and local strikes were met by military intervention. In the light of Chilean history, the dispatch of the military in the same month to repress workers evoked some tragic precedents, but was also a sign of things to come. This was reinforced on 18 August, when the militant shanty town of Lo Hermida, dominated by the far left, was raided by the army ostensibly looking for fugitives and concealed weapons.

The impeachment of Toha may have seemed at the time a fairly marginal dispute. With hindsight it was clearly a test of whether Allende would adhere to the Statute of Guarantees, and respect the independence of the armed forces. The forced resignation of Toha conceded the ground without a fight.

THE MAKING OF A COUP

For Carlos Altamirano, General Secretary of the Socialist Party, the treatment of the armed forces was 'the single most important error made by Popular Unity'.[11] It was a sign of weakness that the right determined to exploit as it moved its attacks to a new level. Yet the government remained conciliatory towards the right and was willing to repress its own supporters as evidence of its continuing commitment to a legal process which the right was systematically ignoring. The role of the armed forces would be, as it always had been, to act against those forces that threatened the stability and maintenance of the existing order and its state.

In May 1972 a right-wing student demonstration was organised in the city of Concepción. A counter-demonstration of the left was banned by the communist mayor, who then called in troops to prevent it. One student was killed. A congress of textile workers in the same month called for workers' control of their industry. At the same time, Allende had resumed negotiations with Christian Democracy and his latest Cabinet reshuffle excluded the independent left Economics Minister Pedro Vuskovic, who was identified with increasing state ownership of the economy and provoked particular odium from the right.

In June, the refusal of a local judge to approve the redistribution of land at Melipilla, just outside Santiago, provoked an angry demonstration in the capital. The demonstrators were joined by striking workers from the nearby industrial area of Cerrillos. Later joint organisations were formed – the *cordones* (literally, industrial belts) – whose first joint declaration demanded a more profound process of change, replacing parliament with workers' assemblies and accelerating the state takeover of the economy. The Communist and Socialist Parties told their members to have nothing to do with the *cordones* and to take their lead only from the official organisations linked to government. Paradoxically, parliamentary and trade union elections in the following months again brought increased support for Popular Unity, which its leadership interpreted as support for its policy of collaboration. For the right, by contrast, the vacillations of the government and the obvious strains between Popular Unity and its supporters were signs of a weakness their strategists were determined to exploit.

While there was common ground in the determination to bring down the government, the right was still divided internally over what strategy to adopt. Within the military, a coup was now being openly discussed, with Pinochet as an increasingly visible advocate of this strategy. Others were arguing for what came to be called 'the soft coup' (*el golpe blando*), which essentially meant laying siege to the government, crippling the economy by hoarding, sabotage and disinvestment, and coupling this with a sustained and vehement campaign of denunciation and disinformation through a press and television still owned and controlled by the right.[12] In reality these were not so much clear alternatives as matters of timing. The use of the armed forces, after all, was central to both strategies.

The armed forces were now increasingly called on to perform their traditional role – the defence of the state against its detractors. Yet their fire was (still largely metaphorically) directed at the grassroots organisations and social movements; the right wing was never the object of repressive action. On the contrary, it seemed that the maintenance of the increasingly fragile consensus on which Popular Unity's strategy rested was dependent on the government's willingness to attack radical initiatives on the ground as evidence of their commitment to gradual change and the defence of the existing state and its institutions.

In July, the military occupied the mining areas in response to a series of strikes. The occupation of Lo Hermida followed a few weeks later, almost certainly as a reaction to events in Concepción, where a Popular Assembly brought together trade unions, local organisations and political parties to discuss the political situation, how to address the assaults of the right and how at the same time to carry forward the promised transition to socialism. The meeting was denounced by the Communist and Socialist Parties, and Allende himself, as a 'counter-revolutionary provocation'. How can you call for a transfer of power to the working classes, Allende asked, when the working class is in power through its elected representatives? Yet what the people at the grass roots could clearly see was that power was not now – and never had been – in the hands of the government, let alone the majority of the Chilean population. Its control of 'a part of power' remained just that.

What is astonishing in retrospect is the blindness of the Popular Unity leadership to these realities. In September the passage of the Arms Control Law marked a critical conjuncture. It was clear that the armed forces were now fully part of the combination of forces ranged against the government. The military presence was more and more visible and its direct intervention in strikes and civil disturbances increasingly frequent. Yet while every previous President of Chile had used the presidential prerogative to reorganise or replace the military high command and relocate officers with clearly political purposes, Allende made no attempt to do so, having surrendered that right before occupying the presidential chair. Instead, he offered high wages and social benefits – and a promise not to intervene in the internal affairs of the armed forces. At key moments he could have intervened to undermine internal conspiracies in the military or bring them under civilian control. Yet he did nothing.

The original Popular Unity programme contained a series of proposals to democratise the military, limit its involvement with foreign powers (specifically the US military, whose aid to the Chilean armed forces had increased considerably under Frei, reaching 10 per cent of the total military budget) and give NCOs and lower ranks the right to vote. These proposals were simply abandoned at the outset. And when, in September 1971, the MIR produced an issue of their weekly paper *El Rebelde* whose front page called for the 'Immediate democratisation of the armed forces and the police', the government removed all copies of the newspaper from the newsstands and arrested its editor, Andres Pascal (Allende's nephew). Yet the demands differed only in details from the original policy of Popular Unity itself. It represented a rare attempt to address the issue of the military in public debate – and it came from an organisation that was largely marginalised and ignored by the 'official' left.

Early in 1972, the army had moved quickly against a demonstration organised by the extreme right-wing Fatherland and Freedom organisation. Perhaps Allende interpreted their action as evidence of their loyalty to the government. However, the events at Concepción and the persistent rumours of internal conspiracies should have challenged that complacency. It clearly did not.

Now, on the eve of a shopkeepers' strike in protest against price controls and shortages, the government passed an Arms Control Law which effectively gave the armed forces the exclusive right to bear arms. In October, the lorry drivers – in a country wholly dependent on freight traffic carried by road – announced that they were calling an indefinite strike. Their lorries were disabled and locked in compounds guarded by armed men. Many professionals – doctors and lawyers among them – joined the strike in sympathy. Factory owners stopped their machines. The extreme right-wing priest Father Habsbun used his TV programme on Channel 9 to call openly for a military coup. In this situation, the Arms Control Law seemed to be exactly the wrong response. It was well known that Fatherland and Freedom was particularly influential among the lorry owners, and it was their armed cadres who guarded the compound gates. Yet the message implicit in the new law was that the military now had *carte blanche* to prevent any attempt by the mass movement to prepare its own armed defence. Patria y Libertad's cadres, by contrast, were now no longer the object of military attentions.

The October strike was designed to bring down the government. If it did not, it was thanks to the massive response from the working-class supporters of Popular Unity. Shops were reopened by force and local committees organised to distribute goods equitably; volunteers drove the lorries once the guards had been overcome; factories were to set to work again by their own workers; volunteers maintained an emergency medical service; and the *cordones* at Cerrillos and elsewhere were mobilised to organise the collective response to the bosses' strike.

At this crucial moment, there were two social forces vying for power; on the one hand, the bourgeoisie was using its economic and political power to destroy any hope of change; on the other, the new organs of working-class power were emerging in the cities and in the countryside to exercise power directly. The struggle was now on the streets. The government was a helpless spectator, having lost its ability to direct events or establish its authority over either of the protagonists, and unable to hold the centre in which it had located itself.

Its solution, at the end of October, was to concede the demand that had first been put forward by the right-wing strikers – to use the armed forces to re-establish order. On 31 October, facing an imminent strike of airline pilots, Allende declared a state of emergency and announced a new cabinet which included three generals. Every left organisation in Chile, including the MIR, welcomed their inclusion; the only exception was the Christian Left, which refused to join the new government, arguing that:

'the advances in working class consciousness don't seem to have reached their political leaders. The base is far richer than the leadership . . . If the social power [of Popular Unity support] were to be organised in a coordinated way at the factory and regional level, *and into organs of defence*, the situation would move forward and be unstoppable.'[13]

This was the critical moment. The October strike had posed in dramatic and concrete terms the issue of power. While the government tried desperately to mediate between the two social forces and re-impose the authority it had clearly lost over the working-class movement, the left parties offered no analysis or orientation, either during the strike or in the aftermath. Later, much later, long after the coup and from exile, Carlos Altamirano, the general secretary of the Socialist Party, an avowedly Marxist, non-Stalinist mass organisation, asked the question that no one seems to have asked at the time: 'Was it possible to argue for a strategy of arming the workers?' He says it was, but nothing was done – and the consequence was the terrible defeat of September 1973.

All parties agreed (with the one exception cited above) that the subject of this process of social change was the government. And while the working class (in the broadest sense) had demonstrated its ability to produce new and independent forms of action in the face of the right's determination to act outside the framework of law and democracy, the government delivered the control of the situation to the armed forces in the continuing belief that they were in some way above politics.

Popular Unity's actions in the wake of the October experience led step by step towards compromise and further reconciliation with the right. The Economics Minister Orland Millas, a communist, proposed a new Economic Plan in January, which included the return of most nationalised factories to their original owners. Renewed talks began at the same time with the Christian Democrats. The reaction in the working-class areas and in the mass movement was one of fury – there were a series of demonstrations, occupations and protests throughout January and February. Yet Congressional elections in March 1973 once again gave an increased majority to Popular Unity candidates.

No significant figures or groups on the left were drawing the political conclusions from the October days – that the struggle between classes had reached a new level, that the bourgeois state had mobilised its forces to defend its existence against the new and more radical direction embedded and implicit in the new forms of independent working-class organisation and government that had emerged in the course of the strike. The right, by contrast, did draw the conclusions. Their political and economic strategies had caused chaos, but they had not undermined electoral support for Popular Unity. By March, the generals left the Cabinet as the opposition finally abandoned the field of politics for the streets, the farms and the factories. The next two months were a period of political confusion. Popular Unity had virtually ceased to function as a political leadership, while new examples of independent radical action pointed to a different possible outcome. But there was neither coordination nor clarity. Nor was there any preparation for the military coup that was now being openly discussed in right-wing circles and in the opposition press.

On 29 June the Tank Regiment under Colonel Roberto Souper rolled onto Santiago's streets and announced the seizure of power. In retrospect it is clear that this was a rehearsal for the coup to come, a test of the capacity of government to act decisively in the face of a military challenge. It was quickly suppressed, leaving a number of military and civilian casualties, the best known among them an Argentine cameraman who filmed his own death when he was shot by one of the coup participants.

More importantly, the response from the militant working-class areas was immediate. But once again Allende chose to speak to the army high command rather than respond to his own mass base and offer political leadership on this final opportunity.

In the days that followed, all the organisations of the left called on the workers to prepare themselves to defend the government. This was disingenuous at best, cynical at worst. As the army now moved quickly to prepare the conditions for the military coup to come, the government still refused to act. Allende relied instead on General Carlos Prats, brought into the government as Interior Minister, to guarantee the constitutional loyalties of the armed forces. The preparations for the coup were hardly secret. A group of MIR members in the air force and the navy publicly denounced the coup preparations and called on Allende to act. His response was to pass the issue back to the high commands – the very people who were about to launch the coup – for investigation. In both cases, the whistle-blowers were arrested and tortured. Yet the reply from the Communist Party to the last-minute argument about arming the workers was unequivocal:

> 'Because the workers took some immediate security measures against the recent attempted coup, and maintained these precautionary measures, some reactionaries have begun to raise a storm, in the belief that they have found a new issue to use to drive a wedge between the people and the armed forces. They are claiming that we have a policy of replacing the professional army. No sir! We continue and will continue to support keeping our armed forces professional.'[14]

By then the preparations for the coup were under way. Officers who were ambivalent were moved. Early in August a group of generals' wives stood outside the home of Carlos Prats hurling abuse at him and his family and demanding he resign from the government. By then the gloves were off. In July, the right had launched a second indefinite general strike. The response from the working-class districts was as militant and determined as it had been in October; but Allende's decision to call on the army to resolve the problem was the final blow. Prats did resign, but he recommended Pinochet as his replacement. With the Arms Control Law as his justification, Pinochet now coordinated a campaign against the popular organisations. By mid-August, hundreds of militants of the *cordones* and the rural organisations were under arrest in military prisons.

All this was taking place against the background of a nationwide employers' strike whose object was to paralyse the economy and make the country ungovernable. The heavily armed fascist group Patria y Libertad was operating with insolent openness in attacking government targets and militant organisations. Most significant of all, the Christian Democrats – the self-appointed representatives of bourgeois democracy – stood by and said nothing, blaming the government for the situation it now faced. And the left, the Communist and Socialist Parties, blamed the activists and the fighters on the ground for the chaos. A famous communist poster proclaimed 'No to the violence of left and right', as if workers' self-defence was equivalent to the systematic assault on the population by the armed forces with the collusion of the most powerful economic sectors and media bosses.

In late July Miguel Enriquez, secretary general of the MIR, called for the workers to be armed. A few days later, Altamirano too raised the call. Yet it was too late. The armed forces were carrying out what was effectively a pre-emptive coup throughout the country. In any event, it was not a matter of distributing arms to a few factories. The problem was the absence of a strategy for taking on the bourgeois opposition and confronting a state which defended their class interests despite the presence of Allende in the presidency. The tragedy of Chile is that, as the moment of the coup approached, both the left in government and the right coincided in their fear for the survival of that state, and while the right actively encouraged the military in their preparations, the official left appealed to a constitutional consciousness in the military which they, and most of the Chilean population, had seen disappearing as the class struggle intensified. General Prats' resignation was a gesture of surrender to the inevitable.

Was there something special about the Chilean military that explained the violence of the coup? The particularities of Chilean history meant that the oligarchy did not for the most part send its sons into the army; the officers came mainly from the lower middle class, though in the course of their Prussian-based training they were quickly isolated from their own class. Ideologically, they were trained as defenders of the nation. The occasions on which the military acted to support socially progressive programmes, as in the early 1920s, are explained by these origins. The modern Chilean army, however, was led by officers inculcated into their role in the United States. Between 1950 and 1972, 4,932 Chilean officers were trained in the United States and from 1968 onwards most officer cadets spent at least two months at the School of the Americas in Panama.[15] Here the dominant register was a virulent anti-communism. As the plots of the late 1960s and early 1970s showed, there were powerful extreme nationalist groups embedded in the armed forces, and particularly in the army, like those around General Roberto Viaux. The force closest to the people were the *carabineros*, not only because its rank and file came from the poorer layers of society, but also because – as essentially an armed police force – it was more regularly in contact with social reality than were the more insulated and isolated armed forces.

There was a commemorative demonstration through the capital on 4 September 1973; but the atmosphere among the marchers was strangely gloomy. One week later, at 9 a.m., British Hawker Hunter jets bombed La Moneda, the presidential palace. Military personnel rooted out the leading cadres of the left, militant workers, peasant leaders, students and prominent Popular Unity supporters like Victor Jara. There were rumours of resistance in the more militant factories such as Ex-Sumar; some said that Prats was mobilising constitutional forces against the coup. We know now that Prats' loyalty was to the army and to the state – not to a defence of Chile's workers, peasants or shanty town dwellers. He had given up weeks before. And the political confusions of the major parties meant that they had made no preparations at all for a coup or prepared any strategy for resistance. There was some resistance at the NCOs school of the *carabineros* – they fought for two days and died there.

Foreign observers spoke with optimism about loyal officers – the myth of the constitutional military persisted to the last – but in reality any officers or men who had displayed doubts or expressed sympathy for the working class had been purged between June and the day of the coup. It is possible, of course, that there were significant numbers of soldiers, particularly in the *carabineros*, who might have been broadly sympathetic to Popular Unity. But the rigid hierarchies of command in the Chilean army could only have been broken had an alternative been available to those who did not want to support the coup – an organised, well-prepared working class that could fight back across the country. As we have seen, no such alternative existed. The MIR fought a rearguard guerrilla action with great courage and selflessness. But they could not substitute for a demobilised, confused working-class movement.

The coup was conducted with ferocity. There was no public division within the armed forces and private reservations were little more than examples of moral cowardice. Activists were arrested, murdered or savagely tortured; leading politicians of the left were sent to concentration camps to be tortured, while others remained in the dreadful basements of the Villa Grimaldi, the torture centre of the security police, the DINA, run by Pinochet's son-in-law, Manuel Contreras.

There was revulsion across the world, and a question: Why was the regime so brutal and violent in its actions? The answer has less to do with psychology than with politics. The Chilean ruling class had seen the workers, the peasants and the poor grow in confidence and organisation. They had seen their strikes broken by collective action. They had, briefly, glimpsed the spectre of revolutionary change.

Their rage was the anger of a class that has seen its power questioned and had looked into the abyss. The Pinochet regime restored their class rule, but it also acted to root out the memory of the struggle for power between 1970 and 1973. Later Chile became a laboratory for an untrammelled and unrestricted neo-liberalism. It was a warning of things to come. Yet the other lesson of Chile – the enormous creativity of workers acting collectively to bring about change – also has much to teach the future.

NOTES

1. See Salvador Allende, *The Chilean Road to Socialism*, Harmondsworth: Penguin Books, 1971.
2. See Irving Horowitz, ed., *The Rise and Fall of Project Camelot*, Boston, MA: MIT, 1967. This was a project using American social scientists to prepare a political campaign 'to assist friendly governments in dealing with active insurgency problems'. Norwegian Professor Johann Galtung called it 'scientific colonialism' and exposed it. The Project was then cancelled. See also chapter 9 in this volume.
3. See C. Kay, in Phil O'Brien and Jacqueline Roddick, *Chile: The Pinochet Decade*, London: Latin America Bureau, 1983.
4. Mike Gonzalez, 'Chile 1970–73', in Colin Barker, ed., *Revolutionary Rehearsals*, London: Bookmarks, 1987, p. 44.
5. Alain Labrousse, in *Chili le dossier noir*, Paris: Gallimard, 1974.
6. The murder of García Lorca and Calvo Sotelo in July and August 1936. See this volume, chapter 6.
7. See Ian Roxborough, Philip O'Brien and Jacqueline Roddick, eds., *State and Revolution in Chile*, London: Macmillan, 1977, chapter 4, and Joan Garces, *Allende y la experiencia chilena*, Barcelona: Ariel, 1976.
8. Roxborough, *State and Revolution in Chile*, p. 77, and Kay, in O'Brien and Roddick, *Chile*.
9. See Andres Wood's lovely film *Machuca*, with its re-enactment of the march. The banging of empty pots thereafter became an increasingly common form of protest in Latin America, used by both left and right.
10. Barker, *Revolutionary Rehearsals*, p. 48.
11. Carlos Altamirano, *Dialéctica de una derrota*, Siglo XXI, Mexico, 1977, p. 153.
12. See Mike Gonzalez on ideology, in Philip O'Brien, ed., *Allende's Chile*, New York: Praeger, 1975, and more generally, Armand Mattelart and Ariel Dorfman, *How to Read Donald Duck: Imperialist Ideology in the Disney Comic*, Amsterdam: International General, 1984.
13. Barker, *Revolutionary Rehearsals*, pp. 63–4, emphasis added.
14. Roxborough, *State and Revolution in Chile*, p. 215.
15. Altamirano, *Dialéctica*, p. 156.

BIBLIOGRAPHY/FURTHER READING

Salvador Allende, *The Chilean Road to Socialism*, Harmondsworth: Penguin, 1971.
J. Ann Zammit, ed., *The Chilean Road to Socialism*, Austin, TX: University of Texas Press, 1971.

Regis Debray, *Conversacion con Allende*, Mexico: Siglo XXI, 1971.

Lee Evans, ed., *Disaster in Chile*, New York: Pathfinder, 1974.

Joan Garces, *Allende y la experiencia chilena*, Barcelona: Ariel, 1976.

Mike Gonzalez, 'Chile 1970–73', in Colin Barker, ed., *Revolutionary Rehearsals*, London: Bookmarks, 1987.

Peter Kornbluh, ed., *The Pinochet File: A Declassified Dossier on Atrocity and Accountability*, New York: The New Press, 2004.

Phil O'Brien and Jacqueline Roddick, *Chile: The Pinochet Decade*, London: Latin America Bureau, 1983.

Hugh O'Shaughnessy, *Pinochet: The Politics of Torture*, London: Latin America Bureau, 2000.

Lubna Z. Qureshi, *Nixon, Kissinger, and Allende: US Involvement in the 1973 Coup in Chile*, Lanham, MD: Lexington Books, 2009.

Ian Roxborough, Philip O'Brien and Jacqueline Roddick, eds., *State and Revolution in Chile*, London: Macmillan, 1977.

Camilo Taufic, *Chile en la hoguera: cronica de la repression military*, Buenos Aires: Corregidor, 1974.

11
Reaction and Slaughter: Indonesia 1965–66

Nathaniel Mehr

When he took office as Indonesia's first President in August 1945, Sukarno was a national hero. He had led the nascent Indonesian nation in successive struggles against Dutch and Japanese occupation, emerging victorious in 1949. Within just over two decades, this internationally revered hero of Third World nationalism had been marginalised by the very generals who had fought alongside him, and by 1967 his populist regime had been supplanted by a right-wing junta.

In order to maintain the fragile unity of Indonesia – a composite nation comprising myriad cultures, ethnicities and political factions, not to mention competing economic interests – Sukarno developed a peculiarly eclectic nationalist ideology, encapsulated in *pancasila* ('the five principles'): nationalism, internationalism, democracy, social justice and belief in God. In the political sphere, this manifested itself in a policy of accommodation towards socialist and Islamist parties; as the Indonesian Communist Party (Partai Komunis Indonesia – PKI) grew in the 1950s, Sukarno increasingly began to align himself with communism. *Nasakom* – an acronym for nationalism, religion and communism (*nasionalisme, agama, komunisme*) – became his new buzz-word to encapsulate his vision for Indonesia. But the political manifestations of *nasionalisme* and *agama* in Indonesia were, and had always been, staunchly hostile to Marxian ideas, notwithstanding the strong current of populism that had pervaded much of Indonesian national life ever since the independence struggle. What began as a pragmatic policy of accommodation gradually crystallised into a stand-off; the tensions between Sukarno and the military were brought into sharp focus when, in May 1965, the President proposed a large purchase of Chinese weaponry to arm the peasantry, who would become a 'fifth force' in the country's security apparatus. The plan did not come to fruition, but the army's leading right-wing generals considered themselves effectively on notice.

As tensions with the military mounted, external factors exerted further pressure on Sukarno. The economy worsened dramatically in the early 1960s; the rate of inflation was around 100 per cent a year in 1961–64; and in 1964 peaked at 134 per cent. From 1962, the country had also been involved in a low-level war against the British in the jungles of newly independent Malaysia. This war, known as 'the Confrontation', was driven by Sukarno's belief that the newly formed Malaysian Federation was simply a front for British imperialist aspirations in the region. The army leadership had initially acquiesced in the venture in the belief that it would help strengthen their position within the government; but while the army continued to accrue large arms loans from the USSR, Sukarno was moving closer to a Chinese-inspired vision of a non-aligned Indonesia leading the Third World against both Soviet socialism and Western capitalism. Sukarno withdrew Indonesia from the United Nations in January 1965, setting up a rival grouping, the Conference of Newly Emerging Forces. By the mid-1960s, the Confrontation had become a burdensome and politically embarrassing distraction to the generals; they wanted out.

Alongside these developments, the meteoric rise of the PKI had led to some significant political gains for the party, most notably the passing of two potentially far-reaching land reform statutes, much to the chagrin of the landowning classes. Against this backdrop of international isolation, economic instability and political division, Sukarno's fragile political equilibrium was shattered in October 1965 when the Indonesian army moved to crush the left and seize power. In a ruthlessly efficient campaign of political mass murder, the military obliterated the PKI, leaving a death toll which numbered in the hundreds of thousands. This chapter is about how – and why – that happened.

HOW THE PKI CHALLENGED INDONESIA'S ELITE

Founded in 1914, the PKI started life as the Indies Social Democratic Association (ISDV) under Dutch colonial rule, changing its name to the Partai Komunis Indonesia in 1920 in tribute to Russia's October revolutionaries of 1917. After a series of revolts in the late 1920s, the party was driven underground by the Dutch authorities and a number of its leaders were imprisoned or executed. The PKI would remain an underground organisation for the remainder of Dutch colonial rule, only emerging as a force in Indonesian politics after the Revolution of 1945–49.[1] During the revolution, the PKI staged an armed uprising against Sukarno in the town of Madiun in East Java in 1948. The uprising was defeated and the PKI was widely denounced by Indonesian nationalists for having betrayed the cause of Indonesian nationalism by staging an internal rebellion at the very time when unity against the common Dutch enemy was seen as paramount.

When Dipa Nusantara Aidit took over the leadership of the party in 1951, the PKI adopted a policy of cooperation with other, non-communist parties and rejected armed struggle in favour of a non-violent strategy, arguing that the nation's unusual geographic and demographic composition made armed struggle unworkable. Aidit believed that the party should be active among the Indonesian masses in order to build a broad united front in its pursuit of political power rather than confining itself to the narrower aim of achieving parliamentary success.[2] The Indonesian proletariat ought to 'build unity with the national bourgeoisie and preserve this unity with all its strength'. Given that Indonesia's bourgeoisie was itself 'being oppressed by foreign imperialism', it could 'under certain circumstances and within certain limits, participate in the struggle against imperialism'.[3] This was a significant departure from the orthodox Marxist perspective, which viewed the proletariat/ bourgeoisie division as something that transcended national boundaries and was fundamentally irreconcilable. This controversial position would form the basis of the PKI's policy under Aidit; at its hub was 'the firm unity between the workers and the peasants, the largest and most oppressed group of the Indonesian people'.[4]

Aidit's approach drew him into open ideological conflict with the USSR, which during this period was pursuing a pragmatic policy of supporting non-communist governments in the underdeveloped world that they were prepared to break ties with the West and establish bonds with the socialist states. The Chinese took the view that this policy, which tended to manifest itself in Russian support for bourgeois and anti-communist regimes, constituted a betrayal of national liberation movements and socialist movements in the underdeveloped world. Aidit agreed, and in 1963 even went so far as to question whether the Soviet government could rightly call itself socialist: 'A socialist country cannot be counted as one if it does not come to the aid of the struggle for independence.'[5] Aidit claimed that the 'progressive aspect' of the Indonesian state had, under Sukarno, become its 'main aspect', superseding the state's repressive and reactionary nature.[6] The PKI's split with the Soviet Union was confirmed when Aidit declined an invitation to a convention of the world's communist parties in Moscow scheduled for 1 March 1965. For its part, the USSR would continue to provide military funding and equipment for the Indonesian army throughout the crisis and mass killings of 1965–66.

Within a few years of becoming leader of the party, Aidit had overseen a remarkable resurgence in the party's fortunes. Although it had been almost completely eradicated in the purges following the Madiun affair of 1948, the party emerged to poll 16.4 per cent of the vote in the 1955 elections. Having resolved to establish a popular support base among the peasantry, who comprised some 70 per cent of the population, the PKI championed the cause of land reform in rural areas. Aidit targeted a number of foreign-owned plantations, especially in Sumatra, describing the system of land tenure as '100 per cent feudalism'.[7] This was tempered by a promise of a degree of protection for the land rights of those among the rich and middling peasants who were prepared to ally themselves with the PKI.[8]

In 1959–60, the party achieved their most significant success at the legislative level, with the passing of two land reform bills with potentially far-reaching effects. The Crop Sharing Law, passed in November 1959, provided for a minimum 50:50 splitting of crops between landlords and tenants, along with other provisions improving the position of tenants.[9] The Basic Agrarian Law, passed in September 1960, aimed at a fundamental overhaul of Indonesia's antiquated landownership system, with the aim of providing greater security for agricultural workers and a stronger position for Indonesian farmers vis-à-vis foreign plantation owners. The law provided for a minimum entitlement of 2 hectares of land per family and included provisions penalising absentee landlords. The effective implementation of the reforms was impeded to a certain extent by inefficient administrative practices, but to a far greater extent by a deliberate policy, on the part of many landlords, of simply ignoring the new legal requirements or actively obstructing their implementation by carrying out the illegal transfer of lands to relatives and 'bogus' buyers.[10] Although the land reform policy had now passed into national law, the landlords, confident that they had strong support in the influential PNI and military circles, were intent on treating the law as an aberration that did not need to be taken seriously. The landlords even had sympathetic friends among the very committees established to oversee and direct the implementation of the reform.[11] A vigorous campaign for full implementation of the laws on the part of various peasant organisations affiliated with the PKI and joined by sympathetic left-wing groups faced determined opposition from the PNI, Islamic groups and the military, culminating in violent confrontations in 1965. In the meantime, the army was becoming increasingly sophisticated in its approach to winning back the popular support it had been losing to the PKI, setting up its own civilian front organisations to rival the PKI's affiliated peasant and trade union groups while continuing with localised suppression of the PKI.[12]

The PKI had made tremendous progress during 1950–65; it had even established itself as an electoral force after a strong showing in provincial elections in 1957. However, the party did not occupy any official positions of note in the various cabinets of the 1950–57 period and thereafter its improved standing was contingent on Sukarno's support in the face of continued opposition from the military. The fundamental policy differences between the army and the PKI were gradually crystallising into a position of unqualified mutual antagonism by 1965. This was a power struggle conducted within an essentially nationalistic framework, as the PKI and the army vied for primacy in the hotly contested national mythology of the young Indonesian state. The PKI saw themselves as the true heirs of the Indonesian national revolution of 1945–49, arguing that the army's role was only related to the primary stages of that revolution, namely the expulsion of foreign occupying forces. They conceived of the Indonesian revolution as ongoing and dynamic: the next step would be to hand more political and administrative responsibility to the people; the PKI's favoured policies – military training for the civilian population, greater civilian involvement in governmental administration and a more prominent role for trade unions – would constitute the next stages in the revolution.[13] The army, by contrast, saw both independence and the prominence of the military in the political and economic life of the country as ends in themselves. Entrenched in a position of privilege achieved and consolidated over the 1950–65 period, the army saw the PKI's reform programme as a direct attack against it.

Sukarno's ruthless suppression of the PKI uprising at Madiun in 1948 had earned him the reputation as an anti-communist. However, the 1957 elections had shown the PKI to be the second largest party in Indonesia and Sukarno took the view that the most effective way to neutralise the party would be to co-opt it, allowing the PKI a significant degree of legitimacy and influence within an overall framework in which the army maintained its role as the most significant political actor in Indonesia. The violent confrontations over land reform in the 1960s showed that this ambitious balancing act was becoming increasingly unstable. For all their progress in the 1950s and early 1960s – they were now the largest communist party outside of the established communist nations – the PKI had been unsuccessful in two important respects: they had failed to penetrate the upper echelons of the state bureaucracy and they had failed to offset the army's adamant opposition to its domestic activities.[14] Sukarno's controversial attempt to break the army's monopoly on armed force by arming the peasantry[15] has since been interpreted as a tacit acknowledgement of the impossibility of persuading the army to set aside their objections to the PKI's programme.[16] The PKI's continued progress was now contingent on preservation of an increasingly delicate balancing act. By the summer of 1965, it was clear that the Indonesian army considered the present arrangement as unsatisfactory, and it was in this atmosphere of mutual suspicion that rumours of an anti-communist coup began to circulate in August and September.

THE MUTINY, OR 'ATTEMPTED COUP', OF 30 SEPTEMBER

In the early hours of 1 October 1965, a group of middle-ranking officers, led by Lieutenant Colonel Untung, attempted to kidnap seven of the army's most senior generals. General Yani and two other generals, Haryono and Panjaitan, were killed at their homes after resisting arrest. Three others, Parman, Suprapto and Sutoyo, were successfully abducted and taken to a secret location at Lubang Buaya, south of Jakarta, where they were killed by members of the PKI youth organisation *Pemuda Rakyat*. Crucially, the most senior of the generals, General Nasution, managed to flee to safety. These killings were the first political assassinations in Indonesia since the war of independence.

Announcing themselves by radio broadcast as the '30 September Movement', the conspirators explained their actions as a pre-emptive measure to prevent the overthrow of President Sukarno by a right-wing, CIA-backed 'Council of Generals'. By the early hours of 2 October, the Movement had been defeated in Jakarta. (There was a more prolonged struggle in central Java, where the Indonesian army took about three more weeks to defeat a rebellion affiliated with the 30 September Movement.) General Suharto, excluded from the conspirators' list of targets in the mistaken belief that he was an apolitical figure who would adjust to the changed circumstances, led the army's strategic reserve in a counter-offensive which quickly outmanoeuvred the rebellious battalions of the Movement. By this point the PKI had apparently thrown its support behind the abortive Movement: a PKI march in Jogjakarta declared its support for Untung's officers, and the party's Jakarta daily newspaper, *Harian Rakjat*, published an editorial endorsing the Movement.

The nature and extent of the PKI's involvement remains unclear to this day. That the PKI offered vocal support for the Movement there is little doubt – Untung and the plotters also received assistance from PKI-affiliated transport and communications unions on 1 October. However, it is significant that the PKI made no attempt to rally its considerable mass membership behind them – a step that would have been eminently sensible if the party had really been behind the 'coup'. It would have been obvious to the PKI that the party was not in a position to take on the army in a physical confrontation and that support for an internal army putsch would risk triggering such a confrontation. The PKI had been making steady gains from its policy of cooperation with non-communist forces and it seems unlikely that the party would deliberately risk all on such a highly dangerous insurrection. The decision to throw the party's weight behind the Movement appears to have been made by a handful of individuals in the very top echelons of the party. It was a gamble that backfired with disastrous consequences.

Notwithstanding the involvement of certain senior PKI individuals and the PKI's sympathetic stance towards the Movement in its immediate wake (this would soon be revised for pragmatic reasons), the conspiracy was primarily an internal rebellion by middle-ranking officers. It comprised two groups: one was composed mainly of young central Javanese officers who were opposed to the corruption and Westernisation epitomised by the Nasution faction, but were also anti-communist; the second comprised older air force officers, opportunists who were concerned about cuts in the military budget and were dependent on Sukarno remaining in power to prolong their careers. Neither group was Marxist, but both were prepared to use the support of the PKI to achieve their respective aims.[17] Evidence put forward at the subsequent trial of the 30 September plotters does not suggest that Untung and his colleagues were conscious agents of the PKI. The initiative for the Movement appears to have come from these 'progressive officers', with the PKI latching on to them at the last moment.[18] Given the uncertainty over the extent of the PKI's connection with the 30 September conspiracy, the characterisation of this conspiracy, which was intended not to change the status quo but to protect it, as a 'coup attempt' seems something of a misnomer, although the right-wing generals inevitably treated it as such. 'Mutiny' might be a more appropriate term.[19] The mutiny ultimately failed because it did not have enough support within the army and Suharto's counter-offensive easily crushed the self-styled Movement.

Sukarno moved to play down the significance of the 30 September Movement, describing it as a mere 'ripple in the ocean of the [Indonesian national] revolution'.[20] The army, however, was determined to seize the opportunity to eliminate the PKI. Army-run newspapers gave the Movement a new label, Gestapu – a tenuous acronym for '*Gerakan Tiga Puluh September*' ('Thirtieth of September Movement'), designed to evoke comparisons with the Gestapo of Nazi Germany. No sooner had Suharto's strategic reserve restored order in Jakarta than a full-blown propaganda campaign was launched with its aim to depict the army mutiny – now routinely referred to as Gestapu – as a Chinese-backed communist attempted coup aimed at overthrowing the Indonesian state and installing a foreign-backed, atheistic and communistic dictatorship. This would provide the pretext for the wholesale destruction of the PKI, which the right-wing generals had long hoped for.

'THE RESTORATION OF SECURITY AND ORDER'

An order of 1 October appointed Major General Pranoto, a Sukarno loyalist, as Army Chief of Staff. This appointment was rejected outright by Suharto, with the support of Nasution. The army leadership had passed to Suharto after the elimination of Yani and the other leading generals on 30 September. Suharto and Nasution had been among the senior officers who had consistently voiced concerns about the rise of the PKI; they did not wish to see responsibility for dealing with Gestapu entrusted to a man so closely associated with Sukarno's PKI-friendly policies. After a five-hour meeting on 2 October, Suharto agreed to accept Pranoto's appointment on condition that the latter's role would be confined to ordinary 'daily tasks', while Suharto would be given responsibility for the 'restoration of security and order'. Matters were now entirely out of Sukarno's hands; the Suharto–Nasution clique was dictating terms. Where once he stood at the fulcrum of a delicate balance of power – with the left-wing PKI on one side and the right-wing general on the other – he was now an increasingly marginal figure. Sukarno's popularity and symbolism as a hero of the national liberation struggle meant that any attempt to oust him from office would be a gamble, but his political weakness enabled the generals to make their move. The PKI, on the back foot in the wake of the 'coup' and with only minority support within the military, was hardly in a position to make a stand on Sukarno's behalf. The erstwhile national saviour and hero of the independence struggle was now reduced to a mere figurehead, President in name only.

The army launched a propaganda campaign portraying the PKI as traitors and thugs, and raising the spectre of a militant atheist takeover in order to spur the country's Muslims into action. The message was not limited to calling for the prosecution of the ringleaders of the Gestapu or to a generic denunciation of the PKI. Instead, the army newspapers called in unequivocal terms for physical violence against PKI members, strongly emphasising a sense of religious duty. An editorial in the army newspaper *Angkatan Bersendjata* on 8 October issued a clear call to arms: 'The sword cannot be met by the Koran . . . but must be met by the sword.'[21] Army newspapers ran stories which featured a host of sordid – and completely false – details about the circumstances surrounding the murder of the generals at Lubang Buaya. Their accounts alleged that, prior to the killings, a number of women from the PKI women's organisation *Gerwani* stripped naked and performed a lascivious dance in front of PKI cadres and air force officers involved in the 30 September Movement, before proceeding to a ritual genital mutilation of the generals.

For the country's zealous (*santri*) Muslim community – already hardly well-disposed towards the PKI – the accounts provided a firm justification to pursue their long-standing vendetta in a more open and violent manner than had hitherto been feasible. In an address to a student gathering, General Nasution called for the destruction of the PKI as a national duty: 'Since they have committed treason, they must be destroyed and quarantined from all activities in our fatherland.'[22] In retribution for the activities of the 30 September plotters, the entire PKI membership – most of whom knew nothing about the 'coup' – 'should no longer be protected by the law', but instead be 'immediately smashed'.[23] This was a party that had, as recently as 1955, claimed a membership of one million people. The Muslim youth groups, who had waited for years for such an opportunity, would comprise the vanguard in the anti-communist extermination, with the army orchestrating and providing essential logistical support for the killings, in a systematic campaign of mass murder which would last several months and leave more than half a million people dead.[24]

The anti-PKI campaign began with a series of administrative measures aimed at freezing the party's political machinery; within a matter of days it progressed to open violence. Assured by the Suharto clique that they could proceed with impunity, anti-PKI civilians launched their first mass action on 8 October 1965, when a mob, mainly composed of members of Muslim youth organisations, attacked the PKI's Jakarta headquarters and set it ablaze. In Java, where a group linked with the Gestapu movement had launched a similar coup on 30 September led by Colonel Suherman, troops from the army's Special Force (RPKAD) section began arming and training anti-communist youth groups for the specific purpose of destroying the PKI.[25] In tandem with the Muslim youth groups, the army tracked down PKI members using membership lists obtained from the ransacking of PKI offices. Party leadership and rank and file alike were targeted. A tide of violence engulfed the archipelago.

The Suharto regime suppressed all discussion of the killings for many decades. In recent years, several studies have pieced together a variety of eyewitness accounts to paint a grisly picture of mutilation, thuggery and savage brutality.[26] Though technologically unsophisticated – there would be no gas chambers in Indonesia, just traditional knives or broad-bladed sickles (where the executioners were civilians) and bullets (where the executioners were soldiers) – the killings were nevertheless carried out with industrial efficiency. A detailed description is beyond the scope of this chapter, but a few examples offer a flavour of the nature of the purge. In the coastal town of Cirebon in Java, residents reported that the killers set up a guillotine which worked steadily throughout the day, day after day.[27] From Salatiga in eastern Java, an American correspondent provided the *Washington Post* with a grim account of a typical massacre:

'At each building, an army captain read names from a list, advising them of their guilt "in the name of the law". Eventually filled with 60 prisoners and piloted by a platoon of troops, the trucks drove six miles through a dark landscape of rice fields and rubber estates to a barren spot near the village of Djelok. The neighbourhood peasants had been ordered by their headman to dig a large pit the day before. The prisoners, lined up at the edge of the pit, were shot down in a matter of minutes. Some may have been buried alive.'[28]

The overwhelming majority of the victims were rural peasants who had joined the party in the hope of improving their lot. Many of their fellow citizens were drawn into the slaughter as a means of militating against possible denunciations or accidental incrimination. As a survivor of the killings, Soe Hok Gie, later recalled: 'Survival is a very strong motive for action. To succeed, one has to cover one's tracks and leave no traces. Killing is the easiest and safest way to do this, because dead people do not speak.'[29] There was some variation in the timing and scale of the violence across the archipelago: the exclusion of west Java was derived from pragmatic concerns about the threat from regionalist movements; and the relatively delayed start of systematic mass killing in Bali is attributable to the late arrival of the army there. Such variations reflect, in the words of Kenneth R. Young, 'the variable speeds at which [different elements of the Indonesian population] have been . . . integrated into the nation'.[30]

One distinctive trait of the entire campaign was the attempt to provide a veneer of legality and procedural propriety to an operation which, being committed to a programme of mass, summary, extra-judicial executions, was inherently illegal and barbaric. The generals included among their number many men who had been educated in the West and they were well aware of the importance of maintaining some semblance of respect for legal norms, however tenuously constructed. The announcement by military men that their actions were 'in the name of the law' should be seen in this light, as should the issuing to detainees of paperwork containing, by way of explanation for their arrest, the stock phrase 'directly or indirectly involved in the September 30th Movement'.[31] Indeed, Nasution's declaration that the entire PKI mass membership had 'committed treason' also borrows from the language of criminal justice in order to give the appearance of legitimacy to the army's subsequent actions. Many years later, the man with overall responsibility for the campaign, General Suharto, would be rather more candid about the nature and aims of the campaign – the strategy, he wrote, was to 'pursue, purge and destroy'.[32] A beleaguered Sukarno protested on 27 October that the army was 'burning down a house to kill a rat'.[33] The capture and killing of Aidit in November did not bring about any abatement of the killing, which carried on until April 1966, by which time the PKI was all but eliminated and Suharto was the county's *de facto* President. His accession to the presidency would be formalised in 1967. Suharto opened up the country to Western (mainly American) business, who jumped at the chance to exploit a large labour force stripped of its rights and prohibited from forming unions, as well as the country's rich natural resource, prompting *Time* magazine to describe the 1965–66 massacres, together with Suharto's rise to power, as 'the West's best news in Asia'.[34] His regime would become synonymous with authoritarianism and human rights abuse, but remained a darling of the West until well into the 1990s.

There is no single reliable death toll for the Indonesian massacres of 1965–66. Suharto's Foreign Minister, Adam Malik, sardonically remarked: 'We'd never taken a census before the coup. We didn't take one after.'[35] Numerous studies by foreign academics have arrived at widely ranging figures. There is general agreement that the lowest estimate – 150,000 deaths (from a study by Washington-based academic Donald Kirk in 1966) – is unrealistically low. There is also some degree of uncertainty at the higher end, with a number of studies arriving at a figure in the region of one million (KOPKAMTIB, the state organisation which organised the killings, claimed this death toll). A figure somewhere around half a million is accepted as realistic by most scholars.

THE ARMY VERSUS THE PEASANTRY: A CLASS WAR?

The massacres were not simply a domestic issue. The archipelago's vast mineral wealth and its geostrategic importance made Indonesia a prime foreign policy concern for the United States; Richard Nixon would later label it 'the greatest prize of all in South East Asia'.[36] Following the failure of a CIA-sponsored regionalist uprising in 1958, US policy-makers decided to play a more patient game, cultivating a strong relationship with the Indonesian army in the hope of toppling Sukarno at a later point. Instead of seeking conflict with the Indonesian military by supporting regionalist rebellions, the United States sought to co-opt the Indonesian military by providing US-based training for Indonesian officers, donating and selling weapons, and providing substantial financial aid. From 1958 to 1965, the United States spent between $10 million and $20 million on military assistance to Indonesia annually.[37] Summing up US policy during this period, the scholar John Roosa observes: 'The consistent US strategy . . . was to help the army officers prepare themselves for a violent attack upon the PKI.'[38]

This policy included an extensive training programme for Indonesian officers in military schools in the United States, such as those at Fort Bragg and Fort Leavenworth. While grooming the military for the eventual showdown with the PKI, the US government sought to destabilise the country by withholding economic aid. In his memoir, former US ambassador Howard Jones recalls the decision of President Johnson, in December 1963, to withhold economic aid, which Kennedy would have supplied 'almost as a matter of routine',[39] thus exacerbating the country's desperate economic problems, and foment anti-Sukarno feeling. By the summer of 1965, the Indonesian military were confident of their strength. Lieutenant General Yani assured the US military attaché, George Benson, that he was not worried about the PKI's apparent political ascendancy: 'We have the guns,' he said, 'and we have kept guns out of their hands. So if there's a clash, we'll wipe them out.'[40] As the killings began, US and British agents spread anti-communist propaganda to stoke up the anti-PKI feeling. Once Suharto was in charge, the aid tap was turned back on in order to give the dictator every chance of achieving domestic stability.

The catastrophe of the massacres prompted Marxists outside Indonesia to reflect critically on Sukarno's ill-fated strategy of accommodating right-wing nationalists and progressive leftists within a broad coalition. In a December 1966 broadcast, Radio Moscow highlighted the strong links between the PKI and the communist regime in China, blaming the 'Indonesian tragedy' on Chinese 'adventurism', accusing China of undermining the cause of Third World nationalism by encouraging the PKI to try to seize power in Indonesia. Expanding on this theme in a March 1967 broadcast, the Russians attacked 'the Peking dogmatists, who seek to play the national liberation movement off against other revolutionary forces', resulting in 'Indonesia's partial departure from the progressive forces of the present and its isolation'.[41] Moscow's policy of backing bourgeois, even reactionary non-communist forces provided that they would break ties with the United States, had been justified on essentially pragmatic grounds but attacked as duplicity by many in the world communist movement. In theoretical terms, the Russian argument is convincing. The PKI's success was always contingent on the support of its petty bourgeois membership; this support had proved ephemeral, as in the months after the 'coup' the petty bourgeois membership ultimately sided with the Suharto campaign, acting as a fifth column to help locate and destroy party members.[42] Echoing these sentiments, Radio Prague announced that the PKI's destruction demonstrated that 'leftist extremism is an immense danger to any progressive movement', because it 'delivers its supporters to the tender mercies of the attacking enemy'.[43]

The remaining PKI supporters were in no position to disagree. In November 1966 surviving party members in exile in China published a self-criticism entitled 'General Line of the Indonesian Revolution'. The document accepted as valid the criticisms levelled at the PKI prior to the 1965–66 period – that their policy of working with the bourgeois and reactionary elements of the state (Sukarno, the nationalists, the army) represented a fundamental deviation from orthodox Marxist thinking. But its authors insisted that the PKI leadership's overall policy was correct, citing the electoral successes of the 1950s. They claimed that the leadership's only major error was its decision to involve itself with the 'adventurist' 30 September affair. The PKI leadership had sought to remove the party's main opposition, the right-wing army leadership, in an 'opportunist gamble', which had failed disastrously.[44] This was nevertheless a significant shift: the remnants of the party were now openly refuting the assertion of their late leader DN Aidit that a 'pro-people' aspect had come to dominate Sukarno's state in the mid-1960s. In failing to recognise that Sukarno's state had remained intrinsically bourgeois and reactionary, the PKI under Aidit had 'made concessions in the theoretical field, wanting to make Marxism, which is the ideology of the working class, the property of the whole nation, which includes the exploiting classes hostile to the working class'. The self-criticism attributed this policy to a 'revisionist shift' which coincided with Aidit's leadership. In attacking Aidit's 'two aspects' theory as being completely different from a 'theory of structural reform', the remnants of the PKI were essentially falling in line with the Soviet approach of seeking to achieve socialism through parliamentary means.[45]

Notwithstanding the conspirators and opportunists in its upper echelons, the PKI was a genuinely popular movement with broad support among Indonesia's rural poor.[46] In destroying the party, the Indonesian military was not merely acting *on behalf* of a bourgeois class; to a certain extent it *was* the bourgeois class. Already at the centre of national life in the wake of the independence struggle of 1945–49, Indonesia's military had become deeply economically engaged ever since the abortive right-wing armed rebellion of 1958. Based in the city of Manado in North Sulawesi province, this secessionist uprising threatened a disintegration of the Indonesian state barely a decade after achieving independence. It was firmly put down by the central government with a series of effective bombing raids by the air force; Sukarno declared martial law and appointed army officers to manage the newly nationalised former

Dutch enterprises. They became the majority of the Indonesian bourgeoisie, alongside the traditional traders and merchants (the latter were usually affiliated to Islamic political groups). The army, therefore, had a direct interest in suppressing PKI-affiliated labour organisations which threatened to erode their profits.

A substantial minority of the officer corps was pro-leftist, but

'by 1965 there is no doubt that a substantial section of the officer corps had become oriented to business and maintaining their new commercial privilege. This factor, and the fact that most came from privileged family backgrounds or had been part of the colonial power structure, meant that their class interests as well as ideology drove them in an anti-communist direction.'[47]

Such antagonism was made all the keener by a climate of economic meltdown, as Roosa explains:

'A lot of business elites were counting on the army to take state power from Sukarno since his rule had really damaged their businesses. Nearly every foreign owned business was nationalised by 1965; workers were occupying Western-owned businesses all over the country; no new foreign investment was coming in. The business elites didn't like it and they grouped behind the army.'[48]

For the minority of officers who sided with the 30 September conspirators, their support for the PKI represented, in Robert Cribb's view, a convergence of political and professional concerns:

'Many people in the army saw the PKI as a sincere force promoting social justice. The PKI was also attractive within the military (as within society more generally) as a vehicle for promoting the interests of those who had missed out on position and power in the post-independence shake-up. Untung was about the same age as Suharto, but he was never going to be more than a Lt. Col. There was a lot of frustrated ambition which easily merged with a sense of broader social injustice.'[49]

For the majority of officers, however, the PKI were little more than upstarts – an obstacle that needed to be removed. The officers came from privileged (or at least petty bourgeois) backgrounds; the PKI's project raised the spectre of a mobilised peasantry pursuing a progressive political agenda.

Moscow may have had its own reasons for denouncing the 'adventurism' of the PKI – the USSR's credibility as a supporter of progressive movements had long been called into question by this point – but the party's vulnerability was painfully exposed after the events of 30 September. Nevertheless it would be a mistake to see the killings as a defensive response to that abortive 'coup'. As Harold Crouch has pointed out, the PKI's agenda was far from radical: prior to 30 September, the party's activities were confined to legitimate parliamentary campaigning and small-scale 'actions' aimed at encouraging the enforcement of land reform laws passed by the central government in Jakarta – the party's programme had been 'in no way "revolutionary"'.[50] In this light, Kenneth R. Young is surely right to remind us that the there was nothing inevitable about the anti-PKI purge; the mass killing was 'more than the climax of years of internal struggle within Indonesian society. It was a political choice deliberately taken by the military commanders who controlled perhaps the only instrument of State policy that could be relied upon – the army itself.'[51] It is significant that the army chose to go as far as it did – rather than merely round up the senior cadres of the PKI, they opted to annihilate the party from top to bottom, which strongly suggests that this was less about defending itself against a PKI 'coup', and more about securing its hegemony in the face of a reformist mass movement.

Indonesia's location within the broader international framework of the Cold War geopolitics, together with the important role played by the United States, means we must tread carefully when treating the Indonesian killings as a case study in the relationship between people and armies. It was clearly much more than a domestic affair. But one thing is certain: the stark imbalance of power between the PKI's defenceless peasants and an efficient and well-armed military. In the carnage that followed the abortive 'coup' or mutiny of 30 September, one can see a state responding to a perceived leftist threat with organised and merciless brutality. In this respect, and for sheer savagery and grossly disproportionate use of violence, the killings evoke the mass executions that followed the crushing of the Paris Commune by the French government in 1871.

NOTES

1. Peter Edman, *Communism à la Aidit: The Indonesian Communist Party under DN Aidit, 1950–1965*, Townsville, Queensland: James Cook University, 1987, pp. 11–12.

2. Ibid, p. 26.

3. DN Aidit, 'The road to a people's democracy for Indonesia', in DN Aidit, *Selected Works*, Volume 1, Jakarta: Jajaan Pembaruan, 1959, pp. 174–5, in Edman, *Communism à la Aidit*, p. 43.

4. DN Aidit, 'The National United Front and its history', in *Selected Works*, Volume 1, p. 54, cited in Edman, *Communism à la Aidit*, p. 43.

5. National China News Agency (NCNA), 6 December 1963, cited in Sheldon W. Simon, *The Broken Triangle: Peking, Djakarta, and the PKI* , Baltimore, MD: Johns Hopkins University Press, 1969, p. 39.

6. Report Developed at Higher Party School of the CP Central Committee, 2 September 1963, Peking: Foreign Languages Press, 1964, pp. 34–7, cited in Simon, *Broken Triangle*, p. 77.

7. DN Aidit, 'The future of the Indonesian peasant movement', *Selected Works*, Volume 1, p. 114, cited in Edman, *Communism à la Aidit*, pp. 69–70.

8. Edman, *Communism à la Aidit*, p. 71.

9. Ibid., p. 77.

10. Ibid., p. 80.

11. Ibid.

12. Simon, *Broken Triangle*, p. 103.

13. D. Hindley, *The Communist Party of Indonesia*, Berkeley, CA: University of California Press, 1964, pp. 286–97, cited in Damien Kingsbury, *The Politics of Indonesia*, Oxford: Oxford University Press, 1998, p. 59.

14. Simon, *Broken Triangle*, p. 103.

15. Senior generals rejected Sukarno's proposal of arming the peasantry to create a 'fifth force'. Instead, Sukarno endorsed an air force programme giving short training courses to civilians from the PKI's mass organisations at the air force base at Halim, in an operation that appeared to the generals to be uncomfortably close to the spirit of the 'fifth force' proposal. By September 1965, some 2,000 civilians had attended these courses. Military suspicions were raised further when the air force chief Omar Dhani embarked on a secret trip to China to discuss a Chinese offer to provide a small arms shipment. The country's most senior army figure, General Nasution, was neither consulted nor given prior notification of the visit, fuelling suspicion that the arms shipment was intended to equip the peasantry in defiance of the military's rejection of that proposal.

16. Robert Cribb and Colin Brown, *Modern Indonesia: A History since 1945*, New York: Longman, 1995, p. 95.

17. Gabriel Kolko, *Confronting the Third World: United States Foreign Policy 1945–1980*, New York: Pantheon, 1988, p. 178.

18. Harold Crouch, *The Army and Politics in Indonesia*, Singapore: Equinox, 2007, pp. 104–5.

19. Damien Kingsbury, *The Politics of Indonesia*, Oxford: Oxford University Press, 1998, p. 62.

20. Suharno's speech, 16 October 1965, cited in Crouch, *Army and Politics*, p. 162.

21. *Angkatan Bersendjata* editorial, 14 October 1965, cited in Geoffrey Robinson, *The Dark Side of Paradise: Political Violence in Bali*, New York: Cornell University Press, 1995, p. 281fn.

22. Cited in John Hughes, *The End of Sukarno: A Coup that Misfired: A Purge that Ran Wild*, Singapore: Archipelago Press, 2002.

23. Ibid., p. 201.

24. In certain regions the killing would be carried out by equally zealous members of other religious faiths – Hindus in Bali, Catholics in Sumatra and the Lesser Sundas.
25. A detailed examination of the 30 September operations in central Java appears in Crouch, *Army and Politics*, chapter 5.
26. These include John Roosa, *Pretext for Mass Murder: The September 30th Movement & Suharto's Coup d'Etat in Indonesia*, Madison, WI: University of Wisconsin Press, 2006, and Robert Cribb, ed., *The Indonesian Killings of 1965–66*, Clayton, Victoria: Monash University Centre for Southeast Asian Studies, 1990. See also Nathaniel Mehr, *'Constructive Bloodbath' in Indonesia: The United States, Britain and the Mass Killings of 1965–66*, Nottingham: Spokesman Books, 2009.
27. Hughes, *The End of Sukarno*, p. 169.
28. Stanley Karnow, 'First report on horror in Indonesia', *Washington Post*, 17 April 1966, cited in Roosa, *Pretext for Mass Murder*, pp. 25–6.
29. Soe Hok Gie, 'The mass killing in Bali', in Cribb, *Indonesian Killings*, p. 255.
30. Kenneth R. Young, 'Local and national influences in the violence of 1965', in Cribb, *The Indonesian Killings of 1965–66*, p. 96.
31. Roosa, *Pretext for Mass Murder*, p. 22.
32. Suharto, *My Thoughts, Words, and Deeds: An Autobiography*, Jakarta: Citra Lamtoro Gung Persada, 1991, p. 114, cited in Roosa, *Pretext for Mass Murder*, p. 23.
33. Cited in Roosa, *Pretext for Mass Murder*, p. 22.
34. *Time Magazine*, 15 July 1966, cited in John Pilger, *The New Rulers of the World*, London: Verso, 2002, p. 35.
35. Cited in Hughes, *The End of Sukarno*, p. 193.
36. Richard Nixon, 'Asia after Vietnam', *Foreign Affairs*, 46(1), October 1967, cited in Roosa, *Pretext for Mass Murder*, p. 15.
37. Roosa, *Pretext for Mass Murder*, p. 183.
38. Ibid., p. 182.
39. Howard Palfrey Jones, *Indonesia: The Possible Dream*, Singapore: AYU MAS PTE, 1977, p. 299.
40. Theodore Friend, *Indonesian Destinies*, Cambridge, MA: Harvard University Press, 2003, p. 102, citing personal account of George Benson.
41. Moscow Domestic Service, 16 March 1967, cited in Simon, *Broken Triangle*, p. 159.
42. Simon, *Broken Triangle*, p. 153.
43. Prague Domestic Service, 9 October 1966, cited in Simon, *Broken Triangle*, p. 163.
44. Fritjof Tichelman, *The Social Evolution of Indonesia: The Asiatic Mode of Production and its* Legacy, The Hague: M. Nijhoff, 1980, p. 244, cited in Edman, *Communism à la Aidit*, p. 114.
45. NCNA 7 and 8 July 1967, cited in Simon, *Broken Triangle*, pp. 164–6.
46. I am grateful to Robert Cribb, Max Lane and John Roosa for their input to the next couple of paragraphs, thanks to a series of email interviews conducted in January 2012.
47. Max Lane, interview January 2012.
48. John Roosa, interview January 2012.
49. Robert Cribb, interview January 2012.
50. Crouch, *Army and Politics*, pp. 155–6.
51. Young, 'Local and national influences in the violence of 1965', p. 86.

BIBLIOGRAPHY/FURTHER READING

Robert Cribb, ed., *The Indonesian Killings of 1965–66*, Clayton, Victoria: Monash University Centre for Southeast Asian Studies, 1990.

Robert Cribb and Colin Brown, *Modern Indonesia: A History Since 1945*, New York: Longman, 1995.

Harold Crouch, *The Army and Politics in Indonesia*, Singapore: Equinox, 2007.

David Easter, *Britain and the Confrontation with Indonesia*, London: Tauris Academic Studies, 2004.

Peter Edman, *Communism à la Aidit: The Indonesian Communist Party under DN Aidit, 1950–65*, Townsville, Queensland: James Cook University, 1987.

Theodore Friend, *Indonesian Destinies*, Cambridge, MA: Harvard University Press, 2003.

Marshall Green, *Indonesia: Crisis and Transformation 1965–68*, Washington, DC: Compass Press, 1990.

John Hughes, *The End of Sukarno: A Coup that Misfired: A Purge that Ran Wild*, Singapore: Archipelago Press, 2002. First published as *Indonesian Upheaval*, New York: David McKay, 1967.

Damien Kingsbury, *The Politics of Indonesia*, Oxford: Oxford University Press, 1998.

Gabriel Kolko, *Confronting the Third World: United States Foreign Policy 1945–1980*, New York: Pantheon, 1988.

Howard Palfrey Jones, *Indonesia: The Possible Dream*, Singapore: AYU MAS PTE, 1977.

John Pilger, *The New Rulers of the World*, London: Verso, 2002.

Geoffrey Robinson, *The Dark Side of Paradise: Political Violence in Bali*, New York: Cornell University Press, 1995.

John Roosa, *Pretext for Mass Murder: The September 30th Movement & Suharto's Coup d'Etat in Indonesia*, Madison, WI: University of Wisconsin Press, 2006.

Peter Dale Scott, 'The United States and the overthrow of Sukarno, 1965–67', *Pacific Affairs*, 58(2), Summer 1985, pp. 239–74.

Sheldon W. Simon, *The Broken Triangle: Peking, Djakarta, and the PKI*, Baltimore, MD: Johns Hopkins Press, 1969.

Sukarno, *Sukarno: An Autobiography*, Hong Kong: Gunung Agung, 1966.

The Civic–Military Alliance

12
'Storming the Ramparts of Tyranny': Egypt and Iraq 1945–63

Anne Alexander

'I imagined that our role was to act as the vanguard, that this role would not last more than a few hours before the masses appeared behind us, marching in serried ranks to the great goal . . . [T]he vanguard performed its task, it stormed the ramparts of tyranny, ousted the tyrant and stood by . . . it waited and waited. Endless crowds appeared, but how different reality is from the imagination: these multitudes were the scattered stragglers from a defeated army.'[1]

This chapter explores aspects of the relationship between 'the people' and 'the army' in Egypt and Iraq through the long period of revolutionary crisis which developed in the aftermath of the Second World War. In both countries popular mobilisation from below fractured the existing state, which was intimately connected to the region's dominant imperialist power, Britain. Thus the anti-colonial struggle was interwoven with waves of strikes and protests for social demands. But it was not the mass movement itself which removed the pro-British kings from power, but revolts by junior army officers in Egypt in 1952 and Iraq in 1958. It did not take long after the military seizure of power for a single leader to emerge from among the 'Free Officers': in Egypt it was Gamal Abd-al-Nasser; in Iraq, Abd-al-Karim Qasim.

The consolidation of Nasser's leadership was a pivotal moment in the history of the Middle East, setting Egypt on a trajectory of state-capitalist development which many other states in the region would soon follow.

In both Egypt and Iraq the army experienced a double fracture during this period. Inside the military institution itself, networks of rebel officers developed as a result of a combination of factors, the most important of which was the impact of the mass movement outside. The fracture in internal discipline was compounded by the temporary breakdown of the army's monopoly over the right to bear arms in the name of the people. This process went furthest in the pre-revolutionary period in Egypt, when civilian groups, particularly the Muslim Brotherhood, led a guerrilla struggle first in Palestine and then against the British occupying forces in the Canal Zone. The Brotherhood, therefore, entered the revolutionary era with thousands of activists with basic military training and a smaller number of highly experienced guerrilla fighters. In Iraq, the emergence of armed civilian movements which claimed at least part of the army's mantle as defenders of the people occurred after the 1958 Revolution with the creation of the communist-dominated Popular Resistance Forces, which mobilised nearly 40,000 men and women by the following May.[2]

Once in power, however, the 'vanguard' of military conspirators outmanoeuvred the civilian mass movement it claimed to represent in order to consolidate a permanent role for itself at the helm of the state. Despite having to negotiate with powerful and apparently independent paramilitary organisations politically dominated by civilians, the ruling officers found it relatively easy to re-establish the authority of the army and the state over sections of the people who had taken up arms to defend the national or revolutionary cause. Eventually, the military regimes in both Egypt and Iraq would embark on a trajectory of state capitalist development which redistributed some wealth from the old ruling class to the workers and peasants. The price for such small steps in the direction of social justice was the destruction of almost all forms of political organisation outside the state.

THE LONG REVOLUTIONARY CRISIS

Egypt and Iraq emerged from the Second World War into a long period of social and political crisis. In Egypt the period 1945–52 can be divided into three protest waves. The first peaked with demonstrations by students and workers calling for the evacuation of British troops from the Nile valley in February and March 1946; the second, in April–May 1948, with a national police strike and outbreak of war in Palestine; and the third is usually seen as beginning in the autumn of 1951 and climaxing with the Cairo Fire on 'Black Saturday', 26 January 1952. Accounts of political events in Iraq 1945–58 usually distinguish three protest peaks: the *wathba* ('leap') of January 1948, the *intifada* (uprising) of November 1952 and the *intifada* of November–December 1956, which was triggered by the Suez Crisis. There was a strong cumulative effect of these waves of protest on both the institutions of the state and the mass movement itself. In both countries the overthrow of the monarchy started as the aspiration of a tiny minority and then was shared by a wide spectrum of political activists. Egypt's and Iraq's rulers found themselves unable to rely on the police to contain protest and became ever more dependent on the army to suppress domestic dissent. In Egypt in 1948 troops were mobilised against striking police officers. At the height of the strike, the police marched with cheering crowds through the streets of Alexandria with loaves of bread fixed on their bayonets to symbolise their struggle for better pay and conditions. Protests, strikes and guerrilla fighting against the British in the Canal Zone intensified through the autumn and winter of 1951–52. November saw probably the largest demonstrations in the country's history until then, with at least 500,000 in Cairo and up to 200,000 in Alexandria joining a protest.[3] In Iraq, the protests in November 1956 mobilised tens of thousands across the country in conjunction with strikes and closures of shops. In some towns the demonstrations assumed insurrectionary proportions, as in Mosul where 3,000 armed protestors tried to storm the police headquarters, and in Najaf and Hayy. Although the monarchy survived – largely because the movement was relatively weak in Baghdad – the British ambassador Michael Wright wrote plaintively to Whitehall on 23 December:

'[i]n the last seven weeks we have had to struggle to prevent a break of diplomatic relations with Iraq. To avert an abrupt dissolution of the Baghdad Pact, to ward off nationalisation or fatal interference with the Iraq Petroleum Company, to keep [Prime Minister] Nuri [al-Sa'id] in power, and to try and maintain the confidence and support of those in authority here.'[4]

Three basic demands emerged from the protests of this era. The first concerned the question of national liberation. Tens of thousands of British troops were based in Egypt, which was the home to one of the British empire's most important military bases. British officials filled senior positions in the police and many government ministries. Although the number of British troops in Iraq was smaller, similarly intimate relationships existed between the Iraqi ruling class and the British establishment. The call on the British to evacuate resonated strongly with the junior officers of both the Egyptian and Iraqi armies, who resented British tutelage which they experienced on a daily basis. The second was the demand for social justice. Strikers and workers fought for better pay and conditions in the face of an inflationary spiral of rising prices and unemployment. The young officers were less sympathetic to the social demands of the era, and most were hostile – or at best suspicious – of politics which sought to erase their hard-won middle-class status through a process of social levelling. The final demand concerned changing the political institutions of the monarchy: corruption and cronyism festered at the heart of government, and the domination of parliament by large landowners allied to the Crown meant there was little scope for reform. Here again there was common ground between the Free Officers and the activists in the civilian mass movement.

THE 'FREE OFFICERS' EMERGE

The network of junior officers which overthrew King Faruq of Egypt in July 1952 was a relatively recent and loose organisation. The core of the group's command committee was linked by ties of friendship and shared political experience on the periphery of the mass movement against the British occupation, but the first leaflet in the name of the 'Free Officers' only appeared in 1949.[5] The future members of the command committee were all born between 1917 and 1922 and entered the Military Academy between 1937 and 1940. Their entry marked the first time that the officer corps, hitherto the preserve of the Turco-Circassian nobility, was opened up to middle- and lower-middle-class Egyptians. The future Free Officers were largely the sons of small landowners, peasant farmers and minor officials.[6] Muhammad Naguib, who was a generation older than the others, was not included in the Free Officers' decision-making structure until after the revolution. He was born around 1901 in Khartoum and entered the Military Academy in 1917. The Iraqi Free Officers were from similar social backgrounds as their Egyptian counterparts. Out of the 15 members of the supreme committee, nine were lower-middle-class, the sons of small landowners, traders, army officers and minor officials, four middle-class from military families, and two upper-class, the sons of wealthy landowners. One, Abd-al-Karim Qasim, was the son of a carpenter.[7] They were similar in age to the Egyptian Free Officers, but took action later and, as a consequence, were more diverse in rank.

Yet, social class also set the Free Officers apart from large sections of the mass movement, particularly the trade unions active within it. Although they were closer to Egypt's and Iraq's impoverished majority than any previous generation of officers, they were not poor themselves. By the 1940s most had achieved a good standard of living, enjoying comfortable homes, cars and other trappings of middle-class existence. Abd-al-Nasser's class prejudices were probably shared by most of the Free Officers' core leadership. On being introduced to 'Comrade Badr' (Sayyid Sulayman al-Rifa'i), the secretary-general of one of the largest of Egypt's communist groups, the Democratic Movement for National Liberation, by his friend and fellow Free Officer Khaled Mohi El Din, he was impressed until he learnt that al-Rifa'i was a mechanic. Later, whenever he wanted to score a point in the Free Officers' debates, he would dismiss Mohi El Din's arguments by saying 'his leader is a mechanic'.[8]

The core demand of the mass movement – British withdrawal – resonated with the Free Officers for a number of reasons. At a personal level, many resented their subordination to the British military hierarchy and were highly sensitive to the subaltern status of Egypt and Iraq in relation to Britain.[9] Moreover, in both countries, events in 1941 and 1942 underlined the inability of nationalist officers to provide military support for political figures who hoped to assert independent policies. On 1 April 1941 four nationalist colonels marched their troops into Baghdad and installed a neutralist government of national unity led by Rashid Ali al-Gaylani. The pro-British Regent Abd-al-Ilah fled the country and only returned after the defeat of the nationalist forces by British troops. The repression which followed left a deep impact: the Iraqi army lost nearly 5,000 men – around 2,000 officers and soldiers killed during the '30 Days War' between British and Iraqi forces in May 1941, and almost 2,900 officers dismissed in the aftermath, most of whom were young.[10] It was also in the aftermath of the revolt that troops began to be supplied with weapons without ammunition.[11] The impact of this purge was one factor in the slow revival of opposition among the armed forces over the following decades.

Most of the leading figures in the Egyptian Free Officers movement looked back to the events of 4 February 1942 as a turning point in their lives, and by extension, a turning point in Egyptian history.[12] On that day, a squadron of British tanks surrounded the Abdin palace in Cairo where King Faruq was conferring with his ministers after receiving an ultimatum from Miles Lampson, the British ambassador, telling him he must appoint a government led by the Wafd Party by 6 pm or 'face the consequences'. The British authorities suspected that the king and many at court were sympathetic to the advancing German army. Following a dramatic confrontation with Lampson, King Faruq agreed. The Wafd Party had been formed in the heat of the revolution of 1919 against the British, and for the historic party of Egyptian nationalism to make a deal with the British was profoundly shocking to many Egyptians, including the growing student movement. In the army, the incident had an even deeper impact, fatally undermining the young officers' confidence that the monarchy had the capacity to resist the British.

PALESTINE

Events in Palestine were another important point of congruence between the emerging networks of Free Officers and the broader national movements in both Egypt and Iraq. The future Free Officers shared the general mood of sympathy for the Palestinians in the Arab world. Moreover, in Egypt, several of the Free Officers were involved with the clandestine military programme organised by the Muslim Brotherhood which trained many volunteers who later joined the fighting in Palestine. The war in Palestine was a formative experience for several of the future leading figures in the Free Officers. Not only was it for most their first deployment in combat, with the conventional Arab forces which entered Palestine following the termination of the British Mandate, but also the humiliation of defeat by Zionist 'irregulars' was a blow to both their national and professional pride. Moreover, events in Palestine acted to intensify the political crisis of the *anciens régimes*, and in the case of Egypt introduced a model of guerrilla struggle into domestic politics.

As tensions rose dramatically following the UN resolution on partition in November 1947, the question confronting the Egyptian Free Officers was whether to join the volunteer fighters mobilising to defend the areas marked out for a Palestinian state. One possible route would have been by resigning from the army and joining the groups of volunteers being organised by the Muslim Brotherhood; by April 1948, its newspaper was running regular reports of the volunteers' involvement in the fighting, including front-page eulogies for young men who had died in action.[13] The decision of several Arab governments to facilitate the recruitment, training and equipment of volunteers in November 1947 provided another, officially sanctioned, avenue for action. Kamal-al-Din Husayn, one of the future members of the Free Officers' Command Council and sympathetic to the Muslim Brotherhood, took this route, joining a group of military volunteers which entered Palestine on 6 May.[14] Abd-al-Nasser hesitated to volunteer so close to the end of his course at the Staff College and remained in Cairo;[15] in the event, Abd-al-Nasser, Zakariyya Mohi El Din and Abd-al-Hakim Amer were among a group of officers who graduated early from the Staff College shortly afterwards and were sent to the front on 16 May with the regular troops. The story of their experiences in the campaign would be told time and again after the 1952 revolution in newspaper articles, speeches and memoirs: administrative chaos, defective weapons, demoralised troops. Muhammad Naguib recounts how 'supply officers, in league with the king and his cronies, had been buying substandard munitions and pocketing the difference between what they had charged the government and what they had actually paid'.[16]

The situation in Iraq differed in some respects from that in Egypt on the eve of war in that there were no civilian groups with paramilitary organisations on the scale of the Muslim Brotherhood, nor had these penetrated the Iraqi army to the same extent.[17] However, the relationship between the national movement and the officers' network over the question of Palestine was driven by the same dynamics. Iraq's rulers, like their counterparts in Egypt, saw the mobilisation of both volunteers and conventional forces in Palestine as a welcome outlet for domestic tensions. If anything, the political crisis in Iraq in early 1948 was more intense than in Egypt, following the massive street protests and strikes of the Wathbah in January and the repudiation of the Treaty of Portsmouth by a panicked Regent. Engagement in the war in Palestine also created a new group of domestic scapegoats – the local Jewish communities and the communist movement, which was condemned as pro-Zionist both because it had attracted a relatively large number of high-profile Jewish members and because of the USSR's support for the UN partition plan and later recognition of the new state of Israel.

The Iraqi cabinet authorised the mobilisation of an initial expeditionary force of 4,500 men and Iraqi forces entered Palestine as the 'junior partner' of the Arab Legion on 14 May.[18] By September the Iraqi force comprised around 18,000 men.[19] Between 15 and 22 May they were involved in failed attempts to capture the Israeli settlement of Gesher and the Crusader fortress of Belvoir, but under pressure from Arab Legion commanders they withdrew to the Jenin area, where they repelled an attack by superior Israeli forces in early June.[20] Despite inflicting a serious defeat on their adversaries at Jenin, Morris argues that the Iraqis lost an opportunity to gain a strategic advantage by pushing on towards the sea across the narrow 'waist' of Israeli-held territory, thus averting a 'nightmare scenario' for the Israelis.[21] The Free Officers who served in Palestine included Abd-al-Karim Qasim,[22] Najib al-Ruba'yi, who would later become president of the post-revolutionary Sovereignty Council, and Rif'at al-Hajj Sirri.[23] Qasim spent just over a year in Palestine (May 1948– June 1949), experiencing many of the same frustrations with the conduct of the war as his Egyptian counterparts; the Iraqi forces were poorly equipped with out-of-date guns and old ammunition, some of which dated back to the First World War.[24] The Iraqi officers returned from Palestine embittered by the experience, believing that their political leaders were at best incompetent, at worst collaborators with their imperialist and Zionist enemies.[25]

The popular mobilisation of volunteers for Palestine did not take place in an historical or political vacuum. The Egyptian Muslim Brothers had organised a wide-ranging solidarity campaign for the Palestinian uprising of 1936–37 and underwent a sharp internal debate about whether to send volunteers to Palestine in 1940, which resulted in some activists who wanted to volunteer splitting from the Brotherhood because of the position of the General Guide, Hassan al-Banna, on the issue.[26] By the end of the same decade, not only the Brotherhood's leadership, but also growing numbers of Egyptians from other political backgrounds had become convinced that the time was ripe for military action to force British evacuation and instigate political change. The mobilisation of volunteers for Palestine played a crucial role in this shift, as the Brotherhood was able to transfer military operations to the Suez Canal Zone after the armistice in Palestine in 1949. The lessons which the officers returning from Palestine drew from their experience should be set against that background.

POLICING THE PROTEST MOVEMENTS

The Egyptian and Iraqi armies were sent onto the streets to contain and sometimes repress protests; in April 1948, they confronted striking members of the police who had 'crossed over' and joined the protest movement. Key members of the Free Officers remained relatively insulated from these pressures, however, and while the social and political tensions generated by the national movements did, in the end, fracture the military hierarchy between junior and senior officers, the seizure of state power by the Free Officers was not the result of a more far-reaching breakdown of military authority.

Egyptian army officers were first confronted with the dilemma of policing large-scale protests early in 1946. Cavalry officer Ahmad

Hamrush, who later played a leading role in the Democratic Movement for National Liberation's military organisation, recalled how officers who sympathised with the protestors did not feel that they could break military discipline and join the demonstrations, but they also resolved to refuse to obey any orders to open fire they might be given.[27]

Al-Arif argues that the Iraqi army's mobilisation to repress the 1952 *intifada*, which was accompanied by the installation of a general as prime minister, had a similarly radicalising effect on the Iraqi officer corps.[28] As speeches to the crowds by activists during the Iraqi uprising of 1948 illustrate, protestors sometimes attempted to sharpen the political tensions within the army and appealed to the troops to side with them against the government – or at least to refuse to obey orders to attack protesters.[29] Reports of the 'Evacuation Day' protests in Cairo on 21 February 1946 also describe the crowds hailing 'the army of the people' and the impact of such slogans on troops patrolling the streets.[30] Some of the core group of the Egyptian Free Officers were insulated, however, from the dilemmas of policing the protest movement by their military roles. Abd-al-Nasser, for example, taught in the Military Academy between 1943 and 1948, then took a position at the Staff College. Loyalty to the principle that army officers should not engage directly in civilian politics exerted a strong influence even on figures such as Khaled Mohi El Din, who was a student at the Faculty of Commerce between 1947 and 1951, seconded from the Cavalry Corps.[31]

THE EVOLUTION OF THE FREE OFFICERS' ORGANISATIONS

The crystallisation of the Free Officers' organisations in both Egypt and Iraq was affected at several levels by the developments in the civilian national movements. Moreover, a number of organised currents within the national movements set out to recruit officers and soldiers and construct networks of their own within the armed forces. There were clandestine groupings of different political hues operating in both armies between 1945 and the July Revolutions. One feature which linked the Free Officers' groups in both Egypt and Iraq was their assertion of political autonomy from the civilian national movement, even while maintaining operational relationships with a range of civilian organisations.

Accounts of the development of the Free Officers' movement in Egypt written in the wake of the revolution tended to present an image of a fully-formed underground network existing prior to the war in Palestine. Anwar al-Sadat, in *Revolt on the Nile*, even claimed the group had been founded as early as 1938.[32] Abd-al-Nasser's memoirs of the war in Palestine referred to the Free Officers' Command Committee as having been in existence for some time before hostilities broke out.[33] Later historians, however, have generally argued that the Free Officers came together as a coherent organisation no earlier than 1949.[34] In his memoirs, Mohi El Din describes how, not long after the end of the war in Palestine, Abd-al-Nasser and a handful of close friends met regularly to discuss the way forward. Five attended the first meeting: Abd-al-Nasser, Abs-al-Munim and Kamal-al-Din Husayn (who were close to the Muslim Brotherhood), Hasan Ibrahim and Mohi El Din. Abd-al-Nasser also added the name of his close friend, Abd-al-Hakim Amr. At first the discussion ranged over the grievances of the national movement – the weak governments, the corruption of the king, the arrogance of the British. But the experience of war in Palestine had thrown these questions into sharper relief. Abd-al-Nasser asked his colleagues, 'If we were defeated by groups of Israeli volunteers, how shall we face the British? How shall we liberate the country?'[35]

It took longer for opposition to crystallise among Iraqi officers than in Egypt. Batatu credits Rif'at al-Hajj Sirri with being 'the real initiator of the Free Officers' movement'.[36] Along with Rajab Abd-al-Majid, on whose memoirs much of Batatu's account is based, Sirri began organising cells of 'Free Officers' in 1952, inspired by the success of the Egyptian revolution. By 1956 a number of key figures had been drawn into their growing network of contacts, including Naji Talib and Wasfi Tahir. The group suffered a temporary setback when Sirri was demoted and placed under surveillance in the summer of 1956 after his activities were discovered by the police. Abd-al-Majid's cells were not affected, and by December 1956 a 'Supreme Committee' had taken shape.[37] At its preliminary meetings the committee appointed a chairman and secretary, and adopted a set of rules for membership. The movement would be organised in clandestine cells and membership was open only to officers.[38]

Simultaneously with the emergence of the group which Sirri initiated, another group of dissident officers began to coalesce. According to Isma'il al-Arif, he recruited Qasim, who was one of his former instructors in the Military Academy, to the group in September 1954, saying that there was a revolutionary current within the army which aimed to overthrow the monarchy and replace it with a 'genuine popular democratic system'. The two groups of officers came together in 1957. The Supreme Committee sent Wasfi Tahir to approach Qasim about joint work in April that year, and the following month Qasim and Abd-al-Salam Arif were co-opted onto the committee.[39] In July 1957 the Supreme Committee agreed that Qasim, as the highest-ranking officer, should become chairman. November 1957 saw the addition of around 80 junior officers to the movement, who brought with them their own organisation and nine-member committee. Between November 1957 and the coup of 14 July 1958 the Supreme Committee's main concern was selecting the opportunity to strike. One problem was the lack of ammunition as the authorities guarded stores carefully, fearing a coup; another was how to ensure the simultaneous capture of the king, crown prince and Nuri al-Sa'id. The possible armed intervention by one of the other Baghdad Pact powers also worried the committee, and, through Siddiq Shanshal of the Independence Party, it approached Abd-al-Nasser and the Soviet ambassador in Cairo for reassurance on this point.[40]

RELATIONSHIP WITH THE NATIONAL MOVEMENTS

The political views of the core group of the Egyptian Free Officers were diverse. Vatikiotis notes that there were 'perhaps as many shades of political belief as there were members of the Free Officers Executive'.[41] Anwar al-Sadat's colourful career as a military conspirator began with his involvement in a failed plot to smuggle the Egyptian Chief-of-Staff, Aziz al-Misry, through British lines to join the German forces led by Rommel.[42] After the war he also worked with the Muslim Brotherhood. Other members of the Free Officers were Muslim Brothers or sympathisers. Another member of the Brotherhood resigned from the command committee after it rejected his proposal to bring the Free Officers' organisation under the control of the Muslim Brotherhood's Guidance Council.[43] On the command committee, Khaled Mohi El Din had briefly joined the Muslim Brotherhood, but later developed a relationship with communist activists in the Democratic Movement for National Liberation.[44] Ahmad Hamrush, another member of the Free Officers, though not of the command committee, had much closer links with the DMNL, as organiser of the group's network of army officers and their representative on the central committee.[45] Abd-al-Nasser was briefly involved with the Muslim Brotherhood's secret military training programme and cultivated extensive personal contacts with a wide range of political activists. Among the Iraqi Free Officers there is less evidence of individual political activity. Some members had participated in Rashid Ali's movement of 1941 and Wasfi Tahir had a personal connection to the Communist Party,[46] but these seem to have been the exceptions.

Relations between the Egyptian Free Officers and the national movement never really developed into formal inter-organisational ties. Rather, there were lines of communication associated with particular individuals. Individuals in the Free Officers regarded these relationships in contrasting ways – Mohi El Din, for example, saw his role in facilitating contacts with the DMNL as of mutual benefit to both organisations. While he accepted the other officers' decision that their organisation should remain independent, he expected a degree of reciprocity in their relations.[47] Abd-al-Nasser, by contrast, was more instrumental in his approach to external organisations. He was prepared to use other groups' practical expertise in propaganda, and accept their support, without feeling any commitment to reciprocate once the Free Officers had taken power.[48] The command committee agreed with Abd-al-Nasser in his insistence that the Free Officers should remain independent of other groups.

It is not clear, however, that the Egyptian Free Officers' suspicions of other parties represented any kind of considered theory that the army should place itself permanently at the head of the national movement and the state. Some of the seeds of this ideology of leadership were present, but they did not germinate until after the seizure of power. Vatikiotis argues that the Free Officers were driven by the collapse of civilian authority in the face of popular protests and rioting on 'Black Saturday', 26 January 1952; their growing dissatisfaction with the competence of the Army Command and, crucially, by the threat to their own safety as the authorities came closer to discovering the identity of their leading members.[49] Joel Gordon suggests that the Free Officers theorised their role as leaders of the nation during their first few years in power.[50]

In Iraq the Free Officers developed a much clearer sense of the role that they should play in the post-revolutionary state. Unlike their Egyptian counterparts, the Supreme Committee approached the revolution having already decided to end the monarchy and form a cabinet in which officers would dominate, or at least control, the key portfolios.[51] Unlike Egypt, the Supreme Committee was able to develop a formal relationship with the National United Front, which was set up in 1957 to bring the major opposition groups together.[52] As in Egypt, the Iraqi Free Officers had no intention of deferring to external organisations and reserved the right to move against the regime as they saw fit. The Supreme Committee rejected the proposal that the National United Front of the principal opposition forces send an observer to the Committee's meetings. In fact, the organisations active in the army, such as the Ba'ath Party and the communists, deferred to the Free Officers' lead. The Ba'athists instructed their members to join the Free Officers and the communists reduced the visibility of the Union of Soldiers and Officers, which they dominated.[53] Although the Supreme Committee attempted to keep the civilian opposition organisations at arm's length, Qasim cultivated personal contacts with both the National Democratic Party and the communists, but there was no assumption on his part that either he or the Free Officers should defer to other groups before making decisions. In fact, in the aftermath of the revolution, Qasim proved effective at playing the civilian opposition groups against his military rivals, while all the time promoting himself as the supreme political arbiter in the new state.

THE JULY REVOLUTIONS

In July 1952 the Egyptian Free Officers seized power in a bloodless coup. Although the streets were empty as the small group of conspirators moved against the army's top hierarchy, they filled with crowds hailing the army's 'blessed movement' in the days that followed. Almost exactly six years later, Abd-al-Salam Arif and Abd-al-Karim Qasim led small numbers of troops to seize the Royal Palace in Baghdad and proclaimed the overthrow of the Iraqi monarchy. Events took a bloodier turn in Iraq than in Egypt, with the killing of the king, other members of the royal household and Nuri al-Sa'id, architect of the Baghdad Pact. Significantly, mass protests played a crucial role in the success of the Iraqi revolution, with huge crowds filling the streets in response to Abd-al-Salam Arif's radio appeal for demonstrators to storm the 'palaces of slavery and humiliation'.[54]

Although the initiative in both countries came directly from dissident army officers, there were broad expectations that political and social change would follow. In Egypt, the Free Officers moved quickly to contain and limit attempts by groups outside the state to force the pace of that change. Within weeks of taking power they crushed a strike at Kafr al-Dawwar, where textile workers had revolted against a corrupt management connected to the palace, despite (or more likely because of) workers' insistence that they were acting in support of the goals of the revolution.[55] Yet a few weeks later they enacted reforms redistributing land to small farmers at the expense of the large landowners, who formed the backbone of the political elite under the monarchy.

In Iraq, expectations of change reached an even higher pitch. In his monthly report for August 1958, the British Consul-General in Basra noted with alarm the widespread belief among Iraqi Port Authority workers that the revolution marked a fundamental shift in the relationship between 'the people' and the state.[56] Moreover, unlike in Egypt, the revolution of July 1958 in Iraq opened a period of massive popular mobilisation from below, peaking with a march on 1 May 1959, which brought hundreds of thousands onto the streets of Baghdad in sympathy with communist demands for a place in government. A key difference from the situation in Egypt was that a split appeared among the dissident officers within weeks of their seizing power. In addition, the conflict between Abd-al-Salam Arif and Abd-al-Karim Qasim mapped onto a major ideological cleavage in post-revolutionary Iraq, with Arif leading the pan-Arab Nationalists who supported Gamal Abd-al-Nasser in Egypt and Qasim heading an 'Iraqist' Nationalist faction.

In both countries the ruling officers reached out to civilian allies in the early post-revolutionary period. In Egypt the Muslim Brotherhood formed a tactical alliance with the Free Officers against its leftist and liberal rivals. In fact, the Free Officers were forced to tolerate the Brotherhood's large paramilitary organisation for several years while they built up alternative, 'official' paramilitary groups and worked on the tensions within the Brotherhood's leadership in order to paralyse the organisation. In Iraq, Abd-al-Salam Arif worked closely with the pan-Arab Nationalists and particularly the Ba'ath Party, while Qasim formed a close relationship with the Iraqi Communist Party. In particular, the emergence of the paramilitary Popular Resistance Forces, which were composed of civilian volunteers, appeared to show a dramatic growth in communist influence during the first year of the revolution. However, in both cases it was the ruling officers who imposed their authority, and the authority of the state, over these 'popular' paramilitary formations.

'BROTHERS-IN-ARMS?' THE MUSLIM BROTHERHOOD AND THE FREE OFFICERS

On the eve of the July Revolution the Muslim Brotherhood had substantial experience in various types of paramilitary activity.

There were small numbers of members organised in the 'Special Section', responsible for bombing campaigns and military attacks on domestic targets during the 1940s, a wider group of fighters who had gained experience in guerrilla warfare in Palestine and the Canal Zone, and a much larger cohort of members and supporters who had attended basic military 'training sessions' and parades. In 1948, the Brotherhood claimed a membership of 40,000 for its Rover Scouts, around the time of a clash with the authorities which saw many of the Scouts arrested. The Rovers were active in guerrilla fighting in the Canal Zone in 1951–52, although their numbers had fallen to around 7,000 in 1953.[57] These bodies of armed men presented the Free Officers with a dilemma. On the one hand, they were determined to avoid sparking strikes, mass protests and uncontrollable clashes with the British. On the other, the Brotherhood's forces could be a useful bargaining chip in negotiations with the British over withdrawal from the Canal Zone and a deterrent to other potential civilian challengers to the Free Officers' authority.

The Free Officers worked quickly to bring the mass paramilitary training of civilian volunteers under state control. They launched a state-sponsored training programme for volunteers in the spring of 1953 with an emphasis on enrolling large numbers and completing their training as quickly as possible, with the likely aim of building up sufficient forces both to impress British officials with Egyptian preparedness for war and to create a counterbalance to the Brotherhood's forces. At the same time, the ruling officers made repeated requests to the Brotherhood's leaders to close down their training camps and use army facilities instead.[58] They also demanded the closure of the 'Special Section'.[59] By the anniversary of the revolution Kamal-al-Din Husayn, the officer in charge of the volunteer training programme, was able to report that facilities were now available to train all young Egyptian men. The army newspaper *Al-Tahrir* announced on 15 July: 'The people will fight the British, and not the army alone.'[60] In the anniversary parade, recently graduated commandos marched with black 'death's head' flags through the streets beside the Muslim Brotherhood's red banners with the symbol of two crossed swords.

Behind the scenes, relations between the Brotherhood and the ruling officers were becoming strained. Abd-al-Nasser was also taking an increasingly proactive role in faction-fighting within the Brotherhood's leadership, backing conspirators within the organisation who planned to overturn the leadership of General

Guide Hasan al-Hudaybi.[61] The fate of the Special Section was a key issue here, with Al-Hudaybi leading moves to rein in its autonomy and reduce its influence. Dramatic events unfolded in the autumn of 1953. The second in command of the Special Section was killed in an explosion at his home, prompting rumours that he had been murdered to prevent him handing over details of the Section's membership to the General Guide.[62] Al-Hudaybi's opponents then attempted to seize the Brotherhood's headquarters and demanded his resignation. However, the Brotherhood's general assembly on 28 November gave vocal support to Al-Hudaybi and several key dissidents were expelled.[63]

October 1953 saw the publication of a law creating the military regime's own paramilitary forces, the National Guard. An official guide to the first year of the Egyptian Republic, published in 1954, shows battalions of National Guardsmen and women parading in the streets with a black skull and cross bones banner similar to that carried by newly trained commandos in the 1953 parades on the anniversary of the revolution. According to the guide, the National Guard had been formed 'not only to act as a rearguard to the regular army, ensuring its supply lines and means of transport, but also to prepare, when necessary, reserve forces familiar with modern weapons'. A second aim was to revitalise Egypt's youth: 'to reawaken their latent energy, mould their character and give them the virile qualities which make a people great'. Enrolment in the Guard would also keep young people occupied 'in activities other than faction fights or street demonstrations, however justified these might appear at times to be'. Volunteers were to be Egyptian, aged between 17 and 40, physically fit and of good character. Young women volunteers were given a prominent place in descriptions of the Guard's activities and, like their male counterparts, took part in parades and were trained to handle weapons.[64]

The first few months of 1954 saw further dramatic ebbs and flows in the Brotherhood's relationship with the Free Officers. In January the Brotherhood was banned, following a clash between its students and supporters of the state-sponsored political party, the Liberation Rally at Cairo University. Among the charges laid by the officers was that the Brotherhood's leadership had sold out the national cause to the British in secret meetings with the British Embassy's Oriental Counsellor, Trefor Evans.[65] In February and March the officers themselves experienced a traumatic split between Muhammad Naguib and Gamal Abd-al-Nasser. The breakdown of unity at the top of the regime opened an opportunity for a resurgence of the mass mobilisations in the streets. The Brotherhood initially appeared to back Naguib, but its followers melted away from the streets after its leadership reached an accommodation with Abd-al-Nasser which left the other civilian opponents of continued military rule isolated. The tactical alliance between the officers and the Brotherhood did not last long, however. As Abd-al-Nasser moved towards agreement on British withdrawal from the Canal Zone, the Brotherhood became increasingly impatient with what it regarded as a shabby deal. By the summer of 1954 it was actively campaigning against the Canal Zone Agreement and had apparently resumed guerrilla attacks on British installations. According to British reports, the Egyptian authorities carried out mass arrests of Brotherhood members, raided the organisation's headquarters and confiscated arms caches.[66]

An assassination attempt in Alexandria on 26 October against Abd-al-Nasser was blamed on the Brotherhood. Six Brotherhood members, including the Deputy General Guide, Abd-al-Qadir Awda,[67] were hanged following a military trial. The General Guide himself escaped the gallows when his sentence was commuted to imprisonment. Although the Brotherhood would outlive Abd-al-Nasser, the organisation took nearly 20 years to recover from the catastrophe of 1954.

IRAQ: 'POPULAR RESISTANCE' AND THE 'SOLE LEADER'

The formation of the Popular Resistance Forces in Iraq was a communist initiative. The danger of external intervention to restore the monarchy weighed on the communist leaders' minds in the early days of the revolution. After the overthrow of the Mussadeq government in Iran in 1953 and the fall of the Nabulsi cabinet in Jordan in 1956 such an action by British or US forces was seen as a real threat. They approached the problem at three distinct levels: first, by privately and publicly appealing to the new government to create a 'Popular Resistance Force' to defend the republic; second, by encouraging citizens to organise themselves into Committees for the Defence of the Republic and Popular Resistance groups; and third, by instructing their own members to lead these groups and ensure that they follow party directives. To get their message across to the government, the Central Committee wrote to Qasim on 14 July warning him:

'We will do well to remember at this moment the government of Mussadeq which, in its eagerness not to provoke the enemy, withheld its confidence from the people and refrained from arming them, lulling them instead into tranquillity, with the result that it fell under the blows of a handful of ruffians and thieves.'[68]

Meanwhile, communist activists were including calls for the formation of Popular Resistance forces in the messages of support for the new government.[69] At the same time Communist Party leaflets urged citizens to organise themselves to defend the republic:

'Multitudes of our heroic Iraqi people: the future of our movement depends on your struggle and your alertness. Start therefore with the formation of Republic Defence Committees in the factories and shops, in the villages and popular institutions. Organise the Popular Resistance Detachments and prepare to face any emergency.'[70]

Recalling the role of the Popular Resistance in Egypt during the Tripartite Attack of 1956, the statement emphasised the need to learn from the mistakes made by Mussadeq in Iran and Nabulsi in Jordan. Finally, an internal party circular argued that the independence of the Popular Resistance Forces from the state would be vital to their success:

'The People's Resistance . . . must shape itself into a kind of popular power, exercising its responsibilities wisely [while] carefully avoiding collision with the government and helping it in every patriotic step. But this should in no way involve an impairment of the authority of its own leading bodies which is decisive as regards the units of the Resistance.'[71]

In fact, both the threat of an internal counter-revolution and the danger of external intervention receded rapidly. There was no serious attempt to organise armed resistance to the revolution, and, despite the landing of US troops in Lebanon, the new republic quickly received international recognition. The government now asserted its control over the Popular Resistance Forces, announcing the creation of an official body with that name on 17 July, but banning the organisation of such forces independently of the state. A proclamation by the Armed Forces General Command announced that 'popular resistance units' would be formed 'to stand side by side with the army in the defence of the homeland', but warned against obeying any call not issued by them.[72] Despite this warning, 'unofficial' popular resistance recruiting centres continued to function for at least several more days, prompting a further, more explicit proclamation by Qasim on 20 July:

> 'Some citizens have begun to open offices for a popular resistance as a gesture of support for the blessed national movement. While appreciating this noble feeling, we warn them against continuing such actions, which demand organised effort and administration, which they cannot ensure.'[73]

A law creating an 'official' popular resistance was published on 1 August. It described the new forces as 'popular military organisations' attached to the Ministry of Defence whose function was to train citizens 'to aid the regular military units of civil defence in the maintenance of internal security and the defence of the country'. Recruitment was open to male and female Iraqi volunteers aged between 15 and 50, and to volunteers from other Arab countries; they would be subject to military discipline and 'to the General Command of the Armed Forces'.[74]

In July 1958, the communists decided against an overt challenge to the government over the closure of the 'unofficial' PRF recruiting centres; instead, activists threw themselves into mobilising support for the 'official' PRF, launched at the beginning of August. An appeal from the League for the Defence of Women's Rights calling for women's enlistment in the PRF was broadcast by Baghdad Radio on 9 August, reminding them that their foremothers had borne arms during the revolution of 1920: 'Women constitute half the people. Let them prove to the people their strength and their desire to participate in the sacred armed struggle. O women citizens, you can carry arms as well as men.'[75]

In Basra, the local branch of the League and the Union of Students called for students to enlist in the PRF.[76] A statement from the National United Front,[77] distributed in the markets and published in the local press at the end of August, demanded that the PRF should begin its operations in Basra immediately.[78]

The launch of the PRF took place in a political context which was rapidly changing. The growing rift between Qasim and Arif meant that both men were manoeuvring to win support within the state and in the wider political arena. At first both were enthusiastic in their support for the idea of an 'official' PRF. Arif told crowds in

Kut, 'Let imperialism know that we shall defend every inch of this blessed homeland. A popular resistance will oppose imperialism, supported by God and the people. A popular resistance organisation with weapons and ammunition will soon be set up.'[79]

A few days later Qasim addressed rallies outside the Ministry of Defence, telling the crowds on 4 August, 'All of you, men and women, will soon learn about the Popular Resistance Forces which will defend the Iraqi Republic alongside the army and the people of this country.'[80]

In the autumn the conflict between Qasim and Arif was temporarily resolved in Qasim's favour; Arif was dismissed from his posts in September and arrested in November, accused of attempting to assassinate Qasim. Leading Communist Party activists, speaking at mass rallies organised by the Peace Partisans across the country, now publicly hailed Qasim as the 'sole leader'.[81] To the communists' pan-Arab nationalist rivals, the presence of PRF checkpoints across Baghdad and the zeal of PRF volunteers in searching for 'spies and saboteurs' were confirmation of the advance of communist influence in the state.[82] The PRF also played a prominent role in the suppression of the attempted coup in Mosul in March 1959 by Colonel Abd-al-Wahhab al-Shawwaf. The murder of leading communist activists, including the peace partisan activist Kamil Qazanchi, by the rebel forces led to violent reprisals. Communist-led forces were accused of the summary execution of 17 people at Damalaja.[83]

In May 1959, Colonel Taha Barimini, commander of the PRF, outlined the current state of the force, saying that its total strength had reached around 35,000 members, including 4,000 women. New recruits went through a training programme of two hours a day for 13 days, during which they learnt how to use a rifle and bayonet, grenades and commando tactics. Women volunteers went through the same course with the addition of first aid. Army officers, assisted by NCOs, were responsible for the training, which also included 'lectures in good citizenship given by army officers, not by civilian politicians; and training in security, including methods of detecting spies and saboteurs'.[84]

The PRF was concentrated in Baghdad and only grew slowly elsewhere. The British military attaché in Baghdad estimated a total force of 37,000 by May 1959, including 25,000 men and 8,000 women trained in the Baghdad area. PRF units were created in the southern area, covering Basra, Ashar and Maqil in August 1958, and by May 1959 around 3,000 men had been trained. A force was set up in Mosul in February 1959 which produced 1,000 trainees. In May 1959 training began in Sa'diyya, and was expected to start shortly in other areas of Diyala province, and PRF units were expected to be set up in Kirkuk and Ramadi.[85]

By early May, communist influence had reached its peak. In the trade union movement, the party appeared to have won both official backing and rank-and-file support. On 1 May, International Workers' Day, vast numbers of trade unionists joined a procession through Baghdad, which was addressed by Qasim. Communist sources claimed that one million marched that day; Batatu puts the figure at 300,000, still a vast number in a city of around one million.[86] The trade union delegations taking part in the march attested to the rapid growth of the labour movement: one source lists 94 organisations, including 19 unions representing manual workers, five unions representing artisans and 22 unions representing service sector workers and the professions. The Communist Party's roots in the state apparatus itself were given visible shape in the form of 18 delegations representing government departments and educational establishments, and 15 delegations from the army, air force and police.[87] Despite this show of strength in the institutions of the state, the Communist Party was still unrepresented in government, and on the 1 May demonstration tens of thousands of marchers could be heard chanting: 'Long live the leader Abd-al-Karim Qasim – The Communist Party in the government is a mighty demand.'[88]

Qasim rebuffed the communists' call for inclusion in government and quickly set in motion a purge, starting with the armed forces, but extending to other state institutions, including the PRF.[89] The party's dependence on Qasim and its energetic promotion of the cult of 'sole leader' made it difficult to break with him. Meanwhile, hostile forces within the state used Qasim's change in position to launch a systematic campaign against the communists.

CONCLUSION

Why did the revolutionary crisis of 1945–63 not result in a deeper shift in the relationship between the army and the people? This chapter suggests there were three main reasons. The first was the relatively limited and shallow nature of the fracture *within* the army: while the 1952 and 1958 revolutions certainly represented a revolt against the military hierarchy by junior officers, the Egyptian and Iraqi armies did not break down further along class lines. This is connected to the second reason: unlike Russia in 1917 or Portugal in 1974, the massive popular protests and waves of strikes did not create institutions which attempted to bind military rebels to the authority of an embryonic alternative state power. In fact, the leaders of the military conspirators insisted on maintaining their independence of the civilian organisations of the pre-revolutionary opposition and categorically rejected any attempts to undermine their authority over the rank-and-file soldiers. The third factor was the perspective taken by the civilian organisations, which allied themselves to some degree with the ruling officers. For different reasons both the communists and the Muslim Brotherhood were unable to maintain an independent political organisation capable of challenging the post-revolutionary regimes. In Egypt the Brotherhood was paralysed by an internal factional struggle, which meant that when it did attempt to break with Abdel-Nasser, its leadership was outmanoeuvred and destroyed. The communists in Iraq built up the cult of Abd-al-Karim Qasim as the 'sole leader', defended him and the revolutionary regime against an attempted military coup in Mosul in March 1959, but retreated from confrontation with Qasim over communist representation in the government, after which their influence rapidly declined.

NOTES

1. Gamal Abd-al-Nasser, *Falsafat al-thawra*, 9th edition, Cairo: Dar al-Sha'b, n.d., p. 22.
2. There were different traditions of civilians taking up arms against the Iraqi state, of course, such as the recurrent rural uprisings in the south of Iraq and the long-running armed struggle by the Kurds in the north.
3. *The Times*, 15 November 1951.
4. Papers of the British Foreign Office, The National Archives, Kew, London (henceforth FO) 371/121647, 'Baghdad Telegram 1646 to Foreign Office', 23 December 1956.
5. Khaled Mohi El Din, *Memories of a Revolution*, Cairo: American University in Cairo Press, 1995, p. 49.
6. P. J. Vatikiotis, *The Egyptian Army in Politics: Pattern for New Nations?*, Bloomington, IN: Indiana University Press, 1961, p. 46.
7. Hanna Batatu, *The Old Social Classes and the Revolutionary Movements of Iraq*, Princeton, NJ: Princeton University Press, 1978, pp. 778–81. Qasim himself frequently referred to his humble origins, particularly when addressing workers.
8. Mohi El Din, *Memories*, pp. 39–40.
9. See ibid., pp. 12–14.
10. Ayad al-Qazzaz, 'The Iraqi–British war of 1941: a review article', *International Journal of Middle East Studies*, 7(4), 1976, pp. 595–6.
11. Ibid., p. 596.
12. See Mohi El Din, *Memories*, p. 16. A different perspective is offered by Ahmad Hamrush, who graduated from the Military Academy in 1942 and

later represented the DMNL's military section on the organisation's central committee. Although he was not yet a member of any left-wing group, he saw the return of the Wafd as 'something natural, because it was the party which represented the majority'. Ahmad Hamrush, interview, Cairo, 8 September 1996, in Arabic.

13. See *Al-Ikhwan al-Muslimin*, 11 April 1948.
14. Gamal Abdul Nasser and Walid Khalidi, 'Nasser's memoirs of the first Palestine war', *Journal of Palestine Studies*, 2(2), Winter 1973, p. 5.
15. Nasser, *Memoirs*, p. 5.
16. Muhammad Naguib, *Egypt's Destiny*, London: Victor Gollancz, 1955, p. 17.
17. There were, however, two models of armed struggle unconnected to the Palestinian question: the guerrilla tactics adopted by the Kurdish nationalist parties and the peasant uprising.
18. Benny Morris, *1948: A History of the First Arab-Israeli War*, New Haven, CT and London: Yale University Press 2008, pp. 246–7.
19. Ibid., p. 248.
20. Ibid., pp. 249–50.
21. Ibid., p. 251.
22. Shamil Abd-al-Qadir, *Abd-al-Karim Qasim, al-bidaya wal nihaya*, Amman: Al-Ahliyya, 2002, p. 31.
23. Ibid.
24. Morris, *1948*, p. 245.
25. Abd-al-Qadir, *Abd-al-Karim Qasim*, p. 34; Al-'Arif, Isma'il, *Asrar thawrat 14 tamuz wa ta'sis al-jumhuriyya fil Iraq*, London: Lana, 1986, p. 71.
26. Abd-al-Fattah Muhammad El Awaisi, *The Muslim Brothers and the Palestine Question*, London: Tauris Academic Studies, 1998, pp. 95–6.
27. Ahmad Hamrush, interview with the author, Cairo, 9 September 1996.
28. Al-Arif, *Asrar*, p. 75.
29. Batatu, *The Old Social Classes*, p. 553.
30. Archives of the Communist Party of Great Britain, National Museum of Labour History, Manchester, CP/CENT/INT/56/03, Untitled report from Cairo, 22 February 1946 (5 pm).
31. Mohi El Din, *Memories*, p. 31.
32. Jean Lacouture, *Nasser*, London: Secker & Warburg, 1973, p. 44.
33. Nasser and Khalidi, 'Nasser's memoirs', p. 5.
34. See Vatikiotis, *The Egyptian Army in Politics*, p. 60; Mohi El Din, *Memories*, p. 34.
35. Mohi El Din, *Memories*, p. 45.
36. Batatu, *The Old Social Classes*, p. 770.
37. Ibid., p. 776.
38. Ibid., p. 777.
39. Ibid., pp. 787–8.
40. Ibid., p. 795.
41. Vatikiotis, *The Egyptian Army in Politics*, p. 68.
42. Anwar al-Sadat, *Revolt on the Nile*, London: Allen Wingate, 1957, pp. 36–8.
43. Joel Gordon, *Nasser's Blessed Movement: Egypt's Free Officers and the July Revolution*, Oxford: Oxford University Press, 1992, p. 80.
44. Mohi al-Din, *Memories*, pp. 26–33.
45. Ahmad Hamrush, interview, Cairo, 8 September 1996, in Arabic.
46. Batatu, *The Old Social Classes*, p. 793.

47. Mohi El Din, *Memories*, pp. 54–63.
48. According to Mohi El Din and Rif'at al-Sa'id, after the Free Officers seized power in July 1952, Abd-al-Nasser arrested the DMNL's printers, whom he knew from his frequent meetings with them to collect the leaflets they had printed for the Free Officers. Mohi El Din, *Memories*, p. 63; Rif'at al-Sa'id, interview, Cairo, 12 September 1996, in Arabic.
49. Vatikiotis, *The Egyptian Army in Politics*, p. 68.
50. Gordon, *Nasser's Blessed Movement*, pp. 191–2.
51. Batatu, *The Old Social Classes*, p. 795.
52. Ibid., p. 794.
53. Ibid., p. 794.
54. *Summary of World Broadcasts*, Part IV, Radio Baghdad, 14 July 1958.
55. Joel Beinin and Zachary Lockman, *Workers on the Nile: Nationalism, Communism, Islam and the Egyptian Working Class, 1882–1954*, London: IB Tauris, 1988, pp. 425–7.
56. FO 371/133068 EQ1015/232, 'Basra monthly summary for August', Consulate General, Basra, p. 1.
57. Richard Mitchell, *The Society of the Muslim Brothers*, London: Oxford University Press, 1969, p. 203.
58. FO 371/108319 JE 1016/12 'The Moslem Brotherhood (Ikhwan el Muslimin) under the Naguib regime', report, n.d., enclosed with letter, Stephenson to Eden, 24 March 1954, p. 1.
59. Mitchell, *The Society of the Muslim Brothers*, p. 115.
60. *Summary of World Broadcasts*, 381, 21 July 1953, Cairo, 1830, 14 July 1953; see also Cairo, 1830, 7 July 1953, *Summary of World Broadcasts*, 379, 14 July 1953.
61. FO 371/102706 JE 1015/129, Letter, Charles Duke, Cairo to Roger Allen, FO, 17 September 1953.
62. Mitchell, *The Society of the Muslim Brothers*, pp. 122–4.
63. Ibid., pp. 122–4.
64. *L'An I de la République d'Egypte*, pp. 137–8. My translation from the French.
65. Evans' account of the discussions with the Brotherhood's leadership is less compromising than the Free Officers charged. See FO 371/102763 JE 1052/75, Letter, Chancery to Dept, 27 February 1953 and Record of Conversation between Mr T. E. Evans and the Supreme Guide of the Muslim Brotherhood, 24 February 1953.
66. FO 371/108314 JE 1013/36 Egy FPS 11–24 August 1954.
67. Mitchell, *The Society of the Muslim Brothers*, pp. 151–61.
68. Batatu, *The Old Social Classes*, p. 847.
69. The letter to Qasim quoted above also protested that Baghdad Radio was ignoring the 'hundreds of telegrams of support' pouring in from their own supporters. By the following day some of these messages were making it onto the airwaves, for example a message from 'youths of Al-Karkh' (an area in Baghdad), who asked to join the Popular Resistance, broadcast by Radio Baghdad 09.45 GMT, 15 July 1958, *SWB*, DS 603, 17 July 1958.
70. Translation in FO 371/133069 EQ1015/247, enclosed with letter, Stewart Crawford, Baghdad to Francis D. W. Brown, Foreign Office, 16 September 1958. According to Crawford the statement was 'issued probably on July 14 and certainly circulating in Basra on July 15'. The main points of the text are identical to those made in the letter to Qasim and the circular to party members

quoted in Batatu, *The Old Social Classes*, pp. 847–8, although in this leaflet the party leadership did not spell out its determination to maintain the independence of the Popular Resistance Forces from the state (see below).

71. Batatu, *The Old Social Classes*, p. 848.
72. Radio Baghdad, 19.00 GMT, 17 July 1958, *SWB*, DS 605, 19 July 1958.
73. Radio Baghdad, 10.08 GMT, 20 July 1958, *SWB*, DS 606, 21 July 1958.
74. Radio Baghdad, 11.00 GMT, 2 August 1958, *SWB*, DS 618, 4 August 1958.
75. Radio Baghdad, 05.15 GMT, 9 August 1958, *SWB*, DS 624, 11 August 1958.
76. FO 371/133068 EQ1015/225, Letter, British Consul, Basra to Chancery, Baghdad, 29 August 1958.
77. The pre-revolutionary alliance between the major opposition parties, including the National Democratic Party, the Independence Party, the Ba'th Party, the Communist Party and the Kurdish Democratic Party. See Dann, *Iraq under Qassem*, p. 13.
78. FO 371/133068 EQ1015/225, Letter, British Consul, Basra to Chancery, Baghdad, 29 August 1958, p. 2.
79. Radio Baghdad, 'Abd-as-Salam 'Arif's speech in Kut', 19.30 GMT, 30 July 1958, *SWB* DS 616, 1 August 1958.
80. Radio Baghdad, 17.20 GMT, 4 August 1958, *SWB*, DS 620, 6 August 1958.
81. FO371/140900, EQ 1015/6, Letter, Chancery, British Embassy Baghdad, to Eastern Department, Foreign Office, 31 December 1958. See also Batatu, *The Old Social Classes*, pp. 808–60.
82. See Batatu, *The Old Social Classes*, p. 857.
83. Ibid., pp. 886–7.
84. FO371/140916 EQ1015/332, Letter, Chancery, Baghdad to Department, FO, 9 May 1959.
85. FO371/140916 EQ1015/332, Memorandum, Military Attaché, British Embassy, Baghdad to Under Secretary of State at the War Office, London, 9 May 1959.
86. Batatu, *The Old Social Classes*, p. 900.
87. LAB 13/1307, 'List of unions and organisations taking place in the Labour Day procession', n.d., received by Ministry of Labour, 3 June 1959. It seems likely that this list was incomplete, for example the Teachers' Union and Port Workers' Union are not mentioned, both of which elected communist leaders in this period. See Batatu, *The Old Social Classes*, p. 952 on the Teachers' Union.
88. Batatu, *The old social classes*, p. 900.
89. Ibid., pp. 890–930.

13
The Civic–Military Alliance: Venezuela 1958–90

An Interview with Douglas Bravo by Mike Gonzalez

Douglas Bravo has played a key role in the political life of Venezuela for more than 60 years. A leader of the Venezuelan guerrilla movement from the 1960s onwards, he continued to have a leading role in the movements of resistance and rebellion in the decades that followed. Until the early 1990s national politics were shaped by the Puntofijista pact between the two mainstream political parties, Acción Democrática and Copei. Signed in 1958, it was effectively an agreement to build a consensual politics around what Bravo describes as 'the political-ideological conception of an oil state integrated into the global strategy of a Western world dominated by the United States'. But this went hand in hand with a consistent and brutal repression of all political forces outside the tent.

The Caracazo of 27 February 1989, an explosion of popular rage against the imposition by the Acción Democrática government of Carlos Andrés Pérez of austerity measures imposed by the International Monetary Fund, ended the consensus. The principal impact of those measures fell on Venezuela's poor, whose proportion of the population more than doubled to 65 per cent as a direct result of these early neo-liberal measures. Their discontent found many different expressions, including the military coup attempt of 4 February 1992 led by Hugo Chavez, a lieutenant colonel of the Parachute Regiment, whose political views owed much to Douglas Bravo, until he broke with him late in 1991.

The foundations of Chavez's political project – Bolivarianism and the 'civic–military alliance' – derive from those early discussions with Douglas Bravo. It was logical, therefore, to explore this critical concept and its relation to the central question of this volume, with its author. We met in 2011 and early in 2012, in various places in Caracas.

DB: The civic–military alliance is a particular feature of Venezuelan history whose origins lie in the struggle for independence when different social sectors united under the leadership of the oligarchy. Yet a black man like Francisco de Miranda could and did emerge as a major military leader at that time.

The Venezuelan armed forces have experienced five historical 'breaks' [cortes] whose effect was to undermine the tradition of continuing aristocratic rule characteristic, for example, of Colombia, Chile and Argentina. The first of these breaks came after independence with the collapse of Bolivar's project for a Greater Colombia when José Antonio Páez, who did not come from the oligarchy, became President of the Republic. Later, in 1859, the leadership of the armed forces passed to Ezequiel Zamora in the course of the Federal War [Guerra Federal]. Zamora, himself of humble origins, had the broad support of the peasantry and an advanced social programme, When Zamora was assassinated his place was taken by Guzmán Blanco who reached an agreement with the oligarchy [the Coche Pact] before his victorious entry into Caracas. And it was during his presidency, in 1885, that the first concession to exploit asphalt was given to a North American. The oil companies then began to take shape.

In 1889, Cipriano Castro, representing the coffee growers of the state of Táchira, seized power through his so-called Liberating Revolution, [la Revolución Libertadora] and replaced the military command. When he was replaced in turn by his Vice President Juan Vicente Gómez, the oil companies came to dominate the economy. It was under their influence that, in 1945, Major Marcos Pérez Jiménez, together with Acción Democrática, a mass-based populist party formed in 1941, led a coup against the democratic government of Isaías Medina. Rómulo Betancourt, head of government, used the new situation to replace the military commanders with appointees more favourable to the interests of the big multinationals.

When he became president in 1999, Hugo Chavez made changes in the military high command that produced considerable confusion. Throughout the last century, and especially in the wake of the Yalta Agreements, Venezuela was firmly located in the western geopolitical camp. But in the first decade of the twenty-first century, and without breaking with its dependence on the US, Venezuela has acquired new dependencies, on Russia and China. Far from achieving our independence, we have diversified and deepened our dependence.

An uncompromising military dictatorship, Pérez Jiménez's regime oversaw the oil boom of the 1950s. Caracas's adventurous modernist buildings and the urban plan that crossed the city with wide avenues for the big American cars that swept through it, are testimony to an era of order and prosperity controlled with exemplary ferocity. Its main beneficiaries were a small bourgeoisie in receipt of petrodollars. The dictator thus faced opposition from several quarters – from those linked to the interests of the big oil companies, and from the mass of the poor among whom the Venezuelan Communist Party [PCV] enjoyed considerable support. Acción Democrática [AD] played a contradictory role in his overthrow, supporting it and enjoying widespread backing from the middle class above all, but also among those working in and for the state.

DB: In 1957, the resistance to Pérez Jiménez's dictatorship began to unify and organise around a political leadership [the Junta Patriótica, created in July 1957] which included AD, Copei [the Social Christian Party] and the Communist Party, to which I belonged. The work of the Junta was organised around four commissions. I was a member of the Workers' Commission (I was a trade union organiser in a cement factory), representing the Communist Party. At the same time the [Communist] Party set up a military commission, whose job was to make contact with sympathisers within the military on the one hand, and to prepare armed brigades for the confrontation to come on the other. It included Eloy Torres, secretary of the Communist Party's Clandestine Regional Committee and a retired colonel, Arráez Morles as well as Teodoro Petkoff and myself.

The essential demand of the Junta Patriótica was for a democratic constitution and parliament. Until the beginning of 1957, the mass resistance movement was on the defensive. In the previous year the military dictatorship had given massive concessions to the Seven Sisters (the major oil multinationals) as well as to smaller independent oil companies. But the Junta had not recognised the contradiction until it became obvious that the Sisters, and the US government, were preparing a confrontation with Pérez Jiménez. The Junta set about organising resistance in different social sectors. The student committee, for example, led an extraordinary action at the Central University in Caracas that led to a military occupation of the campus, the closure of the university and the arrest of hundreds of students. On 15 December, a government-organised plebiscite brought the defeat of the government. The agitation continued and on 1 January 1958 there was a rebellion led by Lieutenant

Colonel Hugo Trejo of the Armoured Division and Lt Col Martín Parada, who commanded a unit of the Air Force. The rebellion was quickly suppressed, but it showed that there was resistance to the dictatorship within the armed forces. At the same time an agreement was signed in New York between Rómulo Betancourt, Rafael Caldera, Jóvito Villalba and the industrialist Enrique Mendoza anticipating the fall of Pérez Jiménez and preparing to challenge the political authority of the Junta Patriótica.

The Junta, led by Fabricio Ojeda, then called a general strike for the 21st. By that time it had built a relationship with army officers and priests who had supported demonstrations in the *barrios,* the poor districts. The government attempted to undermine the strike using the military and the intelligence services; in fact it announced the defeat of the strike on the 22nd while at the same time the dictator was flying into exile. On the following morning the new civilian-military government was announced. The masses took to the streets in huge numbers calling for Fabricio Ojeda to become president. At the same time Hugo Trejo had won enormous influence among officers and soldiers. Yet the leadership of the left wing parties who were members of the Junta did not understand the historic moment we were living through. The first thing they did was call for order and calm, denouncing the people who were looting shops and so on as 'enemies of the people'. What followed was a rebellion from below. Thousands of people took to the streets, while brigades were set up in many of the poor districts. This marked what I called the fourth social uprising in Venezuelan history (the conquest, the struggle for independence and the federal wars were the first three) by which I mean 'that moment when the political, social, military, cultural, and spiritual forces come into confrontation through armed or unarmed social violence'.[1] In some ways we can see it as an early expression of the global uprising of the 1960s.

This mass political offensive continued until January 1962, and at times reached insurrectionary proportions. In 1960, the MIR [Movement of the Revolutionary Left] split from Acción Democrática, the governing party headed by Betancourt, and it was later followed by another split, the URD. In rural areas, some 350 land occupations were organised under the aegis of the Right to Bread Campaigns. And when the oil price fell below 50 cents a barrel, Betancourt responded by cutting the wages of State employees, which intensified the wave of popular protest. According to the intelligence services, there were 70 insurrectionary cells in operation by then. New rebellions followed in December and in

January 1962 a transport strike spread throughout the country. It is clear now that 1961 was a critical turning point that could have marked a definitive creative break with the past.

The opportunity, however, was not taken. There was no concept of seizing power, the masses were growing weary; some officers were arrested and others relieved of their command, while across the country the leaders of the MIR, the Communist Party and the left of the URD were arrested. The mass movement retreated, which meant that the two military rebellions of that year – the revolt in May 1962 at the military base at Carúpano on 4 May and the Porteñazo of 2 June, at the Marine base of Puerto Cabello – were quickly repressed

In April 1964, the Venezuelan Communist Party (PCV) agreed to peaceful co-existence with the government of Leoni, though he was continuing the line of Betancourt who had increased the level of repression after the killing of four guards on the so-called Encanto train at the end of 1963. It was Leoni who was to give the world a new term – 'the disappeared'.

DB: At first Leoni gave the impression of moving to the left, creating illusions in the PCV and the MIR. The consequence was that those of us who argued that armed struggle offered the only way out of the crisis were sanctioned and expelled. The reality was that these parties were following the line of the Soviet Union and the agreements it had reached with the US in the wake of the Cuban Missile Crisis of 1962. The repression against those of us who were continuing the resistance became so intense that the number of the dead and 'disappeared' reached two thousand. The so-called 'Theatres of Counter Guerrilla Operations' created their own law allowing torture, isolation, murder and the continuous violation of human rights.

These were the circumstances in which we founded the Party of the Venezuelan Revolution, the PRV, which brought together revolutionaries like Fabricio Ojeda, the theorists Salvador de la Plaza and others recently expelled from the Communist Party, intellectuals like the architect Fruto Vivas, the poet Victor Valera Mora and military officers including Manuit Camero, Vegas Castejón and Tulio Martínez Delgado, as well as a groups of workers, peasants, students and indigenous people.

The small force of Cuban and Venezuelan guerrillas that landed on the Venezuelan coast in May 1966 was intended to demonstrate the continuing viability of the guerrilla forces. They were quickly located by the Venezuelan air force, though they did survive. That same year, however, Fabricio Ojeda, the charismatic joint leader of the guerrillas was killed. And in April 1967, the Plenum of the Venezuelan Communist Party formally withdrew its support for armed struggle and expelled Bravo.[2]

DB: The expedition led by Ochoa and Petkoff and a group of Cuban officers reached the coast of the state of Falcon in 1966. The PRV had been set up on April 23 1966 and the Soviets had no involvement in it. On the contrary, Fidel Castro and Che Guevara participated in alliances with revolutionary movements and communist parties in power in open defiance of the USSR. I might add that splits occurred in every communist and socialist party after the Cuban Missile Crisis. By this time, in fact, most Latin American communist parties were opposed to the guerrilla movements on the continent, while they were supported by Cuba, China, North Korea, Vietnam and Algeria. Fabricio Ojeda, who was the president of the National Liberation Front [FLN] and of the PRV as well as second in command of Armed Forces of National Liberation [FALN] was murdered by the Military Intelligence Services. The agreements reached between the US and the USSR after the Missile Crisis are the primary cause of the defeat of the Latin American armed revolutionary movements.

Venezuela continued to be an economy dependent on oil. Faced with rising unemployment and the failure of Copei's industrialisation project, there was a new wave of social agitation and protest, especially in the barrios of Caracas. New forms of resistance were evolving under different influences, including the theology of liberation. There were strikes in key industries and new land occupations. Students were taking to the streets again and the first Cultural Congress organised by Bravo in Cabimas produced the early expressions of what Bravo describes as the theory of Marxist Bolivarianism.

The oil crisis of 1973 changed the situation dramatically in Venezuela. The spectacular rise in oil prices under the government of Carlos Andrés Pérez allowed him to present a populist image, opening relations with Cuba and the Soviet Bloc and using the expanding earnings from oil to win allies. It was a time of wild consumerism and a firm belief that the money would never run out. Yet social struggles continued and were met with the usual repressive response – persecution, state terror, political prisoners, unexplained deaths. This was the continuation of the parliamentary democracy with repression established by the Punto Fijo Pact of 1958.

The level of social protest was decreasing, however, especially after the strikes of the banana workers and the student actions of early 1978. The movement underwent a downturn for a decade, though active resistance continued at a local level. A new kind of grassroots democracy was developing outside the structures of the parties which until then had dominated Venezuelan political life.

Bravo, meanwhile, was beginning to develop a concept of revolutionary organisation built around autonomous, grassroots and democratic structures. Its foundation was to be the growth of a parallel people's power [poder popular].³ The movement reawakened with the Caracazo of 27 February 1989.

Hugo Chavez traces his movement back to that 'act of force'. His Bolivarian revolution has its origins in his meetings with Douglas Bravo. They first met in 1982, when the two men were introduced by Chavez's lover Herme Marksman who was a close friend of Bravo's. Chavez at the time was one of a small group of military officers from a working-class background who had come through the Military Academy and were opposed to the corrupt version of democracy they saw in Venezuela. They identified themselves with an anti-imperialist tradition best embodied, as they saw it, in Bolivar and Simón Rodríguez. Chavez maintained contact with Douglas Bravo, as well as Causa R, a split from the Communist Party led by Alfredo Maneiro with deep roots in the industrial working class of Guyana. Two days after the outbreak of the Caracazo, Bravo met Chavez – who was ill and not present in Caracas at the time – together with some liberation priests and others. He was not the only military officer organising against the regime – William Izarra and Francisco Arias had already set up the Revolutionary Alliance of Serving Officers [ARMA]. But Bravo's relationship with Chavez came to an abrupt end in October 1991.

DB: The mass popular rising of 27 February 1989, the 'Caracazo', 'exposed the old contradictions in Venezuelan society and created new ones at the same time. It was the first national expression of a new period of social struggle leading into the twenty-first century. It detonated forces accumulated over 31 years and laid the foundations for profound future social, military, political, legal, cultural and spiritual changes.'⁴ This was the first rising of the masses against neo-liberalism, and its immediate effect in Venezuela was to set in motion social struggles that had been frozen for some time. And this in turn created the conditions for the reactivation of the civic–military–religious alliance.

In 1998, Chavez won the presidential elections with 58 per cent of the popular vote. His involvement in the 1992 coup and his famous promise that the revolution was only over 'por ahora' *[for the moment] made him a hugely popular figure. His first act was to set up a constituent assembly of elected delegates to draw up a new constitution. The new Bolivarian constitution was passed and supported by a massive majority in a referendum.*

DB: A Constitutional Assembly can only be established when it is preceded by 'originating acts of social force.' The masses were not participants in the actions of 4 February 1992, for example, because Chavez himself marginalised them. The civic-military rising of 27 November that year was very different, because arms were distributed beforehand and the project assumed from the outset the involvement of the armed people in Maracay, Caracas and La Guaira. Chavez's conception sees the role of the masses as there to applaud but not to act with their own consciousness, hearts and hands.

Once in the Presidency Chavez called a referendum to approve a Constituent Assembly and since then new laws with a neo-liberal content have been passed. Subsequently the Constituent Assembly, but not one based on mass involvement, was set up and it provided a juridical framework that was clearly neo-liberal in character. And that is increasingly reaffirmed, for example with the initiation of the privatisation of PDVSA (the State Oil Corporation) with the approval by the National Assembly of the Law on Mixed Enterprises on 31 March 2006. We could say that Chavez has carried out the plans of the oil multinationals and others, which is why neither they nor the Employers Organisations nor the Platform of Democratic Unity [MUD] that brings together the old political parties have protested against these laws that violate national sovereignty. This so-called 'twenty-first-century socialism' has guaranteed social peace.

Douglas Bravo's view of the government of Hugo Chavez is deeply critical. He sees it as having betrayed, or misused, the concept of a civic–military alliance because at root, the alliance was directed at building a mass movement in permanent rebellion. Bravo smiles when he says 'What we have in government today is a civic-military alliance ... of the right!'. He returned to the subject in a recent interview.

DB: We have explained here and elsewhere the reasons for our criticism. We are faced with a crisis of power that has deepened the internal contradictions within government and among those who wish to replace it on the basis of neither past nor the present, but a new era. In that debate there emerge many different positions. There are those in government and their external supporters who want Chavez to continue in power even if it violates the electoral rules. It is worth reading the declarations of Merrill Lynch, President Obama, the Bilderberg Group and most recently the declarations of General Douglas Fraser, Head of the US Southern Command, all of whom favour the official candidate. There are others who favour a pact between the government and the MUD in order to avoid the election of a government born out of mass actions from below. The classic military coup-makers are also expressing their intentions. The people, however, do not appear in any of these projects. Their presence would demand popular, mass-based, democratic, civic–military–religious constituent organisations that are united and sovereign and capable of producing the turning point and the creative break that can usher in a new period of genuine emancipation. Nevertheless it is this third force that will slowly but surely create a new grouping founded on philosophical and political ideas that offer an alternative to the capitalist system and open the way to a new civilisation and a new economic, political, cultural, military, social order. The doors are open to the future.

NOTES

1. Douglas Bravo and Argelia Melet, *La otra crisis*, Caracas: Orijinal, 1991, p. 127.
2. According to Teodoro Petkoff, a guerrilla leader at the time, who would soon renounce the armed struggle and eventually become a leading voice of the right, the rural guerrillas were essentially in retreat though they survived because of the sustained support they received from the peasantry. The urban networks, in Petkoff's view, had been severely damaged by state repression. See Richard Gott, *Rural Guerrillas in Latin America*, Harmondsworth: Penguin, 1973, pp. 256–7.
3. See 'Cuál partido, cuál socialismo', in Bravo and Melet, *La otra crisis*, pp. 75–90.
4. Ibid.

BIBLIOGRAPHY/FURTHER READING

Ian Bruce, *The Real Venezuela*: *Making Socialism in the 21st Century*, London: Pluto Press, 2008.

Richard Gott, *Guerrillas in Latin America*, Harmondsworth: Penguin, 1970.

Richard, Gott, *In the Shadow of the Liberator: Hugo Chavez and the Venezuelan Revolution*, London: Verso, 2005.

Bart Jones, *Hugo! The Hugo Chavez Story*, London: Vintage Books, 2009.

Diane Raby, *Democracy and Revolution in Latin America*, London: Pluto Press, 2006.

Gregory Wilpert, *Changing Venezuela by Taking Power*, New York: Monthly Review, 2006.

See also www.venezuelanalysis.com.

Notes on Contributors

Anne Alexander is a Research Fellow at the Centre for Research in the Arts, Social Sciences and Humanities at the University of Cambridge. She is the author of a biography of Gamal Abd-al-Nasser (Haus, 2005), and has written widely on the politics and history of the Middle East. She is currently co-writing a book on the role of the workers' movement in the Egyptian revolution with Mostafa Bassiouny.

Houman Barekat is a London-based writer and critic. He has written for a variety of literary publications including the *Los Angeles Review of Books*, the *Oxonian Review* and *3:AM Magazine*, as well as academic journals like *International Affairs* and *Capital & Class*. He is founding editor of the online literary review, *Review 31*.

Andy Durgan lives and works in Barcelona. He has published in various languages on different aspects of Spanish history, in particular relating to the Civil War, its origins and the labour movement. These include: *B.O.C. El Bloque Obrero y Campesino 1930–1936* (Laertes, 1996) and *The Spanish Civil War* (Palgrave, 2007). He was Historical Advisor for the award-winning Ken Loach film *Land and Freedom* (1996) and a founder member of the *Fundació Andreu Nin*.

Donny Gluckstein is a lecturer in history at Edinburgh College and author of *A People's History of the Second World War. Resistance versus Empire* (Pluto Press, 2012).

Mike Gonzalez is Emeritus Professor of Latin American Studies at Glasgow University. His writings include *Che Guevara and the Cuban Revolution* (2006) and he is joint editor of the *Routledge Encyclopedia of Contemporary Latin American and Caribbean Culture*.(1999) He is a member of the editorial board of the *International Socialism Journal*.

Mike Haynes works at the University of Wolverhampton. He has written extensively on Russia and the former Soviet bloc. He is particularly interested in the social and political costs of change. He is the co-editor of *History and Revolution*, (2007). He is currently researching the history of top level crime and corruption in the history of capitalism.

Philip Marfleet is Professor in the School of Law and Social Sciences at the University of East London. He has written widely on Middle East politics and Society. Recent publications include, with Rabab El Mahdi, *Egypt – the Moment of Change* (Zed Press) and '"Identity politics" – Europe, the EU and the Arab Spring', in Ismael, T., and Parry, G. (eds.) *International Relations of the Contemporary Middle East* (Routledge).

Nathaniel Mehr is a London-based journalist and author of '*Constructive Bloodbath' in Indonesia: The United States, Britain and the Mass Killings of 1965–66* (Spokesman Books, 2009).

Volkhard Mosler, was a member of SDS (1963–69). He studies Industrial Relations in the Institute of Social Research in Frankfurt and is active in revolutionary politics in Germany. Editor of the Marxist journal 'Klassenkampf' (Class Struggle) from 1982–1994 and of 'Sozialismus von unten' (Socialism from below) 1994–1998, he is a member of the Left Party in Frankfurt and of Marx21, Marxist network in the Left Party.

Jonathan Neale is a novelist, playwright, historian, and activist. His books include *Stop Global Warming: Change the World; A People's History of the Vietnam War; What's Wrong with America; Mutineers; The Cutlass and the Lash;* and *Tigers of the Snow*, a history of Sherpa climbers. Jonathan has a BSc in Social Anthropology from LSE and a PhD in Social History from Warwick. He teaches Creative Writing at Bath Spa University.

Peter Robinson went to Portugal in 1975 as a political organiser for the International Socialists (IS) in Lisbon, returning a number of times thereafter to interview activists. He completed his MPhil thesis on Workers' Councils in Portugal: 1974–75. (Open University, 1989). The Socialist History Society published his *Portugal 1974–75, The Forgotten Dream* (1999) and he wrote on Portugal in *Ours to Master and to Own – Workers Control from the Paris Commune to the Present* (Haymarket Press 2011).

Megan Trudell is a PhD student in History at Birkbeck College in London, researching nationalism and revolution in Italy between the First World War and the Fascist seizure of power. She is a member of the editorial board of *International Socialism Journal.*

INDEX